DISRUPTIVE PRISONERS

Disruptive Prisoners reconstitutes the history of Canada's federal prison system in the mid-twentieth century through a process of collective biography – one involving prisoners, administrators, prison reformers, and politicians. This social history relies on extensive archival research and access to government documents, but more importantly, uses the penal press materials created by prisoners themselves and an interview with one of the founding penal press editors to provide a unique and unprecedented analysis.

    Disruptive Prisoners is grounded in the lived experiences of men who were incarcerated in federal penitentiaries in Canada and argues that they were not merely passive recipients of intervention. Evidence indicates that prisoners were active agents of change who advocated for and resisted the initiatives that were part of Canada's "New Deal in Corrections." While prisoners are silent in other criminological and historical texts, here they are central figures: the juxtaposition of their voices with the official administrative, parliamentary, and government records challenges the dominant tropes of progress and provides a more nuanced and complicated reframing of the post–Archambault Commission era.

    The use of an alternative evidential base, the commitment of the authors to integrating subaltern perspectives, and the first-hand accounts by prisoners of their experiences of incarceration make this book a highly readable and engaging glimpse behind the bars of Canada's federal prisons.

CHRIS CLARKSON is a professor in the Department of History at Okanagan College.

MELISSA MUNN is a professor in the Department of Sociology at Okanagan College.

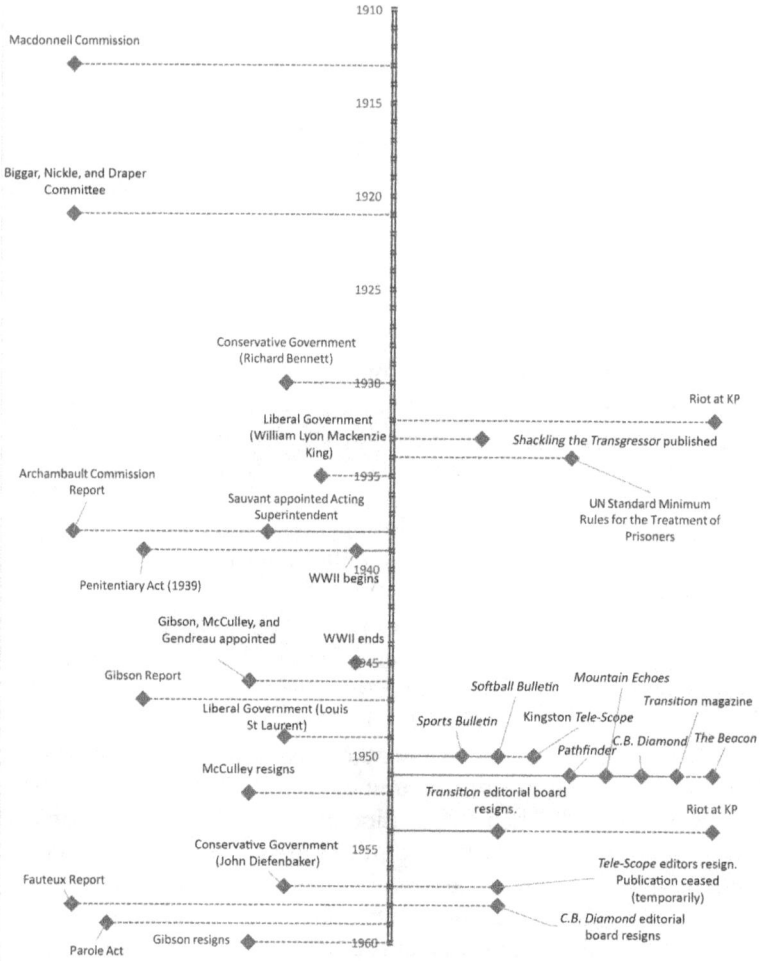

1910	
	Macdonneil Commission
1915	
	Biggar, Nickle, and Draper Committee
1920	
1925	
	Conservative Government (Richard Bennett)
1930	Riot at KP
	Liberal Government (William Lyon Mackenzie King) — *Shackling the Transgressor* published
	Archambault Commission Report
1935	Sauvant appointed Acting Superintendent — UN Standard Minimum Rules for the Treatment of Prisoners
	Penitentiary Act (1939)
1940	WWII begins
	Gibson, McCulley, and Gendreau appointed — WWII ends
1945	Gibson Report
	Liberal Government (Louis St Laurent) — *Softball Bulletin*, *Mountain Echoes*, *Sports Bulletin*, Kingston *Tele-Scope*, *Transition magazine*
1950	McCulley resigns — *Pathfinder*, *C.B. Diamond*, *The Beacon*
	Transition editorial board resigns. — Riot at KP
1955	Conservative Government (John Diefenbaker) — *Tele-Scope* editors resign. Publication ceased (temporarily)
	Fauteux Report — *C.B. Diamond* editorial board resigns
	Parole Act, Gibson resigns
1960	

Chronology of Major Events

Disruptive Prisoners

Resistance, Reform, and the New Deal

CHRIS CLARKSON AND MELISSA MUNN

Foreword by Robert Gaucher

UNIVERSITY OF TORONTO PRESS
Toronto Buffalo London

© University of Toronto Press 2021
Toronto Buffalo London
utorontopress.com

ISBN 978-1-4875-0853-1 (cloth)   ISBN 978-1-4875-3845-3 (EPUB)
ISBN 978-1-4875-2591-0 (paper)   ISBN 978-1-4875-3844-6 (PDF)

Library and Archives Canada Cataloguing in Publication

Title: Disruptive prisoners : resistance, reform, and the new deal /
    Chris Clarkson and Melissa Munn.
Names: Clarkson, Christopher Allan, 1969– author. | Munn, Melissa,
    author.
Description: Includes bibliographical references.
Identifiers: Canadiana (print) 20210232234 | Canadiana (ebook)
    20210232242 | ISBN 9781487508531 (hardcover) | ISBN 9781487525910
    (softcover) | ISBN 9781487538446 (PDF) | ISBN 9781487538453 (EPUB)
Subjects: LCSH: Prisons – Canada – History – 20th century. | LCSH:
    Prisoners – Canada – History – 20th century. | LCSH: Prison reform –
    Canada – History – 20th century.
Classification: LCC HV9507 .C53 2021 | DDC 365/.971 – dc23

This book has been published with the help of a grant from the Federation
for the Humanities and Social Sciences, through the Awards to Scholarly
Publications Program, using funds provided by the Social Sciences and
Humanities Research Council of Canada.

University of Toronto Press acknowledges the financial assistance to its
publishing program of the Canada Council for the Arts and the Ontario
Arts Council, an agency of the Government of Ontario.

Canada Council   Conseil des Arts
for the Arts   du Canada

ONTARIO ARTS COUNCIL
CONSEIL DES ARTS DE L'ONTARIO
an Ontario government agency
un organisme du gouvernement de l'Ontario

Funded by the   Financé par le
Government   gouvernement
of Canada   du Canada

Canada

Contents

Acknowledgments

The writers in the penal press were the first contributors to this manuscript. Without the strength, courage, and innovation of these ethnographers and journalists, this work would not have been possible. Special thanks to André Dion, who took time in his final days to describe the emergence of the press to us, and to his wife, Frances Dion for initiating that never-dreamed-possible moment. Credit for every page in this book belongs to Robert (Bob) Gaucher, who thirty years ago inspired Melissa to recognize prisoners' voices in all of her work. We have endeavoured to follow Bob's historically focussed, prisoner-centric approach in putting together this book, though of course, the shortcomings are ours alone. Thanks also to Bob and Library and Archives Canada for their efforts to preserve the historical documents for us and future researchers. Relatedly, thanks to Cameron Willis and David St Ong (Kingston Penitentiary Museum), Kimberly Bell (Queen's University Library), and Holly Marple for their archival support. Okanagan College, and Dean Robert Huxtable in particular, encouraged this work and the penalpress.com website both financially and through study leaves. The college also funded research assistants (Nicole Arbuckle, Kate Garrett, Brian Garvin, Danielle Lafrance, and Joe Lanaway), who helped us during the early stages of the work. Michelle Doege graciously volunteered to read the manuscript and provided invaluable editorial feedback that pushed us to clarify and reorganize the work; thank you. We also want to thank the two anonymous reviewers for sharing their insights into this work and for validating our approach. Our friends and family have been terrific throughout this process, but we want to note Lee Johnson and Linda Gaucher for particular acts of kindness that kept us moving forward with this project. But *most importantly*, thank you to our spouses, Ruth Clarkson and Al Larsen, for their immeasurable support through the years(!) that it took to put this work together. It simply would not exist without them. They sacrificed time with us, put up with our bitching and moaning, and were the backbone that kept us going. Thanks to Ruth especially for the food and the forced marches and to Al for giving up his dining table for days at a time and sustaining us with his good humour.

Foreword

This study of prison reform in Canada combines the insights and expertise of a criminologist with those of a historian. Their joint effort has resulted in a new interdisciplinary understanding of the post–Second World War federal prison reform initiative. This innovative research introduces two new original sources to the discussion and analysis of the age of penal reform in Canada (1930–60). First, the discovery and inclusion of verbatim wardens' conferences (1949–57) regarding the Archambault Commission (1939) and steps to implement its findings moves the analysis of these initiatives beyond the dominant institutional and academic narrative that has become "accepted wisdom" in Canadian penology. Second, by examining the Canadian penal press, the analysis in this study addresses a glaring lacuna in Canadian penology, that is, the absence of the positions and understandings of federal prisoners on the proposed changes to penal custom in this era. By introducing these two sources into the discussion and analysis of penal reform, this study transcends the dominant institutional and academic narrative on the Archambault Report and how its proposed changes were implemented behind the walls of Canada's penitentiaries. Most striking is the portrayal of the ongoing tensions between management, custodial staff, and prisoners as these played out over the course of the fundamental changes to penal custom proposed and to some extent realized.

As an undergraduate at Queen's University in 1969, I enrolled in a "Sociology of Deviant Behaviour" course taught by a young Englishman, Ian Taylor,[1] which set me on the path to a PhD and a long career in academia. A child of the 1960s, I knew about the inequalities and discrimination that characterized Canadian criminal justice and imprisonment in that era. I knew that our prisons were filled with young men from working-class neighbourhoods and with Indigenous youths from

inner cities and reserves with their histories of subjugation and humiliation in residential schools, and that much of the institutional and public discourse distorted and masked the realities of the focus of social
control. Drawing upon political economic narratives of the left and the
emerging theorization of Western societies' "agents of social control,"
Professor Taylor provided a broad context in which to understand the
dominant and distorting commonsense version of criminal justice and
penalty in Canada. I was introduced to the work of (then) contemporary theorists and researchers. Howard Becker's challenge to rethink
academic "objectivity" in "Whose Side Are We On" (1967) opened my
eyes to the inclusion of the outsider in critical thinking. I found Erving
Goffman's[2] analysis of "total institutions" and processes of disenfran-
chisement and stigmatization of special relevance, as was the work of
David Matza[3] on the transformation of social identity and place. They
cut through the institutional fabrication of individual intentionality and
responsibility that was dominant and especially relevant to my generation. Taylor's lectures and our conversations and the works I read
and engaged fuelled my critical thinking and enlightened my resistance
through the tumultuous late 1960s and 1970s.

My university courses and the encouragement of professors led me
to a lifetime of investigating academic criminology/penology and
Western criminal justice and carceral practices. Initially, there was
very little Canadian-specific work in these fields, and what there was
mainly offered institutional justifications and masking of what was taking place. I was aware of the characteristic inequalities that dominated
criminal justice and carceral practices in Canada; specifically, the mass
incarceration of Indigenous youth and their claims that the penitentiary
was the "finishing school for residential school graduates," which at
least provided better food and fewer daily humiliations for being an
"Indian"; and the dominance of the poor and youthful school "push-
outs" who composed the majority of the prison population. Ian introduced me to the Scandinavian School of socio-legal studies[4] and to the
emerging "New Criminology" in the UK with its focus on the "agencies
of social control" and the politically driven containment of working-
class rebellion and resistance that characterized this era. Most notable
for me was a new study by Stanley Cohen and Laurie Taylor, *Psychological Survival: The Experience of Long-Term Imprisonment* (1972), which
focused on the maximum-security E-wing of Durham Penitentiary in
England. They engaged the prisoners in the unit during the creation
and writing of the study. Amazingly, these authors passed the finished
manuscript over to the prisoners for their comments and corrections
prior to publication. The only other contemporary work I discovered

that presented the views and understandings of prisoners was *The Felon* (1970) by the former American prisoner and then academic John Irwin. Search as I may, I found few Canadian works written by (former) prisoners. The legendary *Shackling the Transgressor* (1933) by Dr Oswald C.J. Withrow stood out. Except for a few biographical works that made passing mention of carceral experiences, including that of a former penal press writer for Kingston Penitentiary's *Tele-Scope*, Harvey Blackstock (*Bitter Humour*, 1967), I uncovered little of note. Blackstock's writing addressed his incarceration in the 1940s and 1950s in Canada and his role as a penal press writer. Living in Kingston, I was familiar with the Canadian penal press, and through my involvements with prisoners in the local penitentiaries I had access to contemporary magazines such as *Tightwire* (P4W). Although censorship and opposition by penal administrators and staff stymied production, it was clear that penal press editorial groups strove to engage the Canadian public and penal administrators with their insights into the failure of prison regimes and their recommendations for positive change.

After years of study, in 1984 I entered the ranks of academia in the Department of Criminology at the University of Ottawa. Determined to use my new position to address the ravages and inequalities that characterize imprisonment in Canada, I became involved with social justice activists like Claire Culhane,[5] whose engagement with criminal justice and carceral practices was grounded in close involvement with prisoners (including an overwhelming amount of correspondence) and constant monitoring of our (primarily federal) prisons. At this time, although others contributed to "prison activism," only "Saint" Claire succeeded in keeping the Canadian public aware of what was transpiring within the walls.

In 1985, along with a contingent of Canadian social justice activists, I attended the second biannual congress of the International Conference on Prison Abolition (ICOPA)[6] in Amsterdam. A major issue we took away from the conference was the absence of (former) prisoner involvement. What sense did it make to have a prison liberation movement that did not involve, front and centre, those subjected to repression and incarceration? ICOPA was a Canadian initiative first held in Toronto in 1983, and our dissatisfaction with what we perceived as an overly academic focus in Amsterdam led our ICOPA steering committee to bring the conference back to Canada in 1987. It was held at the Université de Montréal, jointly hosted by the criminology departments of that university and the University of Ottawa. In light of what we perceived to be a major deficiency of the Amsterdam Conference, we were determined to include grassroots social activist groups/organizations,[7] as well as prisoners' voices, on our agenda. Getting prisoners released or on passes to attend a penal abolition conference was a "pipe dream," so Howard Davidson and I, along with a Boston academic and prison educator, Elizabeth Barker, held a session featuring papers written by current prisoners. Much to our surprise, it was a great success, one of the highlights of the English-language sessions. This led Howard Davidson and I to eventually create *The Journal of Prisoners on Prisons* (1988–2018), an academic journal featuring the writing and analysis of prisoners (and former prisoners) on current criminal justice and carceral issues. It also prompted me to more generally engage prisoners in current academic discourse. At the time, I was working with prison members of the Infinity Lifers' Group at Collins Bay Institution (Kingston, Ontario). That group's dedication to penal reform was opening eyes across Canada, and its instigation of the "prisoner's right to vote" initiative was eventually successful. Its members' intelligent engagement with University of Ottawa students, and a wide variety of Canadian academics and lawyers, spoke volumes about what prisoners could achieve if given the opportunity.

These involvements renewed my past interest in the Canadian penal press as a research source. There were still penal press magazines publishing in Canada, so I contacted editorial groups and started to search for and collect magazines. Notable contemporary "joint" magazines such as *Tightwire* (P4W) and *Terminator* (Stony Mountain), and those produced by specialized groups such as Native Brotherhood groups and lifers' groups, were readily available. I knew that these magazines were a source of prisoners' positions stretching back to the 1950s and the age of prison reform, but they had never been documented or collected. My research into Canada's archival system and university and public libraries, and my contacts with past contributors and (long-time) prison activists, produced a wealth of past issues.[8] At that time, it was clear to me that here was a research source that could be used to address the major lacuna in Canadian penology – the absence the positions of prisoners. In the penal press the basis of prisoner's interrelations and actions, their hopes and aspirations, were available.

From my initial introduction to critical studies in criminology/penology by Ian Taylor (1969–70) I had come to understand that it was not possible to analyse the management and operations of carceral institutions without taking into account the understanding and actions of prisoners and their relationship to penal staff and administrations. Goffman's analysis of total institutions in *Asylums* (1968), the work of Matza (1964, 1969) and Lemert (1967), and the flood of works by the New Criminology illustrated the pertinence of taking into account the understandings and reactions of those subjected to social control measures. In "The Prisoner as Ethnographer" (1988), my "Response" in the first issue of the *Journal of Prisoners on Prisons*, I stated that what the journal aimed to accomplish was "to bring the knowledge and experience of the incarcerated to bear upon ... academic arguments and concerns and to inform public discourse about the current state of our carceral institutions." It is this understanding that characterizes this work. Thanks Chris and Melissa!

This study should be celebrated as exemplifying this goal and for the first time in Canadian history addressing the "age of penal reform" with the vital and necessary inclusion of prisoners' positions and lived understanding of these initiatives. Their input was an essential ingredient in forwarding the reform agenda by their support and their opposition to administrative changes. The discovery of verbatim conference proceedings of the Commissioner's Office and penitentiary wardens adds immeasurably to the analysis of the implementation of the first major penal reforms in Canada. Records of those proceedings provide the debates and musings of the authorities and their reactions to the responses of prison staff and prisoners. Through the unedited discourse provided in these documents we rediscover Goffman's account of the centrality of the social relations of a total institution and the essential dynamics of those relationships. Vigorous archival searches by the authors of this book have unearthed documentation that for the first time reveals the concerns and contradictions that characterize the attempted implementation of the Archambault Report recommendations. These new sources provide a window onto the previously hidden "conversations" among the combatants, and as a result, this work transcends the still dominant institutional and academic narrative on the Archambault Report and the transformation for which it called. The authors' ability to capture this tension energizes the analysis and helps make sense of the stuttering history of penal reform in Canada.

I must complement the authors for their tenacious research into this subject and their strategic use of the new sources they bring to bear on this era, and their study's relevance for addressing the continuing reliance on imprisonment as a response to social conflict and the proven failure of imprisonment. I look forward to their extension of this line of analysis in a second volume that would address the ensuing period of reaction by staff and the subsequent resistance of prisoners.

Prof. (ret.) Robert Gaucher
Ottawa, Ontario
October 2018

DISRUPTIVE PRISONERS

Resistance, Reform, and the New Deal

Introduction

"Telling the truth takes a collective effort."[1] Yet when the story of prison reform in twentieth-century Canada is told, it is usually from an administrative perspective alone. We know what politicians thought; we have the findings of Royal Commissions and government investigations; we have superintendent's reports. These accounts are regurgitated in the extant literature so often that they have become seen as the Truth. Because other voices are seldom heard, there has simply been no counter-narrative. No critique. No disruption to the dominant tale. We argue that telling a more complete story of prisons requires a multitude of voices – those of prisoners, administrators, prison workers, politicians, journalists, and prison reformers. Each adds layers of complexity and nuance to the story. In the case of this research project, prisoners in particular demanded to be heard. They had something to say – something to contribute – and their absence is simply unconscionable if we are to understand the impact of penal reform. Listening to them and grounding our analysis in the documents produced by prison writers and workers, as well as members of the public, has forced us to approach storytelling as a collective effort. This text weaves together their stories and delivers a more comprehensive and complex analysis. With this approach, the dominant narratives of Canadian penal reform fall apart and seemingly linear, straightforward processes are shown to be more layered and multifaceted.

Serendipity: Finding Voices

Why are these voices missing from the extant literature on prison reform? Perhaps the answer lies with the availability of evidence. Past researchers may have wanted to include the experiences and perspectives of Canadian federal prisoners, but the documentary materials available from major repositories were scant. Fortunately, Professor Robert (Bob) Gaucher spent decades collecting Canadian prisoner-generated newsletters. He combed through libraries and archives, talked to prisoners, wrote letters, and catalogued and documented everything he found. His dogged determination resulted in a voluminous collection of a quality that surpassed anything else, anywhere else.[2] But this was his personal collection, and access to it was limited.[3] As many researchers are aware, serendipity sometimes plays a crucial role in academic research. When Bob retired from the University of Ottawa, he donated his collection to a former student and fellow activist/scholar (Melissa Munn), and she shared it with her historian colleague (Chris Clarkson).[4] It immediately became clear to us that these primary documents were a rich, complex, and neglected record of prisoner experience in Canada. We wanted to know whether there were more of them. Armed with a "backpack office" (stapler, staple remover, USB stick, laptop, spreadsheet, and portable scanner), we travelled to Ottawa. We combed through the Public Safety Canada library collection to find and digitize materials that had barely been catalogued (and have since disappeared) and that were kept in a subterranean cage in the parking lot of the PSC building. Again, serendipity would intervene. A few blocks away, in the staid, silent rooms of Library and Archives Canada, we stumbled across a finding aid that read "Warden's Conferences" and, on a hunch, requisitioned those files and others relating to prisoner newspapers and the Archambault Commission. After some months of waiting for the archivists to go through the boxes and remove any "confidential materials," we lifted the lids and a plethora of voices started yelling – well, metaphorically yelling, because, like the prisons of the past, LAC still operates on the silent system. The wardens' meetings – their debates, discussions, and posturing – had been transcribed verbatim. The files documented the moment that the penal press was proposed, and we ran from the room to rejoice aloud in the hallway. We had been reading the prisoners' words, and here were administrators telling the same story from another perspective. And the boxes contained more than just meeting minutes. There were letters from community members (from labour and church organizations, activist groups, political parties, and prisoners' families) declaring what they liked and disliked in the prison newsletters. Clips from newspaper editorials offered insight into how the mainstream media saw their incarcerated brother journalists. There were records from government accountants regarding funding for the prison newsletters. And sure, they were talking about the penal press, but they were also talking about so much more. The variety of source materials exposed voices telling a story of penal reform in Canada that had not been heard before. So, through these serendipitous moments, this book came into being.

Writing a Social History of Prisons

Including these voices changed our understanding of the origin, nature, and outcome of the reform agenda of the 1950s. We no longer saw the Archambault Report and its outcome as the pinnacle of modern penal practice. So this book is not just "contribution history," wherein the ideas and exploits of marginalized groups are added to the existing historical narrative without altering it. Writing a history from below – employing the practices of social and feminist historians – broadens the narrative. Including prisoners' voices in a history of prisons seems so commonsensical that it should need no explanation. But criminology has a history of objectifying and silencing the subjects of its inquiry. As Richards and colleagues have observed, "much of the published work on correctional facilities reflected the ideas of prison administrators and largely ignored what convicts knew about the day-to-day realities of confinement."[5] The penal press and prisoners' writing recast the narrative and influenced the direction of our analysis. Prisoners see things that others do not, and see them from a perspective that is often absent from histories of the prison system. Yet they were not simply recording events. Prisoner-generated documents show that convicts were not just passive recipients of reform: they were active agents who shaped the prison system and the reform interventions introduced during the period under study. Convicts met with commissioners, participated in the training of correctional staff, organized sports, recreation, leisure, and hobbycraft activities for themselves, influenced policy through inmate committees, and through their resistance sometimes set the agenda at warden's conferences. Furthermore, prisoners' writing tells us not only about prison but about the prisoners themselves. In the pages of the penal press, they shared their ideals and aspirations, engaged with prisoners at other institutions, and spoke of events in the outside world. Once introduced to these writers, we could never see them, or prisons, the same way again.

Disruptive Prisoners is a social history of federal prisons in Canada. Charles Tilly has written that social history involves two processes: reconstitution and connection. We have attempted to reconstitute the history of Canada's federal prison system in the mid-twentieth century through a process of collective biography – one involving prisoners, administrators, prison reformers, and politicians. In part, our aim has been "to reconstitute a round of life as people lived it."[6] But to paraphrase Tilly, if we focused solely on reconstructing the daily experiences of ordinary prisoners, we would be missing the opportunity to add to historical debates. We would be producing "many bright fragments of dubious worth and comparability."[7] So we considered it crucial "to connect [prisoners' lives] on the small scale with large social structures and processes."[8] In this book, we hope to connect the personal with the political, both to challenge what has been seen as historically important and to upset the dominant tropes in criminology and history.

The task we set ourselves required us to explore a wide range of primary and secondary sources. Some of these were obvious, including documents produced by government investigations and Royal Commissions, annual departmental reports, and the parliamentary record. But there were also bureaucratic records that shed light on the administrative minutiae of the prison system. These included inspectors' reports, accountants' records, shop instructors' reports, correspondence between colleagues, and reports to superiors. In addition, there were unexpected surprises within the archival files. Among these were large numbers of petitions from social reform groups; letters from family members; inquiries from interested members of the public; newspaper clippings related to key developments; and handwritten notes scribbled into the margins of official documents that revealed the inner workings of the bureaucracy.

Perhaps the biggest surprise during this research project was being contacted by France Dion, the wife of André Dion, founding editor of *Pen-O-Rama*, one of the earliest Canadian penal publications. She had encountered the penal press website and was looking for copies of André's articles and editorials from the early 1950s, to help him write his memoir. André, now in his nineties, viewed his contribution to the penal press as an important part of his personal story. He agreed to meet with Bob and Melissa to share his knowledge of the founding and early history of the penal press in Canada. He died a few months after the meeting. Our two-day interview expanded our understanding of the daily lives of prisoners at Saint-Vincent-de-Paul Penitentiary and gave us insights into the logistical and social intricacies of publishing behind bars. André's story complemented extant prisoner autobiographies, including accounts published by Oswald Withrow, Frank Anderson, and Frank Howard, and prisoner testimony derived from court cases and the penal press.

Of course, none of these individuals existed in a social vacuum. We needed to connect their experiences to the period's zeitgeist. Previous criminological and historical analyses – both contemporaneous works by prison reformers and later analyses produced by academics – helped us understand the social and political context of prison reform; they also illuminated the contemporary analytic frames that shaped the narratives. For example, the works of early twentieth-century prison reformers paint a picture of uneven progress in the Canadian prison system during the 1920s, a time when well-meaning officials with humane and thoughtful plans were stifled by a lack of funding and resources. From their perspective, Canada's prisons were progressing from savagery to civilized conditions, largely due to the wisdom and exertions of great and determined men and women. As should be evident, such works are of great value because they reveal a particular understanding of penology, practice, and achievement; their value as evidential source material is less certain. Recent analyses by historians and sociologists in Canada, the United States, Britain, and Europe offer a more complicated account of prison reform, one that is rife with disagreement among scholars about its extent, purpose, and significance.[9] In sum, in criminologist Bob Gaucher's assessment, the emergent literature challenges us to explore "the tensions between proposed changes, perceived changes, actual changes, and the results of changes."[10]

Study Parameters and Limitations

We felt overwhelmed by the sheer volume of material at our disposal. With more than 10,000 pages of archival materials and more than 2,400 penal newsletters, we needed to establish some working parameters. We had started out with the intention of studying the origins of the penal press. Once we began investigating, however, we became interested in the reforms that made the penal press possible and realized that the press offered both a unique analytic point of entry on the reform program and a visible manifestation of the New Deal for Prisoners. The New Deal began with the release of the *Royal Commission Report on Penal Reform in Canada* (the Archambault Report) in 1938. It was intended to shift the focus within the prison system from punishment to reformation. To accomplish this transformation, changes were proposed at every level of the penitentiary system. The Archambault Report recommended changes to crime prevention techniques, sentencing, conditional release, classification and segregation[11] practices, and vocational and educational programming, as well as improved prison labour standards, the expansion of recreation and leisure opportunities, improved medical services, increased staff training, the reorganization of the administrative bureaucracy, and the improvement of facilities. Choosing a date for the origin of the New Deal was easy. Defining its end was more of a challenge. When does one era of reform end and another begin? Was the next committee on corrections the start of a new era or an extension of the preceding one? In deciding how to bracket our work, we chose to let the politicians, the prisoners, and the Penitentiary Service do it for us. A new Conservative government took office in 1957 and by 1960 had revised the Penitentiary Act. This in and of itself was insufficient to justify an end point. Here, we relied on the prisoners themselves to ground our periodization. In their writing, prisoners consistently conceived of the New Deal as relating to two figures: Deputy Commissioner Joseph McCulley and Commissioner Ralph Gibson – even calling it the McCulley–Gibson Plan.[12] By 1960 both men had left the Penitentiary Service, and there are indications that the tenor of operations shifted under new leadership. That summer saw the tabling of the report of the MacLeod Committee, which had been appointed to "suggest the appropriate restructuring of the entire Canadian penitentiary system, including policy on parole."[13] The committee called for a new set of "large-scale reforms," and a few months later, Chairman Allen J. MacLeod was appointed commissioner, with a mandate to implement his own recommendations.[14] Years later, the MacGuigan Commission looked back on the shift his appointment signalled: "He made it clear that drastic changes would be coming ... He warned those who could not accept his program of justice for all inmates within the prison to look elsewhere for employment."[15]

In addition, several practical considerations limited the scope of our inquiry. The paucity of provincial and French-language publications in the penal press collection led us to utilize primarily English source material from federal penitentiaries. While this permits us to cover the New Deal, which was a federal program, quite well, it hinders our inclusion of the experiences of francophone prisoners. Also, we don't have enough of the voices of female prisoners to explore their experience of the reforms. While there was a "Feminine Features" column in Kingston Penitentiary's penal press magazine, *Tele-Scope*, and the editorial board included members from the women's prison, their contribution to the publications during this era was limited by contemporary gender roles.[16] "Feminine Features" was often granted the same column space, if not less, than was dedicated to pictures of attractive female visitors.[17]

Organization of This Book

With our source materials in hand, and our decisions having been made regarding the approach and scope of the study, we decided to divide the book into two sections. Part I, "Disrupting the Old Order," covers the origins and context of the New Deal reforms. Chapter 1 opens with a riot in 1932, when prisoners at Kingston Penitentiary organized a protest that spiralled out of control. Their actions – and those of the prisoners who rioted elsewhere across the country – drew attention over the following months to conditions throughout the penitentiary system. Chapter 2 explores the resulting investigation. The Royal Commission to Investigate the Penal System of Canada (Archambault Commission), often characterized as a "watershed report,"[18] supported prisoners' accounts of penal conditions and recommended sweeping changes to the system. The report was well-received by the media and the public, and the government came under immediate pressure to implement its recommendations. However, when the Second World War broke out in 1939, government leaders indicated that reforms would have to wait. Minister of Justice Ernest Lapointe announced the indefinite postponement of both the enabling legislation and the appointment of a three-man commission to oversee reforms. The dominant narrative since that time has been one of the war as interlude.

Some scholars have suggested that the war did in fact delay reforms.[19] Yet substantial progress was made between 1939 and 1945, though the public was largely unaware of the penitentiary service's new initiatives. This ignorance, coupled with a wartime panic over juvenile delinquency, motivated social reformers to intensify their campaign to implement the Archambault Report's recommendations. In 1946, Ralph Gibson was appointed Commissioner of Penitentiaries and tasked with developing an implementation strategy. In the years that followed, Gibson and his subordinates, operating on the philosophy that "prisoners are people," would develop a plan of action that would become widely known as "the New Deal" for prisoners.[20]

The implementation of that program – the New Deal – is the subject of Part II of this book – "Disruptive Influences." We begin with the penal press, which was one of the earliest and most visible parts of the New Deal initiatives. Chapter 3 traces the emergence of the press and provides the reader with a sense of how the prisoners organized, planned, and managed the production of the newsletters. The chapter continues by looking at the difficulties of running a free press in a carceral space. Ultimately, we understand the penal press not only as a manifestation of the New Deal but also as a record of its progress. Viewed this way, the New Deal surveilled itself. There are, in the penal press, both indicators and contra-indicators of change. Chapter 4 positions the penal press against other sources to examine the daily lives of prisoners in federal institutions during the 1950s. In this way, a complicated image of prison life emerges. Many new privileges and freedoms are evident. The New

Deal saw the introduction of an improved prisoner pay structure, the inauguration of canteens, new educational and vocational training opportunities, and greater access to sports, leisure, and entertainment activities. But the same documents also reveal continuities. Old problems – like overcrowding – persisted. The lack of sufficient funding and the primacy accorded security undercut the humanitarian impulse. Furthermore, the public and some politicians were slow to embrace the reform program, clinging to older punitive ideals and criticizing the changes that staff and prisoners were making within the penitentiaries. The chapter concludes by examining how, in many ways, the nature of confinement, control, and discipline remained constant despite the New Deal.

No wonder, then, that prisoners were preoccupied with getting out of prison. Propelled by the overcrowding issue, the government was considering ways to release prisoners earlier. Archambault had emphasized the importance of parole, both to encourage prisoners to comply with programming and to ease their transition back into the community. In 1953, the Fauteux Committee was appointed to investigate what would become known as conditional release. Throughout this period, prisoners had uneven access to various mechanisms of early release (ticket-of-leave, "good time," the Royal Prerogative of Mercy, and amnesty); the committee was tasked with devising a more logical and consistent parole process. Chapter 5 argues that though the Fauteux Committee's task emerged from the New Deal, its recommendations reflected a different set of priorities. Progress appeared to be uneven.

In Chapter 6, our focus returns to the penal press. We examine conflicts between administrators and editorial staff over the limits of reform, continuities in the conditions of incarceration, and incidences of prisoner resistance. The Penitentiary Service management was determined to present an image of progressive prison reform to the public. Yet in the pages of the penal press, prisoners advanced their own analyses of conditions and policies and criticized the actions of their keepers, including those at the highest levels of the administrative hierarchy. They also battled over the analysis and implications of key events, including a 1954 riot at Kingston Penitentiary. This led to a struggle over what could – and could not – be published in prison magazines. These censorship struggles reveal prisoners using the penal press as a tool of resistance – and administrators grappling with how to exert control while maintaining an image of enlightenment and benevolence and selling it to the public. This struggle was never completely resolved. It dispirited editors, robbed the press of much of its vitality, and contributed to prisoners' loss of faith in the New Deal.

In our conclusion, we draw on the extant scholarly literature to contextualize our findings. Based on the work of Stanley Cohen, Thomas Mathiesen, and Michel Foucault, we consider whether the New Deal should be viewed as uneven progress, a failed reform program, or a means of achieving something other than its stated objectives. Having deprioritized the administrative history, we conclude that the New Deal reform project cannot be seen simply as progressive. The polyvocal analysis offered in this book points to a more complicated narrative – one in which prisoners played an active role, reforms both succeeded and failed, and the dominant story was disrupted.

PART I

Disrupting the Old Order

1 Riots and Reform: Political Action and the Making of the Archambault Report

On 21 May 1927, Oswald Withrow entered the North Gate of Kingston Penitentiary. He was greeted by a clerk, who recorded his vitals into a file. From there, he was photographed and had his head and face shorn prior to being immersed in a Lysol bath. He was given a prisoner's uniform and fingerprinted before the rules and regulations of the penitentiary were read to him. He may have had questions about these, but he did not ask them, since it was made clear to him that prisoners were to exist in silence. He was then taken to his 5.5 by 10 foot cell, where he first laid eyes on his cot, thin pillow, toilet, cold-water sink (which dispensed non-potable water), shelf, and folding chair. A prison cell was to be his home for the next two and a half years.

Throughout those years, Withrow would retrieve his breakfast (dry bread and tea) and return to his cell to consume it. He would rise on Sunday mornings to go to the chapel for religious service. On the other days he would labour within the prison walls, with a break to retrieve lunch at 11:30 a.m. Following the afternoon's labour, he would be allowed fifteen minutes in the yard before collecting his evening meal tray and returning to his cell, where he would spend the next fifteen hours in silence. Until 9 p.m., Withrow was "free to pace and think, think and pace," until the lights were turned out and he was required to be in his cot, head closest to the bars, until the morning bell rang at 7 a.m.[1]

Given one word to describe his experience as a prisoner in Kingston Penitentiary, Withrow chose "Terror."[2] So when years after his release, he heard that the prisoners had rioted, he was not surprised.

"The wonder is," he wrote, "that it [the riot] was delayed so long."[3]

Withrow's account of his time at Kingston Penitentiary provides a window into prison conditions in the early twentieth century. Using his ethnographic account, government inquiries, prison reformers' publications, superintendent's reports, the parliamentary record, and press coverage, this chapter considers the opaqueness of information during the 1920s and early 1930s. During that era, the Superintendent of Penitentiaries and allied social justice reformers trumpeted the progress made toward a more humane prison system. Reformers relied largely on the official administrative version of events. How could they, and the general public, know what was really happening in the prisons? This chapter considers this question and the ways in which the incarcerated resisted in order to raise awareness of their actual living conditions. Also considered are the state's responses to those efforts, which prepared the ground for reform in the ensuing decades.

The Protest

It was supposed to be a peaceful demonstration.[4] On 17 October 1932, prisoners working in the shops at Kingston Penitentiary went on strike. Their demands were modest: cigarette papers and more recreation time.[5] Yet if these proximate causes appeared simple on the surface, the origins of the disturbance were rooted much deeper in the fabric of prison life. Thomas Mathiesen writes that "seen from the inside, [changes in conditions] which appear small from the outside are often magnified or enlarged and in part receive vital significance."[6] The 1932 strike at Kingston Penitentiary and the riot that followed it were not isolated incidents. Despite the silent system then in force in Canada's federal prisons, the convicts at Kingston had been communicating with one another and organizing an underground resistance for years. The prisoners were critical of prison conditions and had launched protests on more than one occasion.[7] They took great risks to do so.

In the early twentieth century, Canada's penitentiary regulations prohibited prisoners from speaking to anyone "except from necessity or with respect to the work at which [they were] employed."[8] Convicts were also forbidden to write to one another and to gather out of the sight or hearing of officers.[9] Multiple sources indicate that the enforcement of these rules was intermittent and arbitrary and that penalties were unpredictable.[10] A government investigation of the federal penitentiary system in 1921 (hereafter the Biggar, Nickle, and Draper Report) found that the enforcement of the prison regulations varied by institution. Much depended "upon the personality of the warden and the spirit he instils into his staff." The investigators added sardonically that at some institutions enforcement occurred "according to the whim or the condition of the digestion of individual officers."[11] Kingston Penitentiary was one of these.[12] Oswald Withrow recounted that hushed conversations were commonplace in the change rooms and after religious services, but that the guards would subsequently charge prisoners at random for breaking the rule of silence.[13] As a result, a prisoner caught speaking might face no consequences, or he might be brought before the Warden's Court, which was held at noon each day. There the warden would impose penalties ranging from the loss of government-issued tobacco rations to forfeiture of remission (time deducted from the prisoner's sentence for good behaviour), weeks of solitary confinement, and beatings with a paddle specially designed to inflict maximum pain.[14] A prisoner who tried to explain himself almost never succeeded and usually drew a stiffer penalty. It was foolhardy to attempt a defence. Incarcerated men felt the injustice keenly.[15]

Despite the risk and uncertainty, prisoners managed to maintain lines of communication. Even when the prison seemed calm, prisoners exchanged ideas and expressed grievances among themselves. As convict-editor John Brown would explain many years later in the Kingston prison magazine, *Tele-Scope*, by the early 1930s, prison writers "inveighed against the wanton abuses of power, not openly of course, but secretly, by means of crude hand-printed pamphlets denouncing existing conditions and practices, and drawing unfavourable parallels with American penitentiaries, idealized for purposes of propaganda. The pamphlets exhorted their readers to rebel, strike off their chains, and outlined how an effective riot could be carried out."[16]

In July 1932, a prison inspector discovered one of these pamphlets. Its subjects were prison management and prison reform; its authorship and origin were unknown. The pamphlet was number 27 in a series. Neither the inspector nor the warden deemed the discovery worthy of any special action.[17] Perhaps they felt – given the absence of any identifying characteristics – that little could be done. Or – perhaps – it was an unremarkable discovery. There is evidence that prisoners had been circulating messages at least as far back as 1924, and similar practices have been documented in the United States and Great Britain.[18]

Less often, when conditions became intolerable, prisoners organized and protested. In 1927 at Kingston Penitentiary, prisoners rioted to protest the mistreatment of a convict and the quality of the food. Many of those who participated were severely punished. But the rioters did achieve one of their goals: a few months later, the kitchen steward was replaced and the quality of food improved notably.[19] Prisoners and prison administrators alike viewed these periodic outbursts at the prisons as visible manifestations of an ongoing resistance movement. Superintendent D.M. Ormond of the Penitentiary Service and former prisoner Oswald Withrow both drew a connection between the protests of 1927 and 1932 at Kingston Penitentiary.[20] In his report on the 1932 riot, Ormond wrote that the prisoners had been organizing for ten years and perfecting their organizational skills in a conspiracy to overthrow the prison administration.[21] Perhaps Ormond was straining a point for political purposes and exaggerating the preparations for, and intent of, the protest, but even if he was, there was a grain of truth in his analysis. Prisoners had prepared the ground for the protest.

The arrival of several members of the "Toronto Eight" at the prison in 1932 gave the convict resistance a symbol – and a potential leader – to rally around. In 1931, eight officers of the Communist Party of Canada (CPC) were charged with belonging to an illegal organization under Section 98 of the *Criminal Code*, which banned organizations that advocated the use of force to achieve political, industrial, or economic change.[22] All of the CPC officers were convicted and sent to prison. Among them was CPC Secretary Tim Buck.[23] Soon after he arrived at Kingston in February 1932, prisoners working in the laundry began to pin notes outlining their grievances into Buck's clean clothing.[24] Perhaps these prisoners hoped to access the extensive and largely clandestine support network (among both labour militants and political radicals) behind Buck and the Communist Party leadership. Buck was hesitant to be seen as a spokesman for the convicts. Yet he compiled a list of demands for them and advised that they would have to make prison conditions known to the public in order to bring about change.[25] "I am not exaggerating," he wrote, "when I say that in about three weeks, the whole institution was literally pulsating."[26]

While Buck was a reluctant leader, the CPC's presence offered prisoners a convenient ideology around which to structure and legitimate their resistance. One day, while working in the blacksmith's shop, a prisoner passed Buck a note:

> I heard about your answer on the question of reforms in this joint, but I and several others want to know about communism. I, personally, have heard about it, and even heard about Karl Marx, but we want to know what it is, what makes people like you take a chance on such a racket. Would you be willing to write out an explanation of what communism is, how it's organized, and what you hope to do?[27]

In response, Buck wrote a series of letters explaining communism. Prisoners reproduced these and circulated them in secret.[28] John Brown argued that "without such propaganda to shock the feelers rather than the thinkers into action, the riot of 1932 would probably never have occurred."[29] Perhaps inspired by Buck's advice and by a newfound ideology of resistance, convicts began appearing in the Warden's Court, requesting that they be permitted to present their demands to the government. The prison administration took the situation seriously. Superintendent Ormond visited the prison in an effort to discover the ringleaders of the reform movement. According to Buck, he spoke to the wrong people.[30] Meanwhile, the real leaders of the reform movement – among them a prisoner named Bob McRae – began to view a strike as a means of forcing a public investigation.[31]

On 17 October 1932, the prisoners decided to act. Some had played significant roles in the 1927 protest, which achieved a small measure of success.[32] Others had been emboldened by a small protest four days earlier, when convicts in one of Kingston's stone sheds refused to work, demanding that an abusive guard be replaced. Acting Warden Gilbert Smith had agreed to their demand.[33] Inspired by that victory, prisoners began to open new lines of communication. Guards reported that prisoners could be heard tapping out coded messages on the bars of the shops and the cell blocks; this alerted the staff to the possibility of further trouble. The Chief Keeper received several warnings of the impending strike, but he chose not to pass this information on to Acting Warden Smith.[34]

When the strike began at 2:30 p.m., a guard immediately looked to Tim Buck for an explanation. Buck was reluctant to speak for the prisoners and worried that he might be seen as a leader of the insurrection:

Mr. Whitehead came over to me, "What's it all about, Tim?"

"Well, you can see as well as I can. The motors have stopped and apparently, the boys have decided not to work."

"What for?"

"Nobody has said it to me, but I can tell you exactly what it is. They want a public investigation. They want changes in this joint, and they know of no other way to force it."

"You don't know anything about it?"

"Of course, I do. I know as much as the rest of them. The only thing is I think there could have been a better way of forcing the issue than this."

"How?"

"Now look, Mr. Whitehead, you're an officer here. Don't try to involve me, either to corrupt you, to subvert you, or to tell you things which you would be able to repeat, and produce more material for charges against me."[35]

While that conversation was taking place, prison staff began to lock the striking prisoners into the shops, "fastening the steel shutters over our windows and over our doorways."[36] A few minutes later, convict Bob McRae cut the lock from the machine shop door with an acetylene torch.[37] These convicts fanned out and proceeded to free prisoners locked in the other shops and in the stone shed.[38] At least 250 prisoners, half of whom were armed with tools and improvised weapons, gathered together in the shop dome.[39] More continued to arrive as the events unfolded.[40] Yet it seems that the prison authorities perceived no threat of violence. Officers mingled in the shop dome, conversing with the convicts. Acting Warden Smith also entered the area with the intention of defusing the situation. The lead prisoners informed Smith of their demands – for cigarette papers and more recreation time. When other prisoners attempted to add to the list of demands, the leaders reiterated there were only two.[41]

The talks may have been a stalling tactic, given that Smith had already sent for a nearby militia unit. Fifteen minutes later, one hundred militiamen arrived and tensions escalated. The soldiers surrounded the shop dome, and according to Chadwick Marr, who wrote a thesis on riots at Kingston Penitentiary, "this was when the protest turned into a riot."[42] Agitated prisoners began to barricade the doors; some threatened revenge against the staff if any prisoner was injured.[43] To avoid a siege and gain access to the dome, guards backed a truck loaded with stone through the doors. Soldiers and guards clambered through the wreckage. Shots were fired. Most of the prisoners escaped the dome and fled to the shops, where they were ultimately rounded up by armed officers and returned to their cell blocks. A smaller group, after taking Acting Warden Smith and several penitentiary officers as hostages, barricaded themselves inside the mailbag shop, and a tense stand-off ensued.[44] According to Superintendent Ormond, Smith ended the confrontation by promising that no prisoner "would be punished until after he had a proper trial."[45] The prisoners accepted his promise and returned to their cells. At this point, the protest might have ended.

Accounts of the following days differ. Superintendent Ormond recounted that he arrived in the afternoon of 18 October and found the prison officials "dazed" and "nervous."[46] In the meantime, the prisoners had appointed delegates for every shop, hoping to present their grievances to Ormond through those representatives.[47] Ormond, who believed that the prisoners were being directed by communist leaders,[48] replied that "no convict delegates would be recognized and such a system would not be tolerated within the Penitentiary."[49] However, while he was unwilling to meet the representatives of convict groups, he *was* willing to meet with individual prisoners to hear personal grievances. When some prisoners agreed to meet with him on this basis, Ormond recounted, "they were jeered at and threatened by other convicts and from that cause refused to come before me."[50] Ultimately, three convicts did meet with Ormond, and the evidence suggests that they were spokesmen approved by the prisoners. To the superintendent, "it was immediately evident that they were giving their complaints in a pre-arranged manner."[51] In addition to the issues that triggered the protest, they relayed prisoners' dissatisfaction with sanitary conditions, meals, letter-writing and visitation, the censorship of magazines, corporal punishment, guard brutality, and the absence of a reform program in the penitentiary.[52] One prisoner emphasized that these were general grievances and that the immediate demands of the protesters included only cigarette papers and recreation. Another made sure that Ormond understood the importance of the promise that no prisoner would be punished without a fair trial. According to Ormond, the prisoners disagreed as to whether the trials should be held in the civil courts or in the Warden's Court.[53]

All prisoners were sent back to work on 19 October. When a shop instructor reported that the prisoners were difficult to control, ignoring orders and uttering threats, the superintendent ordered a general lock-down. The prisoners remained confined to the cell blocks throughout the remainder of that day and for much of the next.[54] The confinement added to their general dissatisfaction. They viewed the extended confinement as an unwarranted punishment and as a breach of the promise that there would be no punishment without a trial.[55] There may have been even greater punishments than this. Tim Buck alleged in his memoir that prisoners were taken from their cells on the morning of 19 October and paddled.[56] If that punishment did take place, it is not recorded in any official accounts.[57] The prisoners again demanded that Ormond meet with an assembly of their delegates. He refused.[58]

During the afternoon of 20 October, prisoners in the main cell block broke out of their cells. Ormond wrote that they accomplished this using "two planks 12 feet long, 10 inches wide and 2 inches thick [to] ... knock off the cell gate levers and pry out the vertical locking bars."[59] How and by whom this was accomplished is left unexplained in the report.[60] Guards locked the main doors to the cell block to contain the prisoners. Many destroyed the beds, tables, and plumbing fixtures in their cells. Superintendent Ormond again called the militia, who took up positions outside the penitentiary buildings. Meanwhile, reports circulated among penitentiary staff that prisoners were attempting to dig through the brick cell walls and might escape through the ducts. Guards were ordered to enter the ductworks and instructed to fire warning shots through the peepholes into the cells if they found prisoners attempting to dig through walls.[61] That afternoon and evening, guards also began to fire their rifles at the prison's outside walls and windows, with the intention, according to a subsequent penitentiary service investigation, of quelling disturbances.[62] While penitentiary service officials claimed that the guards had intended to fire into the ceilings of the prisoners' cells, a prisoner was wounded and left bleeding in his cell for twenty-two hours.[63] The official report notwithstanding, it is clear that guards also fired into cells in blocks where no rebellion had occurred.[64] At dusk, several shots were fired through the window of Tim Buck's cell, which, because of his political stature and left-wing allies, contributed to demands for an investigation into the riot.[65] The riot petered out around midnight.[66] Exhaustion, hunger, conditions in the damaged cell blocks, and the perceived futility of further agitation undoubtedly combined to render prisoners compliant. Tim Buck and the CPC leaders, whom the penitentiary service suspected of instigating the protest, were transferred to dark cells in the Prison of Isolation (also known as the "East Block") – a section of the prison where prisoners were housed in solitary confinement.[67]

Causes of the Riot

Scholars have advanced a number of general theories to explain what causes prison riots. Among the causes internal to prisons are poor conditions, the accumulation of grievances, a single dramatic spark, the reversal of reforms, changes in prison routines and prison administration, and staffing and administrative failures.[68] There are also external factors. For example, high rates of unemployment can contribute to higher rates of incarceration, triggering overcrowding and leading to deteriorating conditions. The zeitgeist may also stimulate unrest; a general social and political climate critical of social conditions or government authorities may inspire prisoners and lead them to expect sympathy and support for change. Finally, riots at other institutions may have an impact, in that prison riots tend to occur in "waves" or "clusters."[69]

Regarding the Kingston riot of October 1932, a primary motive was to bring prison conditions into the public eye and thereby provoke reforms. The prisoners had reason to expect a degree of public sympathy. By 1932, public confidence in the government of R.B. Bennett and the liberal capitalist order had been shattered. As the country neared the depths of the Great Depression, unemployment and poverty rose to record levels. The widespread and severe human costs of that depression and the obvious dysfunction of the capitalist economy led many to question economic, political, and social values. Across the country,

Canadians were looking for answers and seeking new solutions. On the prairies, the region hardest hit by the economic collapse and the drought, two new political parties advocating radical new policies (the Co-operative Commonwealth Federation and Social Credit) had emerged. Meanwhile, the Communist Party of Canada was experiencing a surge in popularity, especially among the unemployed, relief camp workers, and the Western labour movement.[70] Together, the CCF and CPC gave the political left a coherent voice and inspired new levels of social criticism.

Chadwick Marr has written that "prisons are products of the greater society in which they exist and, as such, they too feel the impact of social upheaval and political unrest."[71] It appears that the 1932 Kingston riot was in part the result of prison conditions and in part the product of a political moment. The social conditions and political developments of the 1930s have been explored in detail elsewhere; prison conditions, by contrast, are less well understood and were obscured in the reports of administrators and prison reformers. Drawing on prisoner testimony and two government investigations of the prison system, in this section we provide the reader with a more complete description of daily life at Kingston Penitentiary during the early twentieth century. In doing so, we hope to contextualize prisoners' motives for resistance and set the stage for a critical re-examination of the published accounts of government officials and prison reform advocates.

This section relies heavily on an exhaustive memoir of prison life. Oswald Withrow's *Shackling the Transgressor: An Indictment of the Canadian Penal System* is one of the most comprehensive first-hand accounts of prison life in early twentieth-century Canada.[72] The book, which began as a series of articles written for the *Globe* newspaper, was a politically motivated exposé of the author's years of incarceration at Kingston Penitentiary. Withrow was a well-educated man, and his meticulous and wide-ranging account of prison life bears the marks of a trained observer who is sensitive to detail and nuance. Withrow, a physician as well as a leader in the Ontario birth control movement, had been convicted in 1927 on charges of manslaughter following the death of patient on whom he had performed an abortion.[73] He entered prison later that year and was released in 1929.[74]

Withrow's account is corroborated by two previous government investigations into the prison system. In 1913, the minister of justice appointed a Royal Commission (hereafter Macdonnell Commission) to investigate charges of mismanagement and corruption at Kingston Penitentiary and to inquire into the methods of prisoner reformation employed at the penitentiary.[75] Seven years later, in the context of two prisoner mutinies at Kingston Penitentiary, the minister launched a second investigation. The committee (the previously referenced Biggar, Nickle, and Draper committee) investigated penitentiary operations and made recommendations to revise the penitentiary regulations and the Penitentiary Act.[76] Again, the government mandate made special reference to the reformation of prisoners.

Context of Resistance

The Macdonnell Commission and the Biggar, Nickle, and Draper Committee reported evidence of serious problems within the penitentiaries. Both had consulted with American prison officials and with representatives of various international prison organizations and their reports found Canada's prisons wanting in comparison.[77] Many of the changes they advocated echoed the reforms put in place at the Elmira Reformatory in New York and at other American institutions during the late nineteenth and early twentieth centuries.[78] The Macdonnell Commission was grimly blunt in its assessment of Canadian penitentiaries: "If the punishment of the offender is the only object society should have in view, the Penitentiaries of Canada fully meet the requirements."[79] Biggar, Nickle, and Draper took a more optimistic tone. As they explained in their introduction, they hoped to create a penal system in which "the principle administrative ideas will not be those of repression and restriction, but rather those of development and cure."[80] Regardless of tone, both investigations advocated a shift from punitive to reformative measures, and together, they laid out a blueprint for change.

Both reports recommended improvements in how prisoners were treated and in their living conditions. The Macdonnell Commission emphasized that prisoners had "certain rights," including the right to sanitary living conditions, education, work, moral training, and discipline.[81] They also argued for an end to the unnecessary humiliation of prisoners, singling out the close cropping of prisoners' hair and the provision of brightly checkered uniforms as practices to be discontinued.[82] Biggar, Nickle, and Draper argued for "the extension to the convicts of all privileges not inconsistent with the restriction of their liberty of movement and association." Elsewhere they termed many of these privileges "convict's rights," frequently using the words "privileges" and "rights" interchangeably.[83] Among other things, their 1921 report advocated improved food and medical services, additional recreational opportunities, more frequent letter-writing and visits, improvements to prison libraries, the introduction of newspapers, and an end to the rule of silence.[84] This would not be the last investigation to recommend these changes.

Read together, Withrow's book and the government inquiries of 1914 and 1921 reveal a great deal about prison conditions, routines, and programs in the early twentieth century. Prisoners were being housed individually in tiny, dingy, dimly lit cells. Withrow wrote: "The only light in my cell came from an electric bulb screwed into a socket in the roof ten or twelve feet from my table. Its strength was only ten watts. Could anyone see well enough with this amount of illumination?"[85] Prisoners who wanted to better themselves through education or private study would strain to read the materials in these dark conditions.

Overcrowding was also a major problem. Between 1923 and 1933, prison populations across the country had risen by 60 per cent.[86] At Kingston Penitentiary, the official capacity was 725, but by 1933 the prison housed more than 900 convicts.[87] At the Prison of Isolation, wooden partitions had been installed in the larger cells so that each could house two prisoners. This makeshift solution meant that only half the cells had plumbing; the other cells were provided with buckets. During periods of extreme overcrowding, Withrow wrote, "one hundred night pails come into commission with the resultant odours and fetidness of the atmosphere. The stench from the night pails might well challenge the sensitiveness of the citizens of Canada."[88] When the numbers swelled beyond even the expanded capacity of the divided cells, prisoners slept in the corridors.[89]

Withrow and both government investigations emphasized the monotony of prison life.[90] Prisoners' movements were tightly regulated according to routines that were repeated day after day, week after week, year after year. "One day is very like another," Withrow wrote. "It is a truism to say that prison life in Kingston Penitentiary is deadly dull and monotonous. The gruelling grind slowly wears away the soul of a man until, if he remain long enough, there is little left."[91] Prisoners left their cells to pick up meals, work, and attend school or religious services, and on very rare occasions, for concerts.[92] They worked in near silence, ate their bland, steam-cooked meals alone, and spent at least sixteen hours each day confined to their cells.[93] Sitting alone in his cell, Withrow "could hear the steady contact of heavy boots with the hard floors. Three paces up, three paces down: so the monotonous movement went on."[94]

Contact with family and friends offered occasional breaks in the monotony. Those prisoners in good standing were entitled to write one or two one-page letters per month. They could also receive letters from home and friends, subject to the approval of censors. Picture postcards, however, were considered transgressive. They were confiscated, and a prisoner was not notified of their existence until his release. The impact of this on the prisoner could be dire:

> Some years ago there was an inmate who had not heard from his wife and family for more than two years. He felt sure they had forgotten him, were estranged from him, had thrown him over. The bitterness engendered by his prison experience was enhanced by this supposed treatment by those he loved. On the day of his release several picture postcards were given him. These had been coming through the years conveying, as best they knew how, the love and caresses of his wife and little ones. He cursed, openly and vehemently.[95]

Relatives and friends could visit every second month.[96] These visits, when they occurred, took place with convict and visitor sitting behind wire screens, separated by a guard who heard – and in effect, limited – all that was said between them. Withrow wryly captured the gulf between the parties: "Relative – wire – censor – wire – convict."[97]

Other opportunities for socialization were limited. In 1913, the Macdonnell Commission reported absolute silence in Kingston Penitientary's shops and cell blocks and worried that "silence and solitude must breed moroseness and resentfulness."[98] While the rule of silence remained on the books, its observance changed in subsequent years, though the reason for the change is unclear. In 1921, Biggar, Nickle, and Draper observed that "in no penitentiary is the rule as to silence rigidly observed," and by Withrow's day, prisoners regularly engaged in low conversations, which he described as "a subdued buzz or hum, as from a beehive on a serene summer day."[99] Enforcement of the rule was unpredictable and varied widely among facilities. Biggar, Nickle, and Draper reported that in some institutions the rule was applied at the whim of individual officers, a practice Withrow's account confirms.[100] "The rule of absolute silence was broken everywhere at all times. But, and here is the cruelty of it, the rule was there, distinct and definite, and if one of the guards 'had it in' for a man, he might and did 'write him up' for punishment whenever it pleased him."[101] Withrow speculated that a kind of quota system was in operation: "Somebody had to be in the warden's court for punishment every day," he opined, so the guards wrote up large numbers of unsuspecting prisoners at opportune moments (in the change rooms or at church, for example), and as many as sixty prisoners at a time might find themselves before the Warden's Court.[102]

At most times, prisoners functioned in isolation. Except for the chapel, the change room, and the workshops, there were few reasons for a

Image 1.1. Photo of the visiting cages at Kingston Penitentiary. Prisoners sat on one side of the mesh and visitors on the other. *Tele-Scope*, August 1959, Gaucher/Munn penal press collection.

prisoner to leave his cell. Kingston Penitentiary had no common dining facilities, the library was a storage facility rather than a reading room, and there were few spaces in the school program. Opportunities to gather for entertainment were rare:[103] Withrow noted that in his two and a half years of incarceration, he saw only three performances.[104] Notably, even in these cases, the monotony was not always broken. For example, prisoners were given the exact same Christmas concert year after year. Withrow notes that he initially enjoyed the performance, but adds that near him sat "men who had been dragged to the warden's concert the year before and the year before that. They told me what was coming next. They remembered. They were correct every time. The same company, the same programme down to the minutest detail. Think of it! It was part of the punishment."[105]

As a doctor, Withrow devoted special attention to sanitation, hygiene, and health care at Kingston Penitentiary.[106] During his incarceration, the prison's water purification system broke down. A slow response – owing to two government departments disclaiming responsibility and the prison doctor's misdiagnosis of the resultant illness – contributed to a minor outbreak of typhus.[107] Inadequate concern for public health was the norm. Withrow, who worked in the prison hospital for part of his stay, reported that 12 per cent of the prisoners were syphilitic, that few were cured, and that no precautions were taken to prevent the spread of the disease. Infected prisoners worked in the kitchen, preparing and serving food; the razors used to shave prisoners were neither changed nor sterilized; and the utensils and clothing of the sick and healthy were interchanged freely.[108] Medical and psychiatric care was also inadequate. The warden boasted to visitors of new hospital equipment and free dental care, yet patients received treatment only in the most pressing cases.[109] Moreover, Withrow recounted several patients who clearly had mental problems (often compounded by physical illness or disability) and who were tormented by guards, repeatedly paddled, or sentenced to solitary confinement.[110] Based on his observations, he concluded "that prevention is not desired … Mentally sick men were not studied or considered. They were brutally punished."[111] Withrow himself was much more fortunate. When he showed signs of illness, his family and friends agitated for his early release, after which a tumour on his thyroid was removed.[112]

As the preceding discussion of the rule of silence makes clear, prisoners could count on fairness and equity neither in guards' application of the prison regulations nor in the dispositions of the warden. With respect to prison regulations, discipline, and punishment, Biggar, Nickle, and Draper called for the institution of clear rules and regulations governing prisoner behaviour, complaints, and punishment. The committee further recommended that each guard and prisoner be provided with a copy of the prison regulations and the Penitentiary Act.[113] All forms of corporal punishment, they contended, should be eliminated. Instead, punishments should be imposed by the withdrawal of "ordinary rights and special privileges," forfeiture of earned remission, loss of pay for labour, or, in the case of work-related offences, transfer to other employment.[114] In specific cases, including escape attempts, offences punishable at law, and persistent misconduct, the committee recommended solitary confinement.[115] Unlike Biggar, Nickle, and Draper, the earlier Macdonnell Commission devoted little attention to the issue of punishment, though it did call for the abolition of some of the most inhumane practices, including the use of the water hose, ball and chain, and solitary confinement in dark cells.[116] Yet they did not oppose the practice of solitary confinement generally. Rather, the commissioners advocated better conditions for those kept in solitude. "The most degraded human being, if he is to be allowed to live," they contended, "is entitled to light and air."[117]

Even so, by the late 1920s, there was little evidence of change in disciplinary procedures. Withrow wrote that at the Warden's Court, a prisoner learned that a guard's evidence was given more weight than his own, he was assumed to be a liar, and "the less he says the better."[118] In cases involving the periodic enforcement of explicit rules, such as the rule of silence, prisoners could at least understand what they were being punished for. However, they often could not understand why the rule was being enforced on that particular occasion. In other cases, Withrow claimed, prisoners were punished for violating rules that had not been explained to them: after recounting his initial introduction to the prison rules, he commented that there "were many dozens more of which we could know nothing but for the infringement of which there were dire penalties."[119] More frustratingly, prisoners were sometimes charged with offences that could be neither defined nor proven: "There was such a crime as dumb insolence," he wrote. "We did not know what it meant, the guard did not know what it meant, the warden did not know what it meant, but it was a gesture deserving some punishment and it was imposed."[120] The range of punishments included loss of privileges, forfeiture of remission, a bread-and-water diet, hard beds, shackling by the wrists to the high cell bars, paddling with a leather strap, and solitary confinement. As sociologist and leading prisoners' aid activist C.W. Topping wrote in his 1929 study of the Canadian prison system, "the Penitentiary Branch can do practically anything short of killing an inmate in order to break him if he shows fight."[121] While some changes may have been made in response to the recommendations of the Macdonnell and Biggar, Nickle, and Draper reports, corporal punishment remained commonplace. In a single year in the late 1920s, 10 per cent of Kingston's prisoner population went under the strap.[122]

The reformation program, comprised of work and education, might have offered prisoners both a diversion and a sense of purpose to break the monotony of prison life. The Macdonnell Report recommended a three-hour schoolday at all institutions for prisoners whose education was deficient.[123] The Biggar, Nickle, and Draper committee went further, calling for mandatory education for illiterate prisoners and for those unable to solve basic math problems. They also recommended that voluntary classroom-based education and correspondence courses be made available to all interested prisoners.[124]

The reports also envisioned the reorganization and modernization of prison industries, calculated to defray operating costs and provide prisoners with marketable skills upon release.[125] Both reports made a connection between work and prisoner satisfaction. Biggar's committee recommended classifying prisoners based on their industrial skills to minimize discontent and to ensure that each prisoner's "activities will harmonize as closely as possible with his capacities"; the Macdonnell commissioners believed that "purposeful, productive work" or "interesting, improving work" would elevate prisoners' spirits and render them more manageable.[126] So would incentives. The reports championed payment for prison labour and early release for good conduct, through alternative mechanisms such as indeterminate sentencing, statutory remission, and supervised parole under the Ticket-of-Leave Act (see chapter 5 for further information on remission and tickets of leave).[127] George Rusche and Otto Kirchheimer argue that this approach should be understood cynically. "The main characteristic of the progressive system," they contend, "is the right of the convicts to make certain material gains by voluntary submission to discipline and not the pedagogical methods of reform."[128]

And indeed, work and educational opportunities were limited, and the prison staff offered little in the way of reformative guidance to prisoners. Notwithstanding the official rhetoric emphasizing the importance of work to reformation, prisoners' and guards' experiences offered a counter-narrative:

> "Work, work, yet more work," says the warden, "is the motto of the institution." He impresses this with measured tones upon every "fish," as he meets him for the first time in the Keeper's Hall. True a percentage of the inmates are overworked ... I have discussed this very subject with several of the more intelligent guards and we agreed that the average working time per inmate would not amount to more than an hour and a half per day. And work, steady, soul-satisfying labour, is the salvation of any man. But the inmates of Kingston Penitentiary, despite the warden's proclamation, have not even the comfort of work.[129]

According to the Biggar, Nickle, and Draper Report, across the country, prisoners were underemployed, except where prison labour was being used to construct new facilities:[130]

> Instead, therefore, of a penitentiary sentence developing the habit of industry, it develops either that of idleness, or, more probably, the much more dangerous habit of going through the motions of work without effecting any result ... That they should not have a chance [to work] is due not so much to intentional cruelty as to traditional prejudice, against

which every penitentiary official inveighs. The results are not only a serious waste of public money, but also a grave menace to society, since the
worst of habits are inculcated in those who have once failed in their social
obligations.[131]

Withrow shared their concern and lamented that "many of the men
deteriorate from idleness."[132] In addition, no attempt was made to
match prisoners' work assignments to their aptitudes, and those prisoners whose tasks required a modicum of skill learned on the job from
their peers. Trades instructors knew little about their trades.[133] Withrow
reported that "if the new man asks a guard or instructor what the proceedings are, he will, probably, be told 'I don't know anything about it.
You'll have to do the best you can ...' So the prison is virtually officered
by the convicts themselves."[134] He concluded that *"no one is ever taught
a trade in that institution."*[135]

The educational program was similarly deficient. The school instructor
served double duty as librarian and engaged in no direct teaching activities. School instruction was performed by prisoner-tutors during the
lunch break. Moreover, school attendance was intentionally curtailed. The
prison staff endeavoured to minimize the number of prisoners attending
classes due to space constraints and their fear of large gatherings of prisoners.[136] The same practical indifference to prisoner reformation coloured
counselling and preparation for release, and prison chaplains were not
permitted to do personal work with prisoners. While Salvation Army
officers made periodic visits to Kingston Penitentiary, and offered much-
needed support, meetings were voluntary and not part of a systematic,
planned effort to aid prisoners in their reformation.[137] Prisoners also had
to request interviews with the Dominion Parole Officer. In the absence of
a request, no personal review of prisoners' progress and no pre-release
meetings would take place.[138] Despite the pronouncements of the official
reform program, the entire system depended on convict initiative.

Given these problems, both government investigations recommended changes to prison administration and staffing. Biggar's committee called for the appointment of an Industrial Director and various
subordinates to reorganize and oversee prison industries. The committee also proposed that two assistant parole officers be appointed to aid
the single officer then fulfilling that role.[139] The Macdonnell Commission hoped to increase the autonomy of wardens and expressed concern
"that in the employment of guards more regard be had to the character and education of the applicant, with a view that the official should
exercise the best possible influence over the prisoner."[140] Each of these
recommendations would later be repeated by investigative bodies.

To ensure that the recommended changes were implemented, both reports suggested penal oversight by a multi-member panel.[141] The Macdonnell Commission, concerned most with the elimination of political patronage and corruption, sought the appointment of a three-member commission; this panel would operate independently of the Department of Justice and have "full power to reorganize the prisons, industrially and otherwise, make regulations for their management, select men for the administrative officers and then hold these men responsible for results."[142] Biggar, Nickle, and Draper took a more moderate approach, suggesting that a Penitentiary Board could have the minister or deputy minister as chair and the superintendent as vice-chair; the remaining seats would be populated by the senior officers of the Penitentiary Service. This committee was to hold many of the management, supervisory, and reporting obligations then conferred on the superintendent by the Penitentiary Act.[143]

The Illusion of Reform

In the 1920s, accounts of progress in Canada's penitentiaries amounted to a convincing illusion. The First World War–era investigations identified problems and recommended solutions. Subsequent annual reports of the Superintendent of Penitentiaries laid out plans for implementation. As the decade wore on, both the superintendent and penal reformers conveyed the impression that the reform plan was being implemented. Anyone interested in prison conditions had reason to believe that the system's failings were being addressed. Because access to the institutions was tightly controlled, the general public had to rely on those published accounts. Even members of Parliament, who had a statutory right to visit the prisons, were taken on carefully guided and staged tours of the facilities.[144] Commenting on a visit by Progressive Party of Canada MP Agnes Macphail (Grey Southeast), Oswald Withrow wondered, "Did she know they were pulling the wool over her eyes? I think perhaps she did and that she has done a [great] deal of thinking and investigating since."[145] After the riots of the early 1930s, which made it clear that serious problems in Canada's prisons persisted, Macphail and other MPs would turn to prisoners and concerned staff members for information.[146] But that was in the future.

In his 1919 annual report, Superintendent William St Pierre Hughes laid out a comprehensive program for the improvement of conditions and reformative programming in the penitentiary system; he placed particular emphasis on education, labour, and parole.[147] Over the course of the 1920s, the superintendent's reports described progress:

new infrastructure, renovated buildings, improved prisoner care, and individual success stories.[148] Yet the superintendent also repeatedly requested money to implement classification and segregation procedures, improve prison industries, and provide adequate assistance to prisoners on release.[149] Clearly, there were financial obstacles to achieving the reformist vision. Yet while much remained to be accomplished, the overall picture created by the Superintendent's propaganda was one of steady improvement and a penitentiary service committed to the humane treatment of prisoners.[150]

Publications by penologists and prison reformers painted a similar picture. Canada's leading prison reformers enjoyed a close relationship with the penitentiary service and a level of access to the institutions few others could secure.[151] Following visits to prisons across the country in the 1920s,[152] Topping contrasted improved conditions in Canadian prisons with poor implementation of scientific observation, classification, and treatment practices.[153] For Topping, these scientific practices entailed surveillance, data recording, and analysis by qualified experts.[154] In stark contrast to Withrow's experience, Topping described largely modernized, sanitary facilities, excellent libraries and schools, "exceptionally thorough" vocational training, and an impressive system of medical care.[155] He characterized the penitentiary service administration as forward-thinking but also frustrated by government.[156] "The first outstanding weakness of the Canadian system," Topping wrote, "is the tendency of the Dominion and of Provincial Governments to regard safe and sanitary buildings as the end of, rather than as the beginning of, a sound penal programme."[157] The result was a series of unmet objectives, among them adequate amounts of work; pay for prisoners; classification and segregation; and a training school for prison staff.[158] Overall, however, Topping described progress, opening and closing his narrative with accounts contrasting existing conditions with those in the past.[159] He concluded that the penitentiary service was meeting international standards of care and that the policies and programs were resulting in the reformation of prisoners.[160]

Ontario's Chief Parole Officer, Alfred Lavell (a penal reform advocate and the son of a former Kingston Penitentiary warden),[161] framed his discussion of prisoner reformation in *The Convicted Criminal and His Re-establishment as a Citizen* (1926) within a progressive narrative. Lavell associated the evolution of human societies "from the savage to the civilized state" with the triumph of humanitarianism over punishment and deterrence.[162] Like Topping, Lavell described conditions at

Kingston Penitentiary in glowing terms.[163] In a letter to Superintendent Hughes, included in Topping's book, he wrote:

> I was delighted to see how the penitentiary at Kingston has come on since my last visit. I never saw it in such efficient shape as now. It has been improved, I think, in every respect. As I passed through it the other day, my memory went back many times to the place as it was when I first saw it, forty-five years ago, and the contrast was very startling.[164]

While Lavell advocated crime prevention measures and alternatives to imprisonment,[165] he observed that prisons were "accepted by practically all countries as an essential in the treatment of most criminals"[166] and were "much improved in humanity, sanity, and efficiency."[167] He also contended that Canada's prisons were far superior to those in the United States. "We saw nothing in Ohio, New York or New Jersey," he wrote, "that was fit to put in the same class with the penitentiary at Kingston."[168] Topping agreed, pointing out that Lavell's assessment had been corroborated by an article in *Collier's* magazine: "No American with any knowledge of the situation in American prisons could fail to see, if he went to Canada, that the penitentiary authorities there are doing more to make penitentiaries count for something and perform their mission properly and profitably, both for society and the inmates, than we are doing in most of our American institutions."[169]

Whether or not this characterization was accurate, when both the Superintendent of Penitentiaries and the leading prison welfare advocates in the country were describing the prisons as greatly improved, few members of the public were likely to question their assessment.[170] But the wave of prison riots in the early 1930s and the revelations that followed shattered that illusion.

Riots and Revelations: Deconstructing the Narrative

The riot at Kingston Penitentiary in 1932 attracted immediate, prolonged, and sensationalized press attention.[171] The sustained interest was the product of three major factors. First, there had been other prison riots both before and after the Kingston Penitentiary protest. Riots at Stony Mountain, Saint-Vincent-de-Paul, and Dorchester penitentiaries suggested that the problems were systemic rather than localized.[172] The press provided exhaustive coverage of Superintendent Ormond's January 1933 report on the Kingston Penitentiary riot, which identified causes and suggested a series of reforms.[173] Despite at least partial implementation, twelve more disturbances took place between

1933 and 1937, providing an ongoing supply of fodder for journalists.[174] *Globe* editor Harry Anderson justified his ongoing coverage by declaring that "the public wants further light thrown on what is going on behind these prison walls."[175] Inspired by that statement, Oswald Withrow began to write.

Second, the events surrounding the gunshots fired into CPC leader Tim Buck's cell generated public interest and sympathy. A.E. Smith, counsel for the Canadian Labour Defence League, a communist front organization, accused Prime Minister Bennett of authorizing Buck's assassination.[176] The editor of the *Ottawa Citizen* opined that "men like Tim Buck are just as certainly political prisoners as the exiles to Siberia were under the Czarist regime."[177] These narratives built on existing criticisms of the government's imprisonment of CPC leaders under Section 98 of the *Criminal Code* and drew attention to Buck's plight and that of his fellow prisoners. More than 450,000 Canadians signed a petition demanding the release of the communist prisoners and the repeal of Section 98.[178]

Third and finally, the trials that followed the Kingston Penitentiary riot played out on front pages across the country. Twenty-nine prisoners were charged and publicly tried for their activities during the riot. Most were convicted, but more importantly, their trials gave many Canadians a startling and disturbing first glimpse of prison conditions, guard brutality, and the use of solitary confinement.[179] The trials also revealed that the government's account of events could not be trusted.[180] In sentencing Tim Buck, Judge George Deroche obliquely critiqued the official narrative: "I believe you, Buck, and the other witnesses, that the intention was a peaceful assembly ... I am satisfied that in the minds of the leaders anyway there was no desire that there should be a riot." He continued: "I know of many of [the prisoners'] grievances, and I know that since the riot they have been largely remedied, which makes your demands look reasonable."[181]

Perhaps most disturbing were the events that followed prisoner Sam Behan's trial. Behan had conducted his own defence against charges relating to the 1932 riot. In his closing arguments, which were reported by the press in syndication, he was thoughtful and eloquent, referring to the miserable conditions in the penitentiary and comparing the riot to a recent demonstration among the unemployed in Kingston. In doing so, Behan linked the plight of prisoners to the suffering endured by average Canadians during the Great Depression:

> We are not humans. We are dogs. It is a living hell, a living grave ... We asked for humane treatment and they locked us up [in the shops] ... Was

it a riot? Right here in the city of Kingston you had a riot of unemployed a few weeks ago. They wanted to see the mayor and committee. What happened? They smashed windows and broke into a meeting. Were there charges laid? No.[182]

Behan explained to the jury that an acquittal meant nothing to him personally. He was serving a life sentence and was unlikely to be granted a ticket-of-leave.[183] His aim was to expose prison conditions and secure justice for prisoners. To the public then, Behan was a selfless martyr and not, as Conservative Minister of Justice Hugh Guthrie characterized him, "of that class of prisoners who are rather dangerous."[184] The jury acquitted Behan, and the judge delighted in delivering the verdict.[185] Yet Behan's story would end in tragedy. A year later, the forty-nine-year-old prisoner died of heart failure. This was followed by reports – initially denied by the Penitentiaries Branch – that at the time of his death, he was being held in solitary confinement and "undergoing special punishment."[186] Agnes Macphail doggedly pressured the justice minister into admitting that Behan had been paddled with a leather strap twelve days before his death and had died in a punishment cell.[187] Despite these admissions, the government refused to appoint an inquiry into Behan's death.[188] Macphail now called into question the reliability of the government's account: "It may be that Behan's death came unexpectedly and that nothing could have been done to save him ... Coming as it does after the very real difficulty in both Kingston and St. Vincent de Paul, it seems to me to be one more strong argument in favour of a careful and impartial investigation into the conduct of our penitentiaries."[189]

Instead, officials in the Penitentiary Service began investigating Macphail and her informants. During a tumultuous interview with a prisoner he was squeezing for information, Inspector Dawson of the Penitentiary Service raged that "Agnes made a ---- fool of herself in the House of Commons, but when we are finished with her she will never be able to lift up her head in the House again."[190] Meanwhile, the Ministry of Justice placed the home of another critic, General Alexander Ross, MP for Kingston, under surveillance. Ross's contacts inside the Penitentiary Service were dismissed.[191]

In his annual report, Superintendent Ormond brushed aside calls for reforms and an investigation, arguing that the prisons were already well run:

The policy presently followed in the penitentiaries gives every convict an opportunity of living a well-ordered life, with the fewest possible restrictions compatible with a reasonable and adequate discipline, which, if accepted according to the spirit of the regulations, is constructive. If a convict uses his powers of reason, he should leave the institution better than when he entered, but certainly no worse.

On the other hand, there will be no relaxation of the standards of good order and discipline, simply to produce well-behaved convicts, rather than to develop the moral and ethical standards required by citizens who are of value to the State.

Penitentiaries treat the convict as individuals who will eventually be returned to society. The training in the penitentiary will be such that the convict should, without difficulty, upon his release adjust himself to the conventions accepted by the citizen of Canada.

Further relaxation in prison rules would only have the effect of making the convicts more comfortable within the penitentiaries, and more easily adjustable to the institutional routine, rather than the statutes and conventions of the freeman public."[192]

Despite these efforts to silence them, the critics persisted. In June 1934, Macphail and J.S. Woodsworth, the leader of the newly formed Cooperative Commonwealth Federation, rose in Parliament to demand an investigation.[193] The demand came in the wake of a series of startling revelations. On 25 June 1934, Justice Minister Guthrie admitted to Parliament that "quiet had not been restored" at Kingston Penitentiary.[194] Disturbances continued. According to Guthrie, "a very noisy outbreak took place. It started with the rattling of trays or aluminum dishes and the flooding of as many cells as they could possibly flood in certain tiers of the building."[195] In one of the protests, prisoners demanded "better food; more letter-writing privileges; safety razors and toilet articles; daily and weekly papers; no reports for minor breaches of rules and regulations; more tobacco; and baseball."[196] The prisoners demonstrated their political savvy by timing a protest to coincide with the governor general's presence in Kingston.[197] The disturbances were accompanied by several incidences of arson, with the fires causing extensive damage.[198] The Penitentiary Service took pre-emptive action. According to Guthrie, physical reinforcements were made in the chapel so that "five or six hundred men, many of whom are desperate characters," could not "overpower the guards."[199] At the same time, discipline was imposed: for their transgressions, twenty-two prisoners were flogged. The minister of justice detailed this corporal punishment for his colleagues in the House: "The first one was sentenced to twenty strokes and eleven were administered; the second was sentenced to twenty strokes and twelve were administered; the third was sentenced to twenty strokes and twelve were administered; the next was sentenced to twenty, twelve strokes administered; the next to twenty, fifteen strokes administered; the next to twenty[…]." He continued through the list, ending with this: "There were five pronounced medically unfit and the strokes were not administered."[200] The situation was so dire that Warden W.B. Megloughlin, appointed in the wake of the 1932 riot, resigned.[201]

After the riots, the trials, and the publication of Withrow's book, politicians, the press, and the public could no longer be confident that Canadian prisons were humane or were developing effective reform programs. In 1935, with the Conservative government steadfast in its refusal to launch an investigation, prison reformers met in Montreal to hold the first Canadian Penal Congress. There, McGill University law professor F.R. Scott, president of the CCF, delivered a speech in which he encouraged the congress to form a national association to address the failures of the legal and penal systems. Those in attendance immediately began organizing the Canadian Penal Association.[202] A few months later, the Conservative Party was defeated. Newly elected Prime Minister William Lyon Mackenzie King, of the Liberal Party, having promised to appoint an inquiry if elected, did so in early 1936.[203] That investigation – the Archambault Commission – would ultimately, and perhaps erroneously, be viewed as a hallmark of penal progress in Canada.

2 The Blueprint for the New Deal: The Archambault Commission Re-envisions Reform

It was a perfect storm. Prison riots, sensational court cases, prolonged media attention, determined political agitation, and the consequent rise in public awareness forced the newly elected Liberal government to take action on the deplorable conditions in Canada's prisons. To *Globe* editor Harry Anderson, it was crucial that a Royal Commission be appointed. In calling for an investigation in November 1932, he wrote that "it will not suffice for the Government to make a secret, internal inquiry and present a statement of the findings to the people." Rather, he argued, "the searchlight should be played on every nook and cranny of Portsmouth [Kingston Penitentiary] and the public made acquainted with both sides of the story … It is a job for a Royal Commission, which can tackle the subject from all sides and make a report and recommendations without fear or favor."[1]

Royal Commission Mandate and Findings

The Royal Commission to Investigate the Penal System of Canada, commonly known as the Archambault Commission, was chaired by Justice Joseph Archambault of the Quebec Superior Court. He was to be joined in the investigation by Winnipeg lawyer and former Manitoba Attorney General R.W. Craig and by journalist Harry Anderson. Before the commission could start its work, Anderson – whose editorials and work with former prisoner Oswald Withrow had stimulated national interest in prisons, and who had led the drive for a public inquiry – died of cancer. His fellow commissioners described him as "a keen student of criminology and penal reform … his untimely death was a great blow."[2] He was replaced by Toronto attorney J.C. McRuer, who was likely to be viewed as a champion and an ally in the struggle for prison reform by critics of the penal system. McRuer had represented MP Agnes Macphail

when the Penitentiary Service attempted to discredit her claims about
Canada's prisons and to undermine her calls for an inquiry.[3]

The commissioners were given a broad mandate, including, but not
limited to, the following issues:

1. The treatment of convicted persons in the penitentiaries, covering the
   investigation and examination of the classification of the institutions;
   The classification of offenders;
   The construction of penal institutions;
   The organization of penal departments;
   The appointment of staffs;
   The treatment to be accorded to the different classes of offenders,
     including corporal and other punishment;
   The protection of society;
   Reformative and rehabilitative treatment;
   Employment of prisoners;
   Prison labour;
   Remuneration;
   The study of international standard minimum rules, and other
     subjects cognate to the above.
2. The administration, management, discipline and police of
   penitentiaries.
3. Co-operation between governmental and social agencies in the prevention of crime, including juvenile delinquency, and the furnish-
   ing of aid to prisoners upon release from imprisonment.
4. The conditional release of prisoners, including parole or release on
   probation, conditional release under the Ticket of Leave Act, and
   remission generally.[4]

They began their work in October 1936, four years after the Kingston riot. Their investigation was extensive, and its scope was unprecedented in the history of the penal system. The commissioners visited
each of the federal penitentiaries and dozens of provincial institutions.
They met with the governments of each province, held public meetings across the country, and conducted *in camera* interviews with 1,840
prisoners and 200 guards. They also toured nine countries, where they
visited prisons and met with officials and experts.[5] Despite the magnitude of their undertaking, their report was released within two years.
It is generally viewed as a turning point in the history of Canadian
prisons: it exposed prison conditions, offered a critical reappraisal of
penitentiary management and methods, and emphasized the primacy
of prisoner reformation.[6]

Prison Conditions

The commissioners used the "Standard Minimum Rules for the Treatment of Prisoners" (SMRTP) adopted by the League of Nations in 1934 as the basis for their evaluation of prison conditions.[7] While not legally binding on any of the member nations, these standards were intended "to define the minimum rights of persons deprived of liberty by decision of the judicial authorities."[8] General points of consideration in the 1934 SMRTP were segregation of prisoners based on sex, age, and the legal reasons for their detention; general attitude; cell and work accommodation; personal hygiene; clothing and bedding; "moral and intellectual reclamation"; food; medical services; exercise and sport; discipline and punishment; instruments of restraint; complaints by prisoners; contact with the outside world; books; religion; illness and transfer; and institutional personnel.[9] The 6 September 1934 report of the Secretary-General to the assembly of the League of Nations noted that Canada's penitentiary regulations were "not less lenient" than the rules of the International Penal and Penitentiary Commission: they complied with some articles (e.g., prison labour and language), and progress was being made in other areas, such as education, religion, remission, and treatment.[10]

Using the existing SMRTP as their guide, the Archambault commissioners examined many of these issues. Their report described cells as modern and sanitary. Even the punishment cells were described as "little different from the ordinary ones, and ... not the dark dungeons some misinformed people would have the public believe. They are not, of course, provided with the comforts of the ordinary cells, but it is not to be expected that inmates undergoing punishment should have the same accommodation as the others."[11]

Food was of "excellent quality, wholesome and plentiful," and better than what was served in European prisons. While the report suggested that "a more substantial breakfast might be given to those who are engaged in heavy outside work," the commissioners were generally pleased with food services.[12] The commission saw no major issues with the regulations surrounding personal hygiene, though they recommended that prisoners be permitted to bathe twice a week (rather than once) and shave daily. Drawing a connection between personal hygiene and moral rectitude, they argued that "all penitentiary regulations should be designed to reform and rehabilitate wherever possible. An inmate who has acquired the habit of keeping clean and neat before he entered the penitentiary should not be discouraged from continuing it, and those who have not acquired the habit should be encouraged to cultivate it ... It is an encouragement to cleanliness."[13]

In *Shackling the Transgressor*, Oswald Withrow levelled a scathing critique of the medical care at Kingston Penitentiary. The commissioners concurred:

> The cells throughout the hospital building are unfit for anyone who is sick; dark, and utterly cheerless. Instead of being the best in the institution, they are without doubt the worst ... The conditions in the hospital were condemned in the report of the 1913 Commission, and, since then, year after year have been reported to the Superintendents of Penitentiaries, but yet no adequate action has been taken to remedy the situation.[14]

Yet in summing up their views on health care, the commissioners softened their criticism: "Medical care is good in some institutions, but bad in others, according to the character and qualifications of the medical officers. Some of the penitentiary hospitals are modern, while others are antiquated and unsatisfactory."[15]

Overall, the report concluded that physical conditions were adequate. But if this was true, what had triggered the riots? Here, the commissioners focused in on prison routines and services. Consciously echoing previous investigations, they emphasized the monotony and boredom of prison life, which they argued was inimical to reformation and should have been addressed decades earlier.[16] Prisoners needed diversions to mitigate the tedium, but opportunities for exercise, recreation, and leisure activities were insufficient. Moreover, letter-writing and visits were unnecessarily constrained. To this, the commissioners added that "the visiting cages are gruesome and humiliating relics of the past."[17]

The report also offered a harsh assessment of prisoner reformation initiatives, which in the commissioners' estimation did not satisfy the international minimum standard.[18] For example, they wrote that "education is neither satisfactory, nor in accordance with the regulations," and they chastised the Penitentiary Service for the low priority assigned to schooling and the low status accorded prison teachers.[19] Guards knew nothing of modern penology, and officers admitted that "no real attempt is made at reformation."[20] The commissioners contended that as a result, "when a prisoner comes out of prison, after the first thrill of freedom, he relapses into habitual lethargy and becomes enveloped in a thick shell of apathy. He is badly handicapped in his efforts at rehabilitation. He wanders aimlessly in the midst of the sharp rivalry and feverish activity of the free world."[21]

Classification practices were also critiqued. The commissioners expressed concern that the classification system was "unscientific and without practical effect."[22] They found that hardened convicts were mixing freely with reformable prisoners, and on this point, they minced no words: "It is hopeless to strive to effect the reformation of a prisoner while, at the same time, exposing him to the destructive association of depraved criminals who have no determination to live anything but degenerate lives of crime."[23] Perhaps the strength of this language was intended to underscore the importance they attached to classification, an issue that had been raised repeatedly by investigators dating back to 1848 but had never been properly addressed.[24]

The system of prison labour came under similar scrutiny. The commissioners stated that prison labour practices met the SMRTP; like Withrow, however, they found that the work available was insufficient and that trades instructors devoted most of their time to custodial duties and paperwork.[25] In connection with these findings, the Archambault commissioners directly and repeatedly criticized Superintendent Ormond. They characterized his annual reports to Parliament as "gravely misleading"[26] and his management style as dictatorial.[27] Ormond, according to the report, failed to consult with wardens or conduct proper on-site inspections, while simultaneously micro-managing all aspects of the system from his office in Ottawa.[28] He issued hundreds of new regulations and policy letters, saddling wardens and their subordinates with large volumes of unnecessary paperwork. According to the commissioners, Ormond constrained his underlings' discretion so thoroughly that experienced wardens had been divested of the authority given them by the Penitentiary Act and were unable to govern their facilities effectively.[29] The commissioners deemed Ormond's authoritarian methods a major contributing factor to the riots during his tenure and called for his immediate dismissal.[30] Yet strangely, the report's major recommendation – the implementation of Borstal-like principles in Canadian penitentiaries (discussed later in this chapter) – was one that Ormond had already studied, recommended, and begun to implement.[31]

It was in this context that the commission addressed the issues of prison discipline and punishment. Here, the commissioners again took the superintendent to task, noting the proliferation of regulations during his tenure and how difficult it was for the prisoners to navigate the byzantine maze of rules.[32] Having observed the Wardens' Courts firsthand, the commissioners reported that prisoners had little chance of a fair and impartial hearing and no opportunity for appeal.[33] Withrow, who had dedicated an entire chapter of his memoir to the Warden's Court at Kingston, offered the following description:

> The warden's court was held every week day, at the noon hour. Twice a week would have been sufficient but the great man seemed to need

victims, daily, and he wanted to be able to use his sarcasm and venom upon those who were obliged to come before him on request. You may think I am writing rashly, but one of the guards informed me that at one time two months had passed without any necessity, as far as he was concerned, of "writing up" any of the men in his gang. The warden called him to his office at the North Gate and asked him if it was not about time he had somebody up for punishment. On another occasion, a man appeared before the warden, on a report for the first time in his seven years within the walls. The warden looked at his record. "I see you have a clean sheet," said he. "Yes, sir," answered the inmate, rather proud of such a finding. "Well, it's about time you had something against you," snarled the great man, highly delighted to be able to impose a first penalty.[34]

The commissioners revealed that acquittal rates for prison offences in individual penitentiaries often dipped well below 1 per cent.[35] An accusation against a prisoner was almost guaranteed to result in punishment since wardens had to accept guards' testimony over that of prisoners or risk undermining the cohesion of their staff.[36] Evidence was also brought forward indicating that the superintendent had ordered prisoners punished without trial.[37] If a prisoner believed he was "unjustly punished without a fair chance to defend himself," the report cautioned, "he will become anti-social, embittered, and uncontrollable. This state of mind is contagious."[38] Faith in justice, the commissioners continued, was essential to reformation.[39] The commissioners also worried about the impact of particular punishments. The report was critical of the implements used for corporal punishment, penalties that deprived prisoners of "all contact with normal life," and the imposition of "permanent" or "indefinite" segregation (i.e., solitary confinement) without explanation or right of appeal.[40] The commissioners focused on discrediting Ormond – echoing the Brown Commission's scapegoating of Warden Henry Smith in 1849[41] – and thus did not plumb deeply into the actions of his subordinates.

Recommendations of the Archambault Report

How, then, should the federal penitentiaries be managed and operated? The commissioners began with basic principles. Like the Macdonnell and Biggar, Nickle, and Draper reports, the Archambault Commission emphasized that "the revengeful or retributive character of punishment should be completely *eliminated*."[42] The most important principle of penology, according to the Archambault Commission, was the protection of society.[43] "The task of the prison," the commissioners argued, "should be, not merely the temporary protection of society through the incarceration of captured offenders, but the *transformation* of reformable criminals into law abiding citizens, and the prevention of those who are accidental or occasional criminals from becoming habitual offenders."[44] To that end, they suggested changes to classification and segregation procedures, new strategies for prisoner reform, a new system of governance for Canada's prisons, and a more comprehensive post-release strategy.

Classification, Segregation, and the Protection of Young Prisoners

The commissioners, who emphasized the financial costs associated with recidivism, blamed increasing reoffence rates on the absence of any serious attempt to reform prisoners. They also argued that the contamination of impressionable prisoners through association with "degenerate and experienced criminals" while in prison, and the failure to provide prisoners with adequate assistance upon release, contributed to recidivism.[45] To address these issues, the report recommended the classification and separation of offenders and a humane and analytical approach to reformation guided by psychiatrists or psychologists. The commissioners contended that those tasked with reformation needed to understand prisoners' motives, encourage their moral development, and build up their habits of industry.[46]

The report called for the classification of the prison population into several categories, each to be segregated and handled in different ways. It recommended that penitentiaries be reserved for reformable adult prisoners and that young offenders, drug addicts, incorrigibles, habitual criminals, and the insane be moved to different facilities. Young offenders were to be segregated in a special system of reformative institutions (discussed below). The rationale for segregating incorrigibles in special institutions was to prevent them from influencing reformable prisoners.[47] Yet strangely, given the importance attached to classification, the report failed to specify how prisoners were to be deemed incorrigible or reformable.

While a definition of incorrigibility was not provided, the commissioners did make suggestions for dealing with easily identifiable "non-reformable" prisoners. Individuals who had been convicted multiple times were seen as unreformable: the report expressed "grave doubt" that such habitual offenders might be reformed.[48] It recommended legislation to permit the courts to designate individuals as habitual offenders[49] upon conviction for their fourth indictable offence and to impose a sentence of indefinite preventive detention.[50]

Likewise, the commissioners presented drug addicts as incurable and "a constant source of irritation and difficulty" within the penitentiaries;[51] as such, they called for their indefinite detention in specialized institutions.[52] Finally, the report urged the transfer of insane prisoners to provincial mental hospitals, where they would be treated at federal expense.[53]

The Archambault commissioners were most interested in protecting juvenile delinquents from the "contaminating influence" of hardened offenders and recommended that young prisoners be classified into two categories: those who were deemed reformable would be sent to new institutions modelled on the English Borstal system; those who were considered "too bad for Borstal" would be sent to the penitentiaries.[54] Borstal facilities were to be as much like schools as possible and less like prisons.[55] The focus was on retraining and resocialization: Borstal prisoners would spend long hours engaged in study, industrial training, and recreation. Idle time was to be kept to a minimum.[56] Prisoners would progress through a grade and merit system based on good conduct and industry. With each promotion in grade, prisoners would gain increased privileges and responsibilities. In the final stages, they would be permitted to work and move about the facilities and grounds without supervision.[57] This recommendation is worth discussing in some detail, because it reveals much about the commission's thinking as to the causes of and solutions to criminality, as well as what they viewed as the key elements in a successful prisoner reform program.

To begin, the desire to segregate youthful offenders stemmed from the commission's views about the influence of older, experienced convicts on "plastic" and "impressionable" youth, and therein, about the importance of environmental influences.[58] The commissioners referred to the heredity-versus-environment debate but avoided weighing in on it. Rather, they asserted that whatever the proportionate influence of each factor, it was "an undeniable fact that the influences of the home, the church, and the school are still the most potent factors in discovering the danger and applying the necessary remedies."[59] They attributed criminality to inadequate discipline, "vicious homes," "defective family relationships," and poverty. Despite the social upheavals and widespread economic hardships resulting from the depression, the commissioners were committed to individualizing the causes of crime – poverty, they emphasized, was the least influential factor.[60]

If these were the causes, what were the remedies? First, the report emphasized the importance of preventative measures, calling on families, schools, churches, and social agencies to assume greater responsibility for children – the "it's your fault" approach. The commission's clearest recommendations in this respect revolved around physical and psychological examinations and supervised leisure activities.[61] The hope was that "problem children" would be discovered and treated before they became "seriously delinquent."[62] "It is more economical," the commissioners wrote, "to save children than to punish criminals."[63] The report recommended that where preventative measures failed, probation should be considered before imprisonment.[64] For youth, incarceration should be a last resort, to be employed only in cases involving recidivism or serious crimes.[65]

Given that the commissioners blamed youth crime on poor socialization, it is not surprising that mentorship was at the heart of the Borstal-style program they recommended. Young prisoners were to be divided among houses overseen by housemasters. The commissioners emphasized that "one of the great factors in training delinquent youths is individual attention given by men of educated minds and sound character."[66] In England, they noted, many housemasters were trained schoolteachers and educated army officers, and their influence was crucial in "establishing a standard and providing an inspiration for each youth."[67] Staff members were expected to give each prisoner "constant attention, and by encouragement, admonition, and regular instruction, help him reshape his life."[68] For the system to succeed, quality personnel would be required, and they would have to enjoy considerable discretion: personal relationships could not be built within a stifling matrix of rules and regulations of the sort found in the penitentiaries.[69] Success would also require the imposition of longer prison terms: little could be achieved, the commissioners suggested, with sentences of less than three years.[70] Longer terms of incarceration might be inimical to many of the commission's other suggested reforms, but with regard to juveniles, they were not seen this way; perhaps the moral panic over juvenile delinquency that emerged during the Second World War overrode any public trepidation (see below).

The final emphasis of the Borstal system was on aftercare. In England, the Borstal system relied on the assistance of voluntary associations, whose operations were fully subsidized by the government.[71] Borstal Association members served as *ersatz* social workers, visiting prisoners prior to release, establishing community mentorships, and investigating homes, family members, and friends, all to facilitate the prisoner's successful reintegration into the community and adjustment to a law-abiding life.[72] Prisoners left the Borstal subject to the terms of a licence, and those who failed to comply with aftercare programming faced substantial penalties.[73]

The Borstal Ascendency in Canadian Penitentiaries

The Archambault commissioners – like Superintendent Ormond – lavished praise on the Borstal ideal.[74] Both the commissioners and Ormond visited England to study the system. While these state-supported visits may have been orchestrated to present a sanitized view of the system's operations, that view was clearly convincing. They returned to Canada with a sense that the Borstal model was the best approach to prisoner reformation and rehabilitation, and its influence bled through the pages of the Archambault Report. The commissioners contended that the adult penitentiaries, once they had been cleared of all non-reformable prisoners through classification, should focus on prisoner transformation through the application of Borstal principles. This would involve mentorship, education and skills training, recreation and leisure activities, and carefully planned and supervised reintegration into the community. The first stages in the new program would involve behaviour modification and mentorship, explicitly inspired by English practice. The commissioners resurrected the age-old proposal that a grade and merit system be implemented in the penitentiaries:[75] "Good conduct and industry," they wrote, "should be allowed to win for the prisoner, not only the reward of a shorter sentence, but increasing privileges and some mitigation of the rigours of prison life."[76] In keeping with the SMRTP, the commissioners recommended that all prisoners have the irrevocable right to libraries, education, letter-writing, and visits. Participation in other prison activities, including "eating in association, games, newspapers, radios, and concerts," should be permitted as privileges, according to the prisoner's status in a conduct-based progressive stage system. Additionally, prisoners should be able to earn early release according to simplified and easily understood rules of remission.[77] Under these rules, prison authorities could revoke earned privileges and accumulated remission as punishment for violations of prison regulations.[78]

If these ideas sounded remarkably Borstal-like, so did the recommendations on staffing. The commissioners emphasized that the success of prison programming depended on the character and attitudes of prison personnel. They suggested that some of the senior personnel in the penitentiary service lacked the necessary qualities and should be forced to retire.[79] Most of the lower-level staff had been selected based on custodial rather than corrective abilities, and few had "either the capacity or training to exert any reformative influence on the prisoners." "They are 'guards,'" the commissioners wrote, "and nothing more."[80] "An orderly reconstruction of the whole personnel" was necessary, and this would entail recruiting in universities, establishing a staff training school, and raising the rates of pay to attract better applicants.[81] The commission recommended that as an interim measure, a group of officers be sent to the British training center at Wakefield, so that the principles taught there might be incorporated into the Canadian system.[82] In discussing the type of officers they hoped such changes would produce, the commission quoted from the Wakefield training centre's syllabus. The ideal officer was a man with a good temperament: a "manly, straightforward, self-reliant man of high ideals, great patience, energy and integrity."[83] He was, in other words, the perfect mentor.

Work was to play a vital role in the reform program. The commissioners – reflecting Weber's discussion of the Protestant work ethic[84] – contended that "the first requirement is that useful and suitable work should be provided *and that there should be plenty of it*."[85] This was nothing new. Thomas Mathiesen argues that this "ideology of work" was hundreds of years old and cites documents from 1589 stating that the treatment of prisoners should make them "used to labour, desirous of holding a good job, capable of standing on their own feet."[86] To increase the amount of work available for prisoners, while avoiding conflict with unionized workers, the commission recommended that the principle of production for state use be maintained[87] (a 1934 report to the League of Nations indicated that "over 99 per cent of the work performed in Canadian penitentiaries" was already part of the regie or "Prison Labour for State Use" system)[88] and called for a survey to determine the needs of government departments. The commissioners argued that to do this work more efficiently, it would be necessary to modernize prison industries and hire qualified and capable trades instructors.[89] The report also recommended the appointment of an agricultural expert to oversee prison farms and improve operations and that guards with agricultural experience be recruited.[90] Prison labour was not intended to be punitive. It was to serve "as an instrument of discipline and reformation."[91] Useful employment, the commissioners wrote, would provide prisoners with a sense of purpose and accomplishment.[92]

While the report discussed trades training, it did not relate the skills acquired in prison industries to post-release employment, which may reflect the primacy given to labour for the institution's operational purposes. Or perhaps it was an oversight. In any case, the commissioners did relate labour to character formation and saw it as a crucial element in the grade and merit system.[93] They also noted with approval that the recently introduced system of pay for prison labour exerted "a distinct reformative influence," besides providing prisoners with a means to acquire "small comforts" during their time in prison and to accumulate modest savings for their release.[94] In keeping with their focus on providing differential rewards for good behaviour, the commissioners argued that prisoners should be paid on a sliding scale, with higher payments awarded for diligence rather than productivity.[95] Character rather than skill was to be the basis of assessment and reward. These principles anticipate the findings of Michel Foucault, who contended that work was a way of disciplining the working class: "the prisoner who could and would work would be released, not so much because he was again useful to society, but because he had again subscribed to the greater ethical pact of human existence."[96]

In addition to trades training, education was a major focus. Mathiesen argued that "an ideology of schooling was important as an addition to the ideology of work" and that both existed "within a very traditional *bourgeois*, frame of reference." He continued: "Diligent work, good schooling, respectable morality and strong discipline, are components which may be found individually in many contexts, but which together, and as a collective system of thought, constitute an expression of bourgeois ethics."[97] The Archambault Report was consistent with Mathiesen's analysis. The commissioners hoped that education would do more than simply counter illiteracy or develop prisoners' academic abilities.[98] They envisioned a holistic educational curriculum that would encompass "religious, academic, vocational, health, cultural, and social training."[99] On one hand, the commissioners wrote, education was intended to counteract the monotony and "mental deterioration inevitably attendant on prison life."[100] On the other, it was to serve as a vehicle for character formation, providing prisoners with healthy activities directed toward their "betterment" and overall "fitness for citizenship."[101] The report called for improvements to school facilities and library collections but focused most intently on ensuring the recruitment of qualified teachers of suitable temperament; cooperation among trades instructors, schoolteachers, and chaplains to develop a complete and coordinated program of education; and the provision of individual attention and encouragement to students.[102] Again, personal relationships and mentorship loomed large, and the commission emphasized that particular attention should be given to younger prisoners, even inside the regular penitentiaries.[103] That being said, these aims, which seem so laudable and generous on the surface, distinctly echoed the educational aims of residential schooling for Indigenous people. As we know from that experience, an education designed to forcibly resocialize the subject could be incredibly traumatizing for the recipient.[104]

The commission's recommendations with regard to recreation, leisure, and communication bore the marks of similar reasoning. To counteract the monotony of prison life, eliminate "time spent in idleness and brooding," and "strengthen [the] soul, mind, and body" of the prisoner, the commission recommended additional time for exercise and recreation. They proposed the expansion of competitive athletics, the introduction of indoor games, and the provision of materials for artistic and craft-based activities in cells.[105] They also recommended that prisoners have better access to books, magazines, newspapers, and radios and that lectures and concerts be held more frequently.[106] Despite this concern to alleviate boredom, the commission recommended that conversation periods in the cell blocks, which had been adopted at some penitentiaries, be abolished. The commissioners argued that the tone of these indoor conversations was so "vile" that the rule of silence should be lifted only during outdoor exercise periods and indoor evening recreation for well-behaved prisoners.[107] It was a telling decision. When confronted with the choice between monotony and character reformation, the commission clearly chose the latter. Prison activities were meant to foster self-improvement, not debasement.

Finally, the commission emphasized the need to ease restrictions on letter-writing and visits. Prisoners should be permitted to write more letters to a wider range of correspondents and to receive longer, more frequent visits from more relatives.[108] At various points in the report, the commissioners emphasized the importance of family and community ties to successful adjustment upon release.[109] Indeed, many of the recommendations surrounding recreation, leisure, and communication were intended to raise morale, improve prisoners' social skills and self-control, and aid them in maintaining connections with the outside world.[110] Ultimately, they were concerned that prisoners subjected to long periods of monotony would be conditioned to lethargy and apathy, which would run counter to their goal of producing good workers – in essence, creating disciplined and docile bodies.[111]

Consolidation of Governance

To put the reform program into place – especially the system of classification and segregation – federal–provincial jurisdictional issues would need to be resolved. To this end, the commission recommended that all levels of prisons be consolidated under federal authority. That change, they argued, would permit authorities to implement a consistent program of classification and segregation across the country and achieve economies of scale.[112] Based on international practice and Canadian concerns, they also argued for the creation of new governance and oversight bodies. Their first recommendation – echoing the reports of

Macdonnell and Biggar, Nickle, and Draper – was to create a board
of prison commissioners; this proposal was justified on the grounds
that "the problem of penal administration is too large in scope and too
serious in results to be left in the hands of one man."[113] The second
recommendation was to create local boards of prison visitors, staffed
by non–penitentiary service appointees, who would include a County
Court judge, a representative from a local social welfare association,
and a physician. The commissioners explained that "under the present system existing in the Canadian penitentiaries, what is going on in
the institutions is shrouded with absolute secrecy, giving rise to suspi-
cions and misgivings, which are further enhanced by extravagant and
biased tales of ex-prisoners and the imagination of sentimentalists."[114]
The prison visitors would act as a check on the prison administration,
inspecting facilities, listening to prisoners' complaints, and hearing
appeals from the decisions of Wardens' Courts.[115]

Centralization was also needed to ensure prisoners' post-release success; the Archambault commissioners attributed increasing rates of
recidivism to the lack of systematic efforts to provide prisoners with
assistance upon release.[116] A number of voluntary prisoners' aid societies across the country offered assistance to ex-convicts, but the commissioners believed that these activities were being hampered by voluntary
private financing, the absence of uniform and coherent programming,
and the intransigence of prison officials, who often hindered their
efforts.[117] As an alternative model, the commissioners referred to the
Central Association for the Aid of Discharged Convicts in England and
Wales. That association was a hybrid government/voluntary body; it
was chaired by the Home Secretary, governed by representatives from
voluntary societies engaged in prisoner rehabilitation, and funded in
part by the Prison Commission.[118] The association's four paid agents
and hundreds of volunteer social workers visited prisoners prior to
release to establish a relationship and a release plan. In the course of
these visits, they arranged for temporary financial assistance, work
placements, and post-carceral housing for ex-convicts. Volunteers also
supervised those on conditional release.[119] The Archambault Commission recommended that a similar "central authority" be established in
Canada. The organization would operate under the direction of the
proposed Prison Commission and incorporate existing prisoners' aid
societies or create new ones if necessary. It would make use of volunteer
social workers, and the government would partly fund their activities.[120]
This tendency to absolve the government of responsibility for adequate
organization and funding for aftercare is not unusual. Mathiesen contends that "in all known societies [the authorities] systematically refrain

from establishing a system at release with sufficient resources for social restoration, or with an apparatus symbolizing the restoration of the prisoner's dignity, rights and honour."[121]

The commissioners emphasized that the "success or failure of any system of rehabilitation or after-care for discharged prisoners depends in the final analysis upon the attitude of the public."[122] In the opinion of the commissioners, public attitudes raised substantial obstacles for released prisoners as they attempted to find work and re-establish themselves in the community. This was something they wanted to change. The report called on governments across the country to lead the way by declaring that a previous conviction should not serve as an automatic bar to employment. The commissioners hoped that by doing so, government "would set an example to all employers of labour."[123]

Reception of the Report

The Archambault Report was released in the late spring of 1938. Even though five years had passed since the riots, newspaper coverage of the commission report was extensive. For example, both the *Globe and Mail* and the *Ottawa Citizen* provided several pages summarizing the report and extensively quoting from it, including specific findings about each prison in the system. Front page coverage in the *Globe and Mail* noted that "in the most colorful and forceful language, the report of the Royal Commission has lifted the lid from the whole penal system and has revealed an ugly situation."[124] Members of Parliament noted that this coverage was favourable.[125] The *Ottawa Citizen* described prison reformer and MP Agnes Macphail as exultant. Macphail characterized the report as "magnificent."[126] She felt vindicated in her efforts to reform the penal system, noting that "all parties are for reform now."[127] While "it took years," she was heartened that "the commission certainly studied the matter thoroughly."[128]

Macphail also applauded the Archambault commissioners' caution against hasty action following the release of their report. The commissioners emphasized the need for gradual, planned, and orderly change. Yet the media dramatized minor changes. For example, shortly after the report was released, Minister of Justice Ernest Lapointe introduced a bill to create the recommended three-member prison commission to oversee the penitentiary system. The prison commission was to play a key role in the orderly reorganization of the Penitentiary Service, and it was instructed to carefully study and consider new policy proposals prior to their enactment and implementation. When the *Globe and Mail* reported on Lapointe's bill, the front-page story described it as "the greatest shake-up in the history of any public institution in the Dominion," opining that it would "affect high and low in the penal system of Canada and will reach into every Federal prison from coast to coast."[129]

Lapointe's bill garnered a mixed response in Parliament. Opposition leader R.B. Bennett objected to the bill. He argued that Parliament had not had sufficient time to study the recommendations of the Archambault Report and had yet to see the evidence upon which it was based.[130] Bennett suggested that Lapointe delay enacting any related legislation for a year, so that parliamentarians could have time to understand what they were being asked to approve.[131] Bennett also took issue with the report's condemnation of Superintendent Ormond, whose actions, the commissioners claimed, "threw the whole penitentiary system into a state of confusion."[132] He argued that in evaluating individual administrators, the Royal Commissioners had ignored basic rules of justice and exceeded their mandate.[133] Indeed, Bennett contested both the assertion that the penitentiaries were mismanaged and the belief that administration by a commission would be superior to management by a single superintendent. "It is one man's direction that always makes for efficient administration in an administrative body," the former prime minister declared.[134] Finally, Bennett argued that the Royal Commission had relied too heavily on the *in camera* testimony of prisoners. Those suffering the results of their own wrongdoing, he claimed, would always complain, and due to the private nature of the hearings, their testimony could not be contradicted.[135]

Agnes Macphail and CCF leader J.S. Woodsworth came to the defence of the bill. Macphail emphasized the need for change in order to prevent further prison unrest and reduce recidivism rates.[136] Woodsworth produced dozens of editorials favouring the bill and argued that crime was often the result of environmental conditions. The "larger number" of criminals, Woodsworth contended, "were the victims of the neglect of society ... I think it is conceded that a very large number of our criminals would have gone straight if they had had half a chance."[137] Woodsworth's comments clearly reflected socialist values and the impact of the Great Depression on public attitudes toward individual responsibility for failure or success. Minister of Justice Lapointe carefully avoided taking such stands. To placate his main political adversary, R.B. Bennett, he admitted that Ormond had "served faithfully" and was "industrious" in office and emphasized that the bill did nothing more than create a prison commission.[138] The work of administering the prisons, said Lapointe, was too much for one man, and the safety of the penal system required a change. Playing further to his audience, Lapointe stated that any major changes thereafter would come before Parliament and that he was not entirely in accord with the Archambault Commission's recommendations.[139] "With some of them I do not agree," said the minister, "and as to many others I have doubts whether they should be carried into practice."[140]

When Lapointe addressed Bennett's concerns, it was for a second audience as well: the Conservative-dominated Senate. He need not have worried. The bill had been introduced late in the session, and the Senate adjourned prior to addressing it. As a result, the bill had to be reintroduced in 1939. By then, Lapointe was under pressure from prison welfare agencies and social service councils to act, and the bill passed through the House of Commons and the Senate without incident.[141] Yet it was never proclaimed. The outbreak of the Second World War in September curtailed any hope of substantive prison reform. Lapointe told anxious prison reformers that the government's energies would be directed to the war effort and that the anticipated reforms would have to wait.

The delay should have been enough to end any hope of reform. After all, most of the major recommendations had been made by previous commissions. The Macdonnell and Biggar, Nickle, and Draper reports had advocated changes to prison conditions, the treatment of prisoners, punishment, labour, and education. Both had also recommended administration by committee. What was different about the Archambault Commission was the nature of its genesis and the reception of its report. After the riots of the early 1930s, widespread pressure from the press, opposition politicians, and reform organizations had led to the commission's appointment. That pressure would be sustained over the following decades. Despite the war, reformers continued to agitate, calling on Lapointe and his successor, Louis St Laurent, to take action.[142]

Postwar Pressure for Implementation

By the time the Second World War ended in 1945, the Archambault Report might have been long forgotten, its recommendations consigned to obscurity alongside those of previous investigations. Almost thirteen years had passed since the riot at Kingston, and seven since the commission's findings had been made public. The intervening war years had been tumultuous, and the federal government now faced major challenges in addressing demobilization and postwar reconstruction. Moreover, Canadian families faced the daunting uncertainties of reunion and the return to civilian life and work. Yet despite all this, the Archambault Commission had not been forgotten, and it would become the blueprint for the "New Deal" in Canadian prisons.[143]

Mathiesen has written that "legislators and the courts may be viewed as 'anxiety barometers,' that is, institutions which, through their decisions, reflect the anxiety level in society."[144] Both during and after the war, officials in the Ministry of Justice and the Penitentiary Service found themselves under sustained public pressure to implement the Archambault recommendations. That pressure came from a wide array of organizations and associations, representing women, religious denominations, social workers, penal reformers, and the political left.[145] Why were so many Canadians determined to see the Archambault recommendations for prison reform acted upon? In part, the answer lies in a wartime panic over rising rates of juvenile delinquency, intensified by anxiety over the changing roles of women.[146] During the early years of the war, juvenile arrest statistics spiked, rising from 9,497 in 1939 to 13,802 in 1942.[147] The increase was due in part to demographic trends and policing practices, but the press attributed the change to the instability of home life during the war.[148] Columnists and editors in several major publications explained that absent fathers and working mothers, though necessitated by the war effort, meant wayward "latchkey" children, who, in the absence of proper guidance and supervision, turned to mischief and crime.[149] The problems posed by unsupervised children were deemed serious enough that in June 1942, the federal government began to subsidize after-school care for the children of women working in war industries.[150] That same concern "confirmed to many Canadians ... that wartime changes in gender roles had to be reversed as soon as the conflict ended in order to reconstitute the type of family stability that would prevent children from going awry."[151] Most importantly for our purposes, many Canadians became convinced that government institutions would have to fulfil the role of re-socializing juvenile delinquents.

Members of Parliament and the boards of voluntary associations maintained pressure on the government to implement the Archambault recommendations throughout the war, but letters and petitions began to arrive at the Ministry of Justice in significant numbers in 1944. The petitioners – including the National Council of Women, the Christian Social Council of Canada, the Canadian Penal Association, and dozens of local organizations – expressed concern over rising rates of juvenile arrests, steadily increasing crime rates, high levels of recidivism, and the possibility of a postwar crime wave.[152] Helen Lewis, writing on behalf of Montreal's League for Women's Rights, explained that

with the present alarming increase in juvenile delinquency throughout Canada and with the approach of the period of readjustment, which after the last war was accompanied by a world-wide wave of crime, it is imperative that the defects in our penal system should be corrected immediately to safeguard the youth of our country and as a measure of reconstruction ... We believe that an opportunity to grow up into an honest, self-respecting citizen is the birthright of every child born in Canada.[153]

The league's representatives wrote that Canada's prisons lacked the necessary "system of rehabilitation" to "reclaim these young people" and that the prisons were ill-prepared to absorb the increasing numbers of prisoners likely to materialize after the war.[154] The executive of Toronto's United Welfare Chest, a social services federation, worried that the unreformed "system of handling offenders is aiding in the creation of a criminal class,"[155] and the Community Welfare Council of Regina, in the context of rising crime rates, added that "the importance of adopting the most advanced criminological and penological concepts and processes becomes very evident."[156] In the New Deal proposed by Archambault, they saw the solution to the problems they had identified.

Reformers' patience with government delays was wearing thin. By 1944, some petitioners were beginning to view the war as a "pretext" for inaction.[157] In November 1945, the Canadian Penal Association took issue with the government's excuse that many of the proposed reforms required federal–provincial cooperation. The association's leaders disagreed, stating that "a great many of the proposed changes in the Archambault Report are exclusively within Federal jurisdiction and require no provincial approval."[158] Most urged the government to do as Archambault suggested and create Borstal institutions to address juvenile delinquency.[159] Borstals were considered so important that the CCF MP E.B. McKay (Weyburn) referred to importation of the Borstal framework as "the main recommendation of the [Archambault] Commission."[160]

Yet the juvenile delinquency scare and the fear of a postwar crime wave do not in themselves explain the campaign to implement the Archambault recommendations. Those who wrote letters and petitions to the Ministry of Justice shared two beliefs: one was that government should take an active, interventionist role in addressing social problems; the other was faith in the efficacy of planned treatment programs. These beliefs – common among women's organizations, church groups, and social workers in Canada in the interwar era – reflect the combined impact of progressivism, the social gospel, and maternal feminism. Each of those influences is evident in their petitions. In these, we see the progressives' methodology of gathering information, analysing the data, and lobbying government to implement solutions; the social gospel effort to save individual souls by reforming the social, economic, and political environment; and the maternal feminist focus on child welfare.[161] Each influence inexorably led to demands for increased government action.

By the end of the war, the public agreed. The CCF advocated the expansion of the social safety net and a planned economy to guarantee jobs for Canadians. As a result, their popularity surged, and the Liberal government responded with comprehensive postwar economic planning and new social security measures.[162] Prison reformer John Kidman connected the struggle for social welfare to legal aid measures: "This is the era of social security measures – security for the family, for the baby, for the aged, for the workman – why not, then, some sign of it in our law courts"?[163] Similarly, interventionist thinking and religious humanitarianism merged in the prison reform movement. In a letter calling for "scientific methods for the re-establishment of first offenders[,] ... the permanent suitable care of recidivists," and the creation of a Borstal system to rehabilitate young offenders, the General Synod of the Church of England in Canada continued to press for improved social security measures throughout society.[164]

Under this pressure, the government acted. Late in 1945, Minister of Justice Louis St Laurent introduced an amendment to the Penitentiary Act (1939), which still had not been proclaimed and put into effect. The amendment allowed cabinet to appoint a single commissioner prior to the proclamation of the act. This appointee was to assess the progress already made toward achieving the Archambault Commission's recommendations and formulate a strategy for future action. In April 1946, General Ralph B. Gibson was appointed to the temporary position.[165] Gibson was a lawyer and – like many who worked in the prison service – a military man. He commanded a militia regiment during peacetime, served in both world wars, and attained the rank of Vice Chief of the General Staff in 1944. His wartime background, knowledge of the law, and management background made him a reasonable choice to set up a plan to implement prison reform.[166]

The Gibson Report

In 1947, Gibson released his report. He had organized the Archambault Commission's recommendations into two groups of four topics each. The first group, which could be addressed in the near term, involved conditions within the penitentiary system: reorganization of the penal administration; classification and segregation; reformative and treatment services; and specific recommendations for improvements within individual penitentiaries. The second group of recommendations, Gibson wrote, were not within the exclusive jurisdiction of the federal government or were explicitly excluded from his terms of reference. On these, he could recommend no specific recourse. Thus, no action could be taken on the centralization of prisons under a single administration, special institutions for young offenders, and recommendations regarding juvenile courts, family courts, and adult probation. In addition, Gibson had been instructed not to consider the Archambault Commission's recommendations surrounding ticket-of-leave and the supervision of parole, which fell under the purview of the Remission Service, and thus outside the scope of the Penitentiary Branch. Within a decade, the federal government would appoint another group of men to study and make recommendations on this subject (see chapter 5).

Sauvant's Progress

Gibson reported that while the war had resulted in delays, more than one hundred reforms had been effected. While often overlooked in accounts of the implementation of the Archambault recommendations, the Acting Superintendent, G.L. Sauvant, had been working on the reforms, and as such, Gibson's report should be viewed as an interim progress report – and a comprehensive plan for future implementation – rather than the origin of the new era. Sauvant knew the system well, having worked as a Librarian School Teacher, then as a Warden's Clerk at Saint-Vincent-de-Paul Penitentiary during the 1932 riot. In his role as Inspector of Penitentiaries, a post he had taken up in July 1934, he had visited every penitentiary in the country before becoming the Acting Superintendent in July 1938.[167] While the wartime reforms could be seen as piecemeal, they were significant. For example, in terms of physical conditions, efforts had been made to improve prisoners' hygiene, kitchen sanitation, and cell lighting.[168] As well, numerous renovations had been completed and new buildings erected; this included improvements to schoolrooms, shops, farm buildings, hospitals, and cell blocks.[169] Significant changes had been made to the prison regulations. Prisoners were allowed to shave and bathe more frequently. Conversation was permitted during specified periods and during outdoor recreation. Letter-writing and visitation privileges had been expanded and were no longer curtailed as punishment. Libraries were improved, and daily radio news reports were broadcast over prison loudspeaker systems.[170] Prisoners were given cigarette lighters. The remission regulations had been simplified, and some small changes had been made in the area of prison discipline.[171] Many of the reforms may seem inconsequential to the non-incarcerated, but they constituted significant changes in prisoners' daily lives.

With respect to work, Gibson reported substantial progress on prison farms: "The acreage usefully employed for farm purposes has been increased from 3127 acres in 1937 to 4918 [acres] in 1946."[172] He bragged that "the value of production from farming operations increased from $68,232.20 for the fiscal year ending March 31st, 1936 to $223,947.88 for the last fiscal year [1946]."[173] At the time of his report, prisoners were producing all the vegetables for the penitentiaries, and the Acting Commissioner reported that dairy and beef herds had been established. Prisoners were also involved in egg production and canning operations.[174]

In the shops, Gibson reported that employment and production levels had increased significantly over the course of the war. Between 1936 and 1946, revenues had increased by over 300 per cent, from $54,266.47 to $187,412.43, and the total value of production had risen to $436,038.22 annually. Still, Gibson noted problems in the industrial department. Several inspections by the Department of Labour identified shortcomings and specified remedies, including the modernization of obsolete equipment, training for instructors, and the introduction of a vocational program.[175]

Gibson's report should not be read as the definitive account of conditions in the Penitentiary Service in 1947. It is clear that he did not present all initiatives undertaken since the Archambault Report. Some initiatives had been omitted in their entirety or received cursory treatment. For example, Gibson contended that vocational instructors were not adequately trained, but internal memos prepared in response to questions by MPs paint a different picture. In a December 1943 memorandum to the deputy minister of justice, Assistant Superintendent W.S. Lawson wrote:

> Job Instructor Training courses have been held in all Penitentiaries and practically all the instructors and Plant Engineers are now in possession of Job Instructor Training Certificates certifying that they have completed training as a war production job instructor and have pledged to apply the principles of good job instruction in their daily work. These courses were held under the supervision of the Department of Labour and lectures were given by expert instructors of that department.[176]

Gibson's report also paid limited attention to efforts to revise the penitentiary regulations, conduct mental testing, compile prisoner case histories, segregate youth job training at several penitentiaries, modernize shops, and plan postwar industrial activity to supply government departments.[177]

Gibson's Plan

Commissioner Gibson's vision for reform prioritized the "reformative training and treatment of the convicts," which, he wrote, was "the main theme of the [Archambault] Commission's Report."[178] On the subject of prisoner rehabilitation, he focused on industrial, educational, and medical services as well as prison discipline. Gibson, following Archambault, wrote that "continuous and useful employment is a potent instrument of discipline and reformation."[179] Yet he added to Archambault's concept of work as an inherently reformative instrument, suggesting that the Penitentiary Service should refocus industrial development to combine production with "training value for employment after discharge."[180] While this utilitarian principle may have been implicit in many of the Archambault recommendations, it was not stated explicitly in the report. Gibson emphasized that to develop such a training program, the Penitentiary Service needed to modernize its industrial plant and take full advantage of the federal policy permitting prison-industrial production for state use. This would require "the fullest cooperation of other government departments in placing orders."[181] Money for modernization was provided in the estimates.[182] However, securing government orders would prove to be an ongoing difficulty.

Gibson commented little on the subjects of education and medical/psychiatric services. Yet the brevity of his comments should not be construed as disinterest. Rather, he understood the magnitude of the changes required in these areas and the need for dedicated administrative expertise to oversee and implement reforms. As he explained, improving prison education would require the skills of an "experienced educationist."[183] He recommended that one of the two deputy commissioners be appointed to supervise the educational branch, survey prisoners' educational needs, and cooperate with universities and experts in the field to devise a program of adult education.[184] As will be made clear in chapter 4, educational and vocational opportunities for prisoners remained limited through the 1950s. The other deputy commissioner would oversee the medical branch and conduct a survey of medical arrangements in order to recommend further changes.[185]

Regarding classification and segregation, the commissioner recommended that classification officers be hired at each institution and that prisoners be transferred to appropriate facilities based on their evaluations. The penitentiaries in Kingston and Manitoba were to house "incorrigible and intractable prisoners whose conduct and anti-social attitude makes it desirable to separate them from the normal prison population in other institutions."[186] The penitentiaries in Collins Bay and Saskatchewan would serve as "institutions for the treatment of young convicts and the reformable type of prisoner," with special facilities for vocational training.[187] Gibson recommended the construction of a third institution of this type in Quebec, operating on "the principles of the Borstal system."[188] Once the system of classification, transfers, and segregation was in place, the commissioner envisioned the introduction of the Archambault Commission's proposal to implement "a grade and merit system modelled on the system in use in England."[189] None of these recommendations would be implemented.

The commissioner reported that some minor changes had already been made on the issue of prison discipline. In a remarkable shift from the top-down approach taken by former Superintendent Ormond, Gibson proposed that before undertaking further revision of the penitentiary regulations, discussion with the wardens should occur: "Your Commissioner considers it essential that the Wardens, who are responsible for the administration of discipline, should be consulted and given the opportunity of expressing their views upon proposed changes in methods before they are taken into effect." He recommended that a wardens' conference be held in the near future for that purpose.[190] In this respect, Gibson concurred with Archambault, suggesting that change be implemented cautiously, through "a gradual, well-planned reconstruction" of the prison system. In his estimation, "precipitate action without proper preparation would invite failure."[191] Criminologist Bob Gaucher has written that these consultations reflected "the conundrum [of] resistance to change [that] characterized institutional authorities (from keepers to guards), while (cautious) desire for change characterized Headquarters."[192]

With regard to the reorganization of the Penitentiary Service administration, Gibson's hands were tied. The Archambault Commission had recommended the creation of a three-member commission to oversee the prison system. This proposal was premised on the federal takeover of all jails, reformatories, and penitentiaries in Canada. Since no arrangements for centralization had been worked out with the provinces, the federal cabinet had decided that a single commissioner would oversee the penitentiary system with the aid of a number of deputy and assistant commissioners.[193] Whether Gibson supported that decision or not is unknown, but he did accept the permanent position of commissioner on 5 April 1946.[194] Two deputy commissioners, Joseph McCulley (to oversee education, recreation, religious activities, and staff training) and G.L. Gendreau (to oversee medical and psychiatric services and "the development of research and statistics to assess the adequacy and results of present and proposed methods of correctional treatment") were appointed.[195] On the surface, the work of these two men was equally necessary, but as we will see in subsequent chapters, neither the commissioner nor the prisoners paid much attention to Gendreau, while tremendous and detailed accounts of McCulley and his work are available.[196] So it is important that McCulley's background be given some consideration so that we can later understand how his ideals came to serve as the backbone of the New Deal reforms – tellingly referred to by some prisoners as the McCulley–Gibson plan.[197]

McCulley, formerly headmaster of Pickering College, had been recommended to Commissioner Gibson by prison reform advocate Alex Edmison.[198] McCulley and Edmison had known each other since their days as staff members at a YMCA children's camp in Ontario in the 1920s.[199] McCulley has been described as Christian, democratic, and socialist in outlook, and his ideals were shaped by both progressivism and the social gospel.[200] In a piece written for *Canadian Forum* in 1934 and a speech on education written in 1945, McCulley expressed concern that power over politics, the economy, and institutions – including churches and schools – was becoming concentrated in fewer and fewer hands, thus threatening democracy and economic liberty and producing inequality.[201] He argued that individuals and governments had an obligation "to change the unideal, to bring it nearer to the ideal, to bring nearer to realization the prophet's dream of a kingdom of God on earth."[202] For McCulley, the ideal was "the Beloved Community in which *the welfare of each is the concern of all*,"[203] and he repeatedly emphasized "the infinite worth of every human soul."[204]

At Pickering College, McCulley was permitted great latitude. There, he led a Dewey-ite progressive experiment in education, which he hoped would imbue students with a sense of "moral equality" and influence them to favour democracy and social justice.[205] The school was operated by a joint student/staff committee that oversaw administration and operations. McCulley emphasized cooperation rather than competition and coercion.[206] Project-based assignments took precedence over formal examinations. Corporal punishment and formal discipline were discouraged.[207] McCulley believed that students were more likely to respond to kindness than punishment and hoped to create an atmosphere in which they could be encouraged to make sound choices.[208] The headmaster argued that all individuals sought to fulfil five basic "urges" – for "recognition, experience, affection, power, and security" – and that it was better to provide legitimate outlets for those urges than to repress them.[209] Yet he was not, as Joel Kropf has emphasized, willing to "live and let live." Rather, he expected teachers to exercise an influence over their students' character and ideals. The aim was to inculcate a specific set of values through a combination of sympathy, idealism, and persuasion and to cultivate those values in students through the development of self-discipline.[210] Regarding the latter process, McCulley argued that "you cannot learn to be good or how to make good choices in an environment where there is no chance to be bad. Character comes from choice and choices are only possible in an atmosphere of freedom."[211]

Joel Kropf has argued that the ideals that McCulley championed at Pickering College "served as significant ingredients in the perspective to which he adhered" during his postwar stint in the Penitentiary Service.[212] His energy seemed boundless. A colleague described him as "a real pusher, a real dynamo," and he played a key role in introducing new vocational and academic opportunities in the penitentiaries, in the development of training courses and a staff college for penitentiary officers, and in organizing recreational and leisure activities for prisoners.[213] As Kropf has explained, McCulley expected that providing such opportunities "would help to highlight inmates' humanness, showing 'that the administration recognizes them as human beings with normal human needs.'"[214] Moreover, McCulley justified the changes he pursued (but did not always achieve) by arguing that the reformation of prisoners would contribute to the protection of society.[215] In sum, the values that McCulley brought with him to his work as deputy commissioner created the New Deal's main refrain: "Prisoners Are People."

By 1947, the way forward seemed clear. Some work had already been done; a leader and his assistants were in place; they had a slogan and a plan. Now they faced the daunting tasks of restructuring the Penitentiary Service and implementing the New Deal. It was by no means clear that they could achieve these goals. The recommendations of the Macdonnell and Biggar, Nickle, and Draper inquiries had gone largely unfulfilled. Was Archambault similarly fated to remain unfinished? In Part II of this book we examine the reforms – both their successes and their failures – and consider whether the lauded place in criminological texts that the Archambault Report occupies is merited.

PART II

Disruptive Influences

3 "Men Who Beefed":
Writing the New Deal

The Archambault Report provided the government with a blueprint for reform. The first Commissioner of Penitentiaries needed to build from there. The New Deal offered a comprehensive approach operating under the mantra "Prisoners Are People." Reformation, rather than discipline and punishment, was to guide the Penitentiary Service's actions. The first section of this book documented the origins of the New Deal; the following chapters examine its implementation. Much has been written on this topic, but no research has integrated the voices of the subjects of those interventions – the prisoners. Current texts are saturated with an administrative history that simply does not account for how the reforms were experienced and engaged with by those behind the bars and consequently cannot account for the course of the New Deal. Fortunately, one of the first initiatives undertaken as part of the New Deal provides us with a primary source grounded in the lived experience of prisoners: the penal press. Part II of this book uses these materials extensively to provide a critical analysis of prison reform between 1935 and 1960. However, before considering how the penal press exemplified the New Deal and offering an analysis of it rooted in lived experience, it is important to explain and document the provenance of these records.

The Creation of the Penal Press in Canada

Deputy Commissioner Joseph McCulley first asked Commissioner Ralph Gibson to give the idea of starting a penal press[1] "serious consideration" on 19 May 1948, contending that it could boost prison morale.[2] McCulley was drawing on his knowledge of the long history of the penal press in the United States.[3] He argued that prison newspapers would "touch all members of the convict population."[4] He was not wrong.

McCulley was dogged in his efforts to get the press started. On 7 December 1948, he wrote to Gibson again, stating that staff at Collins Bay Institution and Kingston Penitentiary were keen to create a prison magazine. He suggested that perhaps they could launch a general four-page joint paper (no pun intended) with a specific insert for each institution. McCulley's tenacity was evident when he wrote to the warden at Collins Bay in June 1949 to remind him that a penal press was "not out of line with the developing programme."[5]

However, it was not the warden at Collins Bay who accepted the challenge. Instead, on 14 July 1950, Warden Allan of Kingston Penitentiary wrote to Gibson to say they wanted to replace their *Softball Bulletin* with a "permanent prison newspaper." Allan claimed that "the interest which has been displayed in the softball bulletin justifies an enlargement of this paper to the point where regular issues can be made throughout the year."[6] He noted that there were two prisoners at Kingston who could do the work, that the facility had space to house the publication, and that the costs would be minimal. In a handwritten note at the bottom of this memo, Gibson stated that the press was "a worthwhile innovation"[7] and gave approval in principle.

A week later, Gibson wrote to Warden Allan requesting more information as well as assurances that there was adequate staff support for supervision. He also wanted confirmation that the convict editors were up to the task and that there were replacements for them in the event they were released. He also requested details on the format and cost of publication. While Gibson's requests may sound bureaucratic, his approach tracked closely with Russell Baird's view of the penal press in the United States: "The most common source of difficulty with penal publications – dispute over policy – are minimized," Baird claimed, "if reasonable policies are established and inmates know in advance of application, if the editors are carefully selected, and if competent supervision is provided."[8]

In his letter to Warden Allan, Gibson's concluding rationale was prophetic: "A project of this nature, once approved, becomes very difficult to discontinue."[9] Allan, unable to anticipate the impact the penal press would have on the prisoners, disagreed with the commissioner, arguing that publication could be discontinued at "any time without any unfavourable reaction from the convict population."[10] Interestingly, a handwritten notation appears at the bottom of this memo: "if the paper serves it's [sic] function, it's [sic] discontinuance *should* cause some convict reaction. Once instituted on a satisfactory basis, however, I see no

Image 3.1. *Tele-Scope* prototype cover, 1950, LAC, Correctional Service of Canada fonds, vol. 105, file 4-11-26, pt 1.

reason why it should be necessary to discontinue it, if present basic policies [i.e., the New Deal] are to be continued."[11]

On 11 August 1950, Allan provided written assurances to Gibson and enclosed a prototype of *Tele-Scope* (see Image 3.1). Informal discussions had by then taken place, for Allan anticipated publishing the first issue the very next month. Indeed, the editors had already been chosen. In an 8 August 1950 handwritten letter to his warden, editor-elect Gordon Marr noted that it would be good to have a message from the commissioner for the front page "as soon as possible, as we now have considerable parts of this edition ready for press."[12]

Soon after this, McCulley recommended to Gibson that $500 be allotted to Kingston Penitentiary to publish *Tele-Scope* for the 1950–51 fiscal year.[13] He also indicated his acceptance of the suggested editors. A few weeks later, in September 1950, the first issue of *Tele-Scope* was published. Warden Allan estimated an annual circulation of 24,000 copies at a cost of $0.34 per issue based on 16 to 20 pages per edition.[14] This inaugural issue included introductory messages from the administration, sports news, and columns on hobbycraft, education, and trades, as well as an editorial inviting prisoners to become contributors.[15]

Even before the launch, Gord Marr, nascent editor of *Tele-Scope*, saw the power of the medium to provide information and opportunity. In a handwritten letter to Warden Allan, he stated that the penal press would offer "the inmate body the opportunity to learn to express themselves in a constructive, orderly and appreciative manner."[16] He also believed that *Tele-Scope* could "establish a permanent link between the Commissioner, the Administration and the inmate body,"[17] a sentiment consistent with McCulley's practices at Pickering College (see chapter 2). To this end, Marr wanted the first two pages to be "permanently reserved" for the commissioner and administration (see Image 3.2) so that they could demonstrate an interest in the publication and use it to communicate correctional policies and directions; this was not to be.[18] Over the next decade, the administration's submissions to the penal press were mostly "well-wishes" when publications launched, or they were anniversary or holiday greetings. Gibson wrote on the first page of *Tele-Scope* that the publication was "a history making event. It is the first time in the history of Canadian penitentiaries that an opportunity has been provided for the expression of the inmate opinion and for an exchange of views between the Administration and the population."[19] These claims notwithstanding, neither he nor his underlings would contribute much writing in the subsequent decade.[20] In fact, there is evidence that the wardens believed they could not rebut assertions in the penal press.[21] While exchanges between prisoners and administrators may not have manifested themselves in the way Marr envisioned, it is clear that the penal press generated discussions between administrators. For example, in a November 1955 letter, the commissioner asked the warden at Saskatchewan Penitentiary about an article he had read: "In the November issue of 'The Pathfinder' there is an article at page 9 and 11 written by inmate CAPSTICK in which reference is made to an alleged cut in the periods allotted for outdoor recreation by two-thirds during the

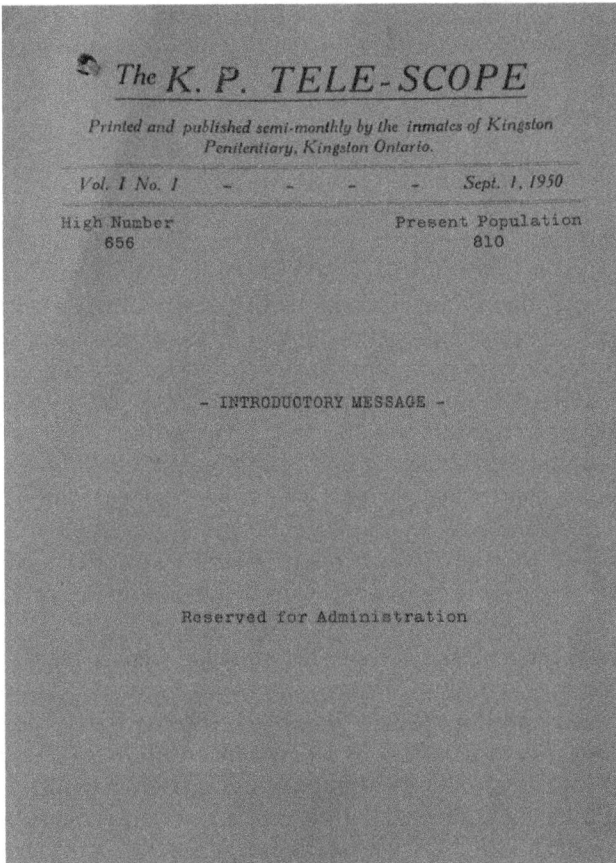

Image 3.2. *Tele-Scope* prototype inside page, 1950, LAC, Correctional Service of Canada fonds, vol. 105, file 4-11-26, pt 1.

past two or three years ... [Have] available [exercise periods] in fact been cut from 240 minutes to 60 minutes per day?"[22] In his response, the acting warden was forced to concede that the allegations made in the press were "correct to a certain extent"; he then went on to justify this reduction.[23] Here we see the penal press being used to keep the commissioner apprised of what "was really happening" inside and forcing an exchange between him and his underlings. No wonder then that prisoners' letters to the commissioner were blocked by at least one warden; the concerns over the correspondence were neatly summarized by the deputy commissioner, who stated that "there is a continuing 'battle of wits' in which the Editors [of *Pathfinder*] hope to have the Commissioner as an ally."[24]

The Penal Press Expands

As Table 3.1 shows, *Tele-Scope* was not to be an only child for long. As Robert Gaucher noted in his documentation of the Canadian penal press, by 1952, five other institutions had started their own publications. When prisoners at Saskatchewan Penitentiary began publishing *Pathfinder* in February 1951, *Tele-Scope* acknowledged its launch: "The K.P. Tele-scope has stiff competition. The initial edition of the Saskatchewan Penitentiary *Pathfinder* dropped into our office this week and it's a swell effort. Congratulations to the *Pathfinder*'s editorial staff for a commendable start. We know that the *Pathfinder* shall help us to lead the way to foster better understanding by the Canadian public of the inmate and his problems. Welcome to the penal press."[25] In this simple statement, we see the emergence of a friendly rivalry.

The press pushed farther west. *Transition* began publication at BC Penitentiary a month after *Pathfinder*'s launch. It moved east when, after a naming contest was held, the bilingual *Pen-O-Rama* replaced the *Sports Bulletin* at Saint-Vincent-de-Paul Penitentiary in May 1951. Dorchester Penitentiary's *Beacon* commenced weekly publication in the summer of 1951, making the penal press a truly national undertaking. The name *Beacon* generated comment almost immediately. One prisoner indicated that he liked it because "from the point of view of location; a watch tower [sic] of observation and its guiding light piercing the heart of darkness so that others may see beyond – [it is] an excellent choice."[26] Another pointed out that "it has a different meaning when you put it this way: BE-A-CON!"[27] *Mountain Echoes* from Manitoba Penitentiary appeared on the circuit in September 1951. Collins Bay Institution, which McCulley had years earlier envisioned being the birthplace of the Canadian penal press, finally converted its inside-directed sports flyer into an outside-directed magazine, *C.B. Diamond*, in January 1952.[28] The rapid spread of the penal press suggests its importance to prisoners. Michael Marks has emphasized the importance of prisoners' sense of community and group identification as mechanisms for coping with the pains of imprisonment, and as we will see, the penal press served this purpose.[29]

Table 3.1. List of penal press publications in print, 1950–1960

Publication	Penitentiary	Dates of publication
Sports Bulletin	Saint-Vincent-de-Paul	May 1950–Sept. 1951
Tele-Scope	Kingston	Sept. 1950–1968
Pathfinder	Saskatchewan	Feb. 1951–1966
C.B. Diamond	Collins Bay	Apr. 1951–Apr. 1968
The Beacon	Dorchester	July 1951–Jan. 1971
Pen-O-Rama	Saint-Vincent-de-Paul	May 1951–Dec. 1968
Transition	BC	Apr. 1951–1963
Mountain Echoes	Manitoba	Sept. 1951–June 1965

Source: Gaucher, "The Canadian Penal Press."

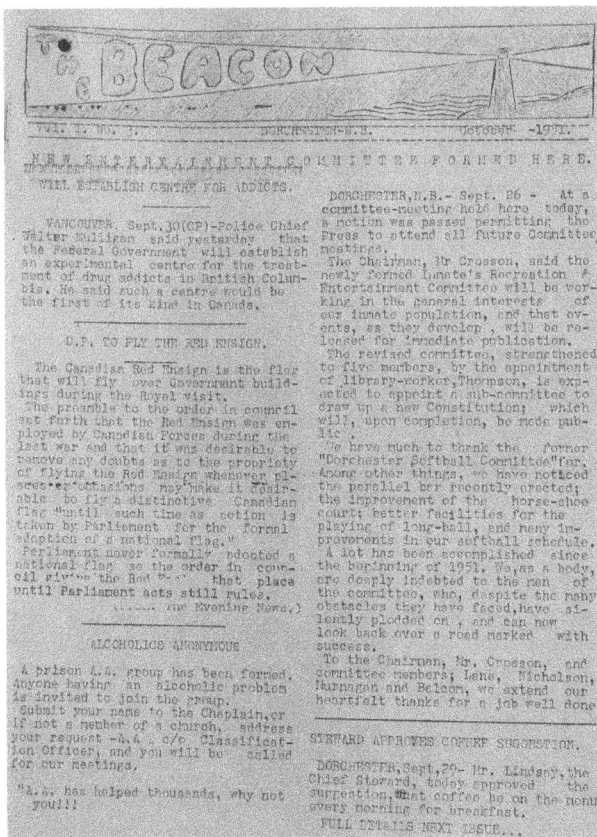

Image 3.3. *The Beacon* cover, October 1951, vol. 1 no. 3. Gaucher/Munn penal press collection.

Image 3.4. *Transition* cover, May–June 1958. Gaucher/Munn penal press collection.

Image 3.5. *Mountain Echoes* cover, September 1951. Gaucher/Munn penal press collection.

Image 3.6. *Pen-O-Rama* cover, January 1953. Gaucher/Munn penal press collection.

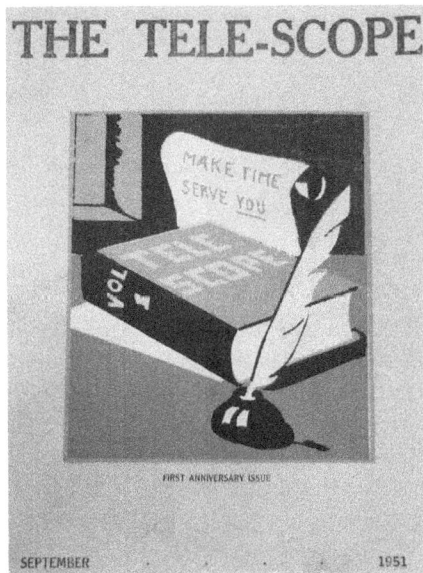

Image 3.7. Cover of the *Tele-Scope*, First Anniversary Edition, September 1951. W.D. Jordan Rare Books and Special Collections, Queen's University Library.

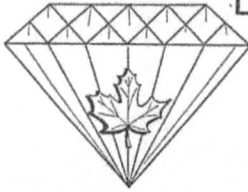

May 1956

C.B.

DIAMOND

∝ *I Favour Hanging*

∝ *A Helping Hand*

∝ *The Case For Parole*

∝ *Editorial*

Image 3.8. *C.B. Diamond* cover, May 1956. Gaucher/Munn penal press collection.

Taking Shape: The Technical Aspects of the Penal Press

While the press's function was fairly consistent at a superficial level, its form varied considerably (see Images 3.3–3.9). Some of the publications had access to full printing and silk-screening services and won awards for "best cover design of all penitentiary periodicals."[30] Others relied on donated typewriters[31] or old gestetner and mimeograph machines.[32] In the penal press's first decade of existence, it was not uncommon to see requests for donations of necessary equipment appearing on the pages. Often their pleas were heard. Members of the public, printing houses, and companies like Pepsi donated paper, type, cuts, engraving, and cash. In 1952, *Pen-O-Rama* even received a full printing press from the Gazette Printing Company of Canada.[33]

PATHFINDER

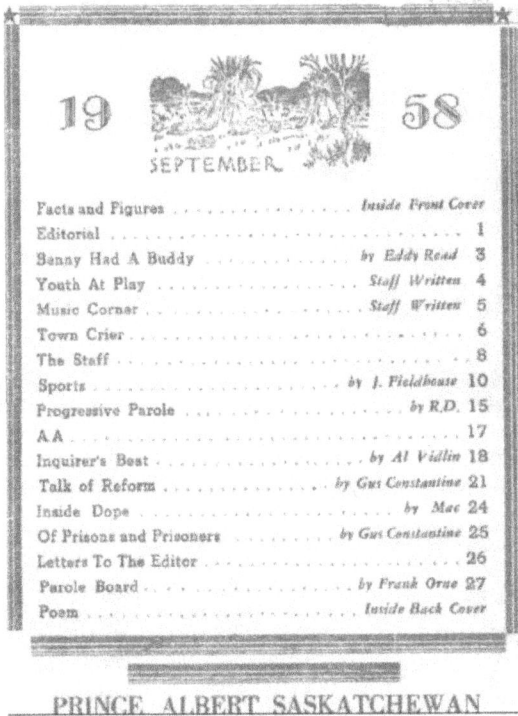

19   58

SEPTEMBER

PRINCE ALBERT SASKATCHEWAN

Image 3.9. *Pathfinder* cover, September 1958. Gaucher/Munn penal press collection.

Production costs and equipment were early but persistent issues. Some publications were allotted start-up costs, others were not. Early on, the lack of funds was pointed out to McCulley by managing editor W. Lake of *Mountain Echoes;* following this meeting, the deputy commissioner authorized $100 for that publication. He asked that this decision be communicated to the editorial staff in part to "indicate in a tangible way the cooperation of the Commissioner and the interest of the Headquarters staff."[34]

The founding editors recognized that a broader subscription base would bring them a stronger voice and more influence, besides providing more financial stability. They lobbied for permission to accept outside

Image 3.10. Prisoner at printing press, unknown date, Kingston Penitentiary Museum, Accession No.2012.032.02.

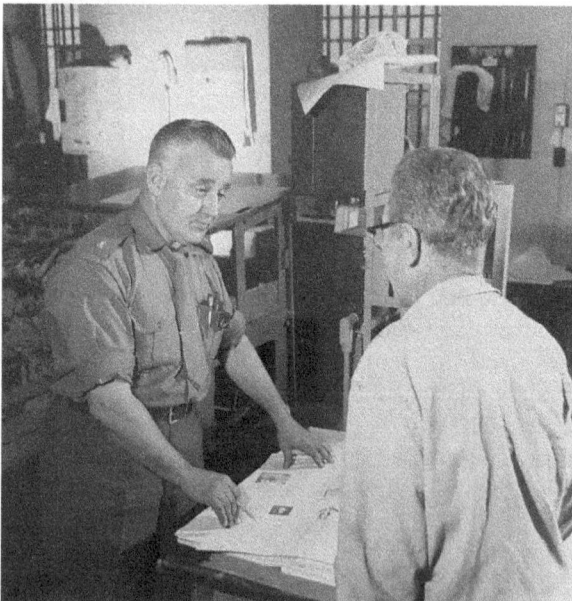

Image 3.11. Penitentiary Services worker reviews copy with prisoner for *The Tele-Scope*, unknown date, Kingston Penitentiary Museum, Accession No.2012.032.02.

subscriptions because there was an "evident need to inform the taxpayer what goes on inside these walls and hold up for his inspection the new rehabilitation program currently unfolding in this and other Canadian penal institutions. So far, the reaction to this 'propaganda' has been, for the most part, healthy and encouraging."[35] Subscriptions were opened to the public in 1951, and by the end of the decade, the penal press had a diverse local, national, and international readership. While there was an expectation that convicts' family members would subscribe, their audience was in fact much broader than that – it included clergy, medical personnel, teachers, labour unions, parents' groups, community-based service agencies, guards, public and university libraries, newspapers and magazines, corporations, politicians, lawyers, and housewives, among others. Administrative records indicate that there was a great deal of controversy over outside subscriptions. For example, Commissioner Gibson and Deputy Commissioner March disagreed on the issue of whether prisoners should be able to purchase subscriptions for others. March argued that prisoners could use subscriptions to communicate with people with whom other forms of communication were forbidden. Gibson did not object and saw prisoners' desire to send subscriptions to others as an example of "pride in their magazine."[36]

Favourable reviews in the mainstream press spurred the rapid growth of the penal press during this early period. For example, in November 1952, *Pen-O-Rama* had 900 English and 1,925 French subscriptions.[37] One month later, they printed 3,400 copies of the December edition.[38] This far exceeded the predictions of the liaison officer, who in August 1952 had anticipated perhaps 300 subscriptions![39] By March 1953, *C.B. Diamond* had 700 subscribers.

While penal press magazines only charged outside subscribers $1 to $2 per year, the funds did, for the most part, cover the costs of publication. In some cases, they made a profit. In a document titled "Policy for Financing Inmate Prison Newspapers," Penitentiary Service accountants revealed that only 36 per cent of the monies received for *Tele-Scope* were needed to cover costs. The balance was deposited in the convicts' recreation and welfare fund.[40] At Saint-Vincent-de-Paul, $1,100 in proceeds were given to purchase books for the prison library.[41] This publication further solidified its finances by selling advertising space to local businesses as well as larger companies like Pepsi-Cola, Carling Brewery, Eaton's, Player's Tobacco, and Snap-On Tools Canada[42] (see Images 3.12 and 3.13 for examples of advertising that appeared in the penal press). By 1953, *Mountain Echoes* was able to buy its own printing press at a cost of $175.[43] However, in some cases, operating costs were not covered. These magazines tried to cut their expenses by publishing

Enjoy Coke...ice cold

Right from the bottle

"Coke" is a registered trade-mark.   COCA-COLA LTD.

Image 3.12. Coca-Cola advertisement, *Tele-Scope*, August 1959, back cover. Gaucher/Munn penal press collection.

less frequently or with less content, by lowering subscription costs (to increase circulation), or by borrowing from Inmate Welfare Funds.[44]

Physical space, or lack thereof, was another problem. In August 1950 the editor of *Sports Bulletin* wrote:

> Your editor is compelled to work in his cell with two typewriters, one for editing text and one (smaller face type for stencils. He had to buy a typewriter especially to make these stencils.) [sic] It is somewhat awkward to have two big typewriters in one cell. The Committee is hoping that the authorities will soon find a place to establish a permanent office, where editorial and technical work will be done at ease and on time. As soon as we get this office, the editor will install his typewriters there, the secretary will store his files there, and the Committee will appoint an assistant to work exclusively on summaries, stencils and correspondence.[45]

Player's "MILD"

LA CIGARETTE
LA PLUS DOUCE, LA PLUS SAVOUREUSE

Plus populaire

Auprès des ménagères

Que toutes les autres

Marques réunies.

ROBIN HOOD FLOUR

MILLS LIMITED

Image 3.13. Advertising by Player's and Robin Hood in *Pen-O-Rama*, December 1958. Gaucher/Munn penal press collection.

We know that the administration was eager to show its support. At Saint-Vincent-de-Paul, by the time *Pen-O-Rama* was officially launched, editor André Dion and his illustrator had been given space in the library and allowed free movement throughout the prison in order to conduct their business.[46] Even so, the adequacy of facilities continued to be a problem. In 1958, the editorial board of *C.B. Diamond* resigned when their space was given to the classification department.[47]

To make use of extant equipment and skills, some penal press publications relied on others for their printing. For example, *C.B. Diamond* was printed by prisoners operating the industrial press at Kingston Penitentiary, where government forms were produced.[48] This worked well until there was a disturbance at Kingston Penitentiary that closed the print shop down, albeit temporarily. *Pathfinder* also relied on the prison's industrial print shop, which prioritized the printing of government forms. This arrangement affected the editor's ability to produce a nicer layout or increase the amount of material:

> Publishing of the magazine must not interfere with the production of the print shop. If no industrial job is to be run on the larger of the platen presses, it may be used to print the issue being assembled. Although the type used in the printing of this magazine belongs to the print shop, it is assigned exclusively to The Pathfinder. There is sufficient type to set six pages. These must then be printed and the type distributed back into the cases before any more pages can be set.[49]

It was only to be expected that the state enjoyed the inside position regarding use of the press. According to the commissioner's report, the print shops were a significant industrial activity, printing six million pages of government forms annually; the penal press was characterized as an informal educational activity.[50] In essence, institutional requirements trumped the interests of the penal press, which was seen as an interesting, if tangential, experiment in the larger context of prison reform.

The Penal Press Finds Purpose

Not surprisingly, Joseph McCulley, who had done so much to launch the penal press, took great interest in its development. He provided the following advice to the editors of *Mountain Echoes* in November 1951:

> It is interesting to note that each of the prison papers is developing all on its own individual lines. This is, I think, as it should be inasmuch as there

are fairly wide variations in each of our seven penitentiaries although we are, of course, endeavouring to implement a similar general philosophy in all them. If I might make a suggestion to your Committee, therefore, it would be that they should work to make your paper satisfy the needs of their own Institution, its inmates, its staff in your own local public, rather than it should necessarily be patterned after any of the other inmate papers.[51]

It seems that the editors concurred with McCulley, for each magazine developed its own principles and practices.[52] Every magazine positioned itself as "the voice of the inmate," but beyond that basic premise, they differed.

The back cover of the inaugural edition of *Tele-Scope* stated: "Kingston Penitentiary Tele-Scope is published for the purpose of providing an outlet for individual expression and a link for establishing unity in thought and action that may prove beneficial to everyone in promoting good fellowship. Also a medium to stimulate a personal interest in the educational, industrial, hobbycraft, sports and entertainment fields."[53] Within a year of launch, the prisoners at Kingston Penitentiary were also using their magazine to help newcomers adjust to prison life. As James Carleton recounted,

that first night in the cell one of the chaps near me was kind enough to send me down six copies of the Tele-Scope. I could hardly put them down once I started to read them. They were so filled with truth, written by men and women just like myself, men who were inside, beyond that wall of separation from loved ones and from a way of life all of us long for, but probably never fully appreciated until we were deprived of it ... It is good to see a publication that reflects so much work, ability and heartfelt realism.[54]

Other publications used their pages in a similar way, to orient new convicts to prison life. *C.B. Diamond* offered a full-page piece titled "The Prisoner's Ten Commandments" (see Image 3.15), which was reprinted in *Transition*.[55] This type of material may also have been a means to mitigate the pains of imprisonment by creating group cohesion through "vehement vocal support of the inmate code."[56] However, as Erving Goffman pointed out, adoption of such a code is always tentative within a total institution: "The individual is formed by groups, identifies with groups, and wilts away unless he obtains emotional support from groups. But ... we always find the individual employing methods to keep some distance, some elbow room, between himself and that with which others assume he should be identified."[57] Later in this

For Unity of Expression

The K.P. TELE-SCOPE is published for the purpose of providing an outlet for individual expression and a link for establishing unity in thought and action that may prove beneficial to everyone in promoting good fellowship.   Also a medium to stimulate a personal interest in the educational, industrial, hobby-craft, sport and entertainment fields.

This is your paper, and the Editorial Staff requests you to take a personal, active interest in its publication by submitting your art, poetic or inventive talent, your inside news and views of daily interesting happenings around you.

Let your expression be governed by:

1.   Interesting ideas and news,
2.   Sensible, helpful suggestions,
3.   Constructive criticism,
4.   Clean humour

Keeping in mind to express yourself as briefly as possible and to the point.   Space is limited.

———◇———

"Do Not Serve Time,
        Make Time Serve You."

Image 3.14. Statement of purpose appearing on back cover of *Tele-Scope*, vol. 1, no. 1, September 1950. LAC.

The Prisoner's Ten Commandments

I

Thou shalt respect the rights of thy fellow prisoner, giving unto him the same consideration which thou desireth thyself.

II

Honor the rules and regulations, lest thy time be over-long in this land to which the judge hath sent thee.

III

Thou shalt mind thine own business, lest thy proboscis be scarred by the blows of wrath of thy fellow man.

IV

Thou shalt not bear false witness against thy neighbor, lest thou be branded all the days thou dwellest here.

V

Thou shalt not covet thy neighbor's weed, nor his books, nor his pipe, nor his blankets, nor his job, lest thou wake up some morning to find thyself stripped of all thy dearest possessions.

VI

Thou shalt not cry, 'Bum Rap!' lest thy fellow prisoners shun thee like the plague.

VII

Thou shalt not force thine aggressions upon thy fellow man, for verily, his adversities are as great as thine own.

VIII

Do well the work allotted thee, lest thou find thyself held accountable for thy laziness.

IX

Incur not the wrath of thy keepers, lest thou be cast into the darkness of the dungeon.

X

Honor these Commandments and refute them not, lest thou suffer great disappointments toward securing an early departure.

Image 3.15. The Prisoner's Ten Commandments, *C.B. Diamond*, July 1957. Gaucher/Munn penal press collection.

chapter, we will consider the tensions inherent in representing captives in a total institution.

Mountain Echoes stated its goals as follows: to "provide inmates with an opportunity for self-expression and a medium for discussion of public problems, to foster better understanding between the inmates and the Administration, and to serve as a medium for the promotion of useful thought and activity within the institution."[58] The administration and staff both recognized the internal communication potential of the penal press; in marking the first anniversary of *Tele-Scope*, Deputy Warden S.C. Davidson at Kingston Penitentiary noted that it had "been a means of bringing about a better understanding between officers and inmates."[59]

These goals were sensible when these publications were in-house organs only. But as an outside readership began to develop, the stated goals of the press changed: editors assigned greater importance to the education of the free masses and those involved in the criminal justice system. Thus, in the March 1952 edition of *C.B. Diamond*, the editors offered the following statement of the magazine's purpose: "It aims to be a home magazine to encourage moral and intellectual improvement among the inmates; to acquaint the public with the true status of the inmate; to disseminate penological information; and to aid in dispelling the prejudice which has been the bar sinister to a fallen man's redemption."[60] The shift in focus was noted and lauded by members of the administration. The following statement from the Classification Department at Kingston Penitentiary both describes and prescribes the new tenor of the press: "Your magazine is an organ of criticism, public relations, news, entertainment and education all at once. There will be shifts in emphasis from time to time as you find need to give importance to one or the other of these features. We see a trend now to emphasize public relations as education. This is good and you are to be congratulated."[61]

"Prisoners Are People" and the "New Deal" Materialize

The editors of *Transition* wanted their magazine to become "a publication with intrinsic merit as well as novelty appeal."[62] Those last words are important. The penal press repeatedly acknowledged that part of its role was to help humanize the incarcerated for the public, but it also realized that subscriptions relied, to some degree, on salacious interest – readers wanted to know what actually *happened* in prisons. Ginny A., a female prisoner writing for *Tele-Scope*, said: "No longer does the public have to believe that we are confined to cage-like cells with nothing to do but time. Now they can realize that we are thinking individuals, and not an army of sad, grey-looking women with our days and nights occupied in mulling over past sins and mistakes and in counting off the hours in the oft believed prison fashion."[63]

There is strong evidence that the penal press did help the public see prisoners differently. Bob Blackburn of the *Ottawa Citizen* wrote that "the first effect of reading through the Tele-scope was a sudden and rather startling realization that the contributing writers are people. People like you and I."[64] Similarly, in a 1958 letter to *Tele-Scope*, Doris McDonald wrote: "I am one of the many who have a very distorted view of the inside of our federal prisons. You are to be complimented on your achievement in being able to reach out and enlighten the public on such an important matter."[65] The editor of the *Edmonton Journal* wrote of *Pathfinder*: "Productions of this quality are striking reminders of the valuable human material that often becomes involved in crimes and winds up in prison."[66] Others saw the penal press as a mode of deterrence for young people; one police officer bought a subscription to keep his son behaving well![67] A teacher suggested that the government provide subscriptions to *Pathfinder* for all schools because he saw it as "more beneficial than large volumes of social studies, etc."[68]

Beyond the "Prisoners Are People" rhetoric, outside readers and writers made the link between these publications and the New Deal's rehabilitative focus.[69] In the House of Commons, Liberal-Progressive MP William Weir (Portage-Neepawa), commended the government on the changes happening in the prison system. He concluded:

> I happen to have in my hand another little innovation which I thought indicated a very useful effort on the part of the institution. It is the publication of a little pamphlet in the form of a monthly news bulletin known as the *Mountain Echo*. It is a well prepared booklet having to do mostly with the institution, the life therein and some of the personnel. I look upon it as a creditable effort, and one in which those who are associated with the institution, particularly those within it, can take pride. The publication is in my opinion something that should be commended.[70]

Sidney Katz of *Maclean's* magazine saw the role of the penal press thusly: "They give the outside public a revealing and intimate picture of prison life. They must also play an important role in the rehabilitation of the prisoners concerned with their production."[71] Prisoners too advanced this argument. In a 14 November 1957 letter to the commissioner, the editor of *Mountain Echoes* described two former editors of that publication who had left the prison and found work in the free press.[72] The same rehabilitative connection was made by Alex Edmison, Principal of Queen's University, in his address to the Canadian Psychological Association:

> Here is another example and it concerns a former inmate of Kingston Penitentiary. He was a man with a long record, several jail sentences and three or four terms in the penitentiary. You would look at his dossier and say – "Here is a professional criminal, quite beyond reform." Yet, during his last term in Kingston he became Editor of the Kingston Penitentiary "Telescope" – a splendid monthly magazine written and printed by inmates. (Send one dollar to the Warden and you will receive 12 interesting issues of this fine publication!) When he was discharged from prison I saw him

in my capacity as a representative of the John Howard Society of Ontario. He said – "This time I won't go back. As Editor of the K.P. Telescope I'd be letting the other boys down." That was two years ago. Two weeks ago he brought his bride to see me ... It was appropriate that he and his wife should be motored to my home by Mr. Joseph McCulley, now Warden of Hart House – but formerly Deputy Commissioner of Penitentiaries. This combination of circumstances would have been quite impossible only a few years ago. In fact, had it not been for the "Telescope" and other reformative aspects of our penitentiary system, our man would assuredly have been back, long since, in prison, at the considerable expense of the Canadian taxpayer.[73]

Strength in Numbers: The Penal Press Goes International

As previously noted, the first magazines were in-house only[74] and outside subscriptions were not permitted.[75] The members of the penal press, however, could receive copies of one another's publications.[76] On its first anniversary, *Tele-Scope* acknowledged and commended these other magazines on the circuit: "We are confident that much good has been accomplished in this past year and a greater measure of enlightenment and an understanding has been provided the general public in regard to prisons and to prisoners."[77] It also noted the importance of learning from its American counterparts:

> When the Tele-scope was born its field of readers was limited almost entirely to the prison population; but when permission was granted to establish an exchange with penal publications in the United States, a whole new realm of interest came into being. Our creative efforts were penetrating beyond other walls of stone and steel, and kindred thoughts and feelings were being returned to us in the form of papers and magazines of the American Penal Press. From these fine publications – some of which have been in print for more than fifty years – the infant Tele-scope had much to learn. We learned, among other things, the need of variety and illustration; we learned that the penal press is critical – quick to praise when praise is merited, but equally quick to chastise where chastisement is due.[78]

The editors of *Pathfinder* wanted an opportunity to learn from a broader group and requested permission to correspond with other free press editors. In a letter to their warden, the editorial staff argued that seeking "advice and guidance" from other editors would help their newly launched magazine create "a better understanding between ourselves and the general public" by learning the rules "and other points of journalism."[79] Immediate approval was not granted, but discussions between the warden and the commissioner continued.[80] Perhaps as a result of their contact with other penal publications, the Canadian penal press writers and editors found the courage to use the press to advocate for change. In his March 1953 editorial, John Brown wrote:

> The Tele-scope has never forgotten its duty to the inmates. Not long after it drew its first breath, it began shouting for needed reforms. It shouted for things inmates now take for granted – newspapers, pay increases, shaving outfits, longer exercise periods, and so on. And the Tele-scope will keep on fingering anachronisms, even if it must fight on alone. The Tele-Scope, moreover, has tackled social and legal problems of vital importance to the inmates – drug addiction, the Habitual Criminal Act, corporal punishment, capital punishment, and others too numerous to mention. It has usually led the way, sometimes handling "dynamite."[81]

By 1957, *C.B. Diamond* too had taken a more proactive political stance. Its editors stated that their purpose was now "to aid, inspire and cultivate intellectual improvement among prisoners; to assist in overcoming arbitrary social bias wherever it is met; to discuss, advocate and encourage further penological improvements, and to champion the cause of prisoners everywhere."[82] Where their 1952 statement had emphasized prejudice, morality, and the redemption of fallen men, they now conceived of their role as advocates for structural change. The writers and editors well knew that by strongly advocating for change, they ran the risk of being read as a "beef sheet," but in a January 1958 editorial, *Tele-Scope* argued this was necessary: "The history of penal reform is a succession of tales of wrongs that were righted by men of vision and the courage to act on that vision – in short, men who beefed."[83]

The editors of the critical press were certain of their influence and sought to extend it. In 1954, *Pen-O-Rama*'s editors wrote:

> In its ensemble, the Penal Press, doubtless has a certain influence. Although the various publications that are part of it may differ in the details of their policies, the editorial aims of most of them are parallel. Therefore, some 150 periodicals work at propagating what are fundamentally the same ideas. If we place the average outside circulation of each at 800 units (to be very conservative) we obtain a total of 120,000, which is a respectable figure. Now, admitting (still conservatively) that at least three persons read each copy sent beyond the walls, we get an idea of its combined strength.[84]

By the time this was written, the earliest effort to organize the penal press had already been thwarted. In the spring of 1952, Penitentiary Service officers became aware of the organizing efforts of American prisoner and penal press editor Clint Sanders of *Alabama Pen Point*. Sanders was attempting to organize an International Prisoners Association. He had written to the editors of each prison publication in Canada and had named Emile Zarbatany, the editor of *Pen-O-Rama* at Saint-Vincent-de-Paul Penitentiary, vice-president of the association.[85] Zarbatany claimed to have no knowledge of the organization or his appointment, and the matter was quickly dropped.[86] Yet it raised the spectre of inter-institutional prisoner communication and the threat it posed for prison administrators. As Warden Cleeton of Collins Bay Institution wrote, the proposed prisoners' organization "could have perhaps far reaching effects not altogether on the right side, especially in bringing about a 'closer association of prisoners' as stated in the article."[87] The commissioner's office took no chances, advising wardens not to permit prisoners to receive correspondence from Sanders or copies of *Alabama Pen Point*, a directive that was successfully enforced.[88]

It is no surprise that the government sought to vanquish the prisoners' association. What *was* startling was the existence of the penal press in the first place. "Perhaps, in the final analysis," Russell Baird has written, "it is the willingness of prison administrators to foster newspapers and magazines in their institutions that is the most unusual aspect of the prison press. The penal press is an anomaly; authoritarian rule and the printing press historically have been incompatible."[89] Yet as the Zarbatany incident makes clear, authoritarian rule and the press could indeed coexist.

"Keeping It Real" or "What to Write about in the Penal Press"

In terms of general content, the early Canadian penal press differed little from its American counterparts. Russell N. Baird's description of American penal magazines applies equally to those north of the border:

> Most of the attention of a prison newspaper is devoted to inmate activities: sports events, movies and other entertainment, personal items, blood banks, school and organizational activities, hobbies, and the like. Sports events are thoroughly covered; movie schedules complete with typical ads and reviews are standard fare; inmate variety shows get profuse preliminary and follow up coverage; personal recognition varies from "gossip column" notices to laudatory items for participation in blood drives and school activities; alcoholics anonymous, Synanon, Junior Chamber of Commerce, and the various religious organizations are subjects of many stories.[90]

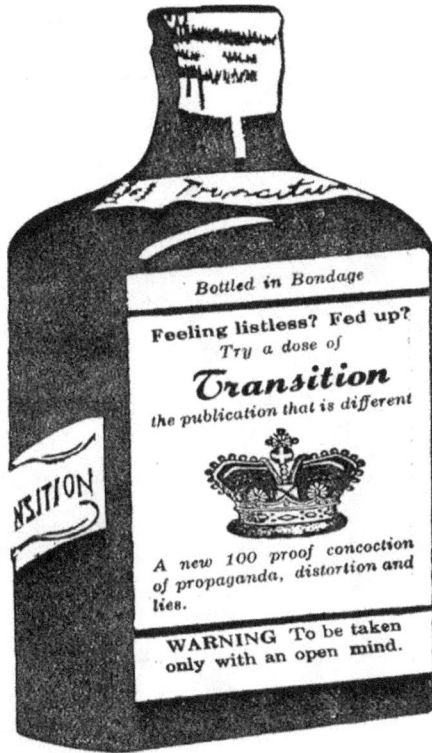

Image 3.16. Humorous image from the back cover of the December 1956 issue of *Transition*. Gaucher/Munn penal press collection.

Perhaps the one oversight in Baird's description is the inclusion of humour sections. Several of the Canadian magazines included satirical pieces, joke columns, cartoons, and other pieces meant to make the reader smile. While some were simply jokes of the regular kind (setup followed by punchline), others took on a certain gallows humour. Images 3.16 to 3.18 provide examples of this type of material.

Sports and events coverage dominated the Canadian penal press, and editors chafed at the limited scope afforded them. Their "beat" was no accident: it was the legacy of early policies formulated by the commissioner. The editors of the original *Sports Bulletin* explained in 1950 that they had been instructed to "remain within a limited scope, featuring sports." Yet even at this early date, they expressed optimism "that this scope will be widened in the near future, which will permit the publication of matter that will sustain reader interest."[91] The focus on

Image 3.17. Cartoon from back cover of *Tele-Scope*, June 1960. Gaucher/Munn penal press collection.

"Stop sulking an' eat your supper; if beans are good enough for me, beans are good enough for you, see!!"

Image 3.18. Big Paul cartoon by G. Riendeau from back cover of *Pen-O-Rama*, vol. 2, no. 11, June 1956. Gaucher/Munn penal press collection.

Image 3.19. The Men Behind the Diamond, *C.B. Diamond*, December 1953, Gaucher/Munn penal press collection.

sports became a source of ongoing tension in the press. The contributors' primary concern was that by providing too much written and photographic coverage of their new athletic opportunities, the public was being given an inaccurate image of life behind bars:

> If one were to judge an institution by the content of its penal publication, the worst oftentimes is made to look like the best ... and not a few over-zealous prison writers portray contemporary gaol as little less than plush country clubs wherein pampered felons languish in perfect socialism ... And despite a growing trend toward portraying prison life circa 1957 as one big round-relay of ball games, schoolwork, shop training, hobbycraft, movies, stage shows, ad infinitum, a convict is still very much a convict.[92]

While editors understood this criticism and desperately did *not* want their publications to be seen as "front magazines," they also offered various justifications, such as the one below:

The truth is that sports and entertainment form the only true bright spots in a pervasive darkness of monotony, routine, discipline, and regimentation, little drops of cheer which we take out of context in a sea of unhappiness and exaggerate out of all reasonable perspective.[93]

Other publications attempted to balance this coverage by providing contextual information:

Now look at it this way. Out of a possible 744 hours in the month of May and using these three events [boxing, musical revue, and softball league openings] as a yardstick, the inmate assisted at 4 ½ hours of entertainment during the month. Not much is it? Other than this diversion, systematic routine is in effect at all times."[94]

In 1957, *Tele-Scope* even went so far as to publish a 7-page pictorial that the editors hoped would "convey the deadening monotony and drab atmosphere of prison life" (some of these pictures appear in chapter 4).[95]

The Difficulties of Being THE Voice of Prisoners

Battles over content, which were not unique to the penal press, placed editors under pressure to perform. The papers were minimally staffed, which meant that tremendous responsibility to be "THE voice of prisoners" – as diverse a group as one can imagine[96] – fell to only a few men,[97] who besides, had to live in close quarters with those they represented.[98] This was a problem from the very beginning, when wardens chose the editors (see Image 3.19, a photograph of the *C.B. Diamond* editorial board from December 1953). In August 1951, Deputy Commissioner McCulley sent a suggestion to the warden at BC Penitentiary:

Growing out of our experience at some of the other institutions it has seemed preferable that the responsibility for the paper, as far as the inmates are concerned, should be delegated to a committee and that no one inmate should be designated as editor-in-chief. You will easily see that in the event of criticism from the inmate population this enables the responsibility to be spread rather than focused primarily on one person.

We know that some institutions heeded his suggestion. *Beacon* formed its first editorial board in November 1951 and did not refrain from giving out titles;[99] that paper's staff, for example, was comprised of an editor-in-chief, a sports editor, and an art person, all of whom met every Monday for the purpose of "considering material, discussing suggestions and hearing complaints."[100] Some publications, like *Tele-Scope*, expanded their boards (from four to eight people in this instance),[101] but despite these efforts, conflict over content persisted even when the prison population elected their own editorial boards.

The strongest tension between the editorial boards and those they represented was around the level and tone of the content. Regarding the first point, some prisoners expressed concern that the sophistication of the writing alienated some of the less literate prisoners:

> We understand fully that it is nice to convince the public that we're not all morons and half-wits to be sure, but let us not convince them at the majority of the inmates' expense. As it stands now a person has to have his Webster close at hand (if he owns one) in order to get by many of the educated words used in nearly all the articles in our Tele-Scope today. The motto "By and for the men" seems to have gone the way of all flesh.[102]

The press was also perceived as being too cozy with the administration. Some accused the penal press of being a "house organ," which Alex Younge defined as follows: "It reflects the views of the administration, contains considerable religious material, has a tendency to preach and often censures. It is usually distributed free and serves no practical purpose. It is unread by the majority of the inmate body and is uninteresting to outsiders. Like most frauds it is easily detected."[103]

Instead some prisoners wanted an inmate publication that emphasized the convict/guard dualism and was "prejudiced in the inmate's favor and at no time discusses his faults; it never preaches and is not sycophantic towards the administration."[104] Of course, like most binaries, this division was overly simplistic. Editorial boards found themselves in a "diplomatic struggle between two firing squads"[105] – between what the administration would allow to be published and what the prisoners thought should appear in their magazines. In May 1954, the editor of *Tele-Scope* commented that while the warden could stop an article from going to press, he could not dictate what should be published. He concluded that "the content of any given penal magazine, therefore, reflects the degree of official tolerance prevailing within the prison."[106] Indeed, as Erving Goffman contended, the "house organ" was no mere mouthpiece for the administration:

> Inmates who make this compact with the staff [to follow the official ideology in the institutional press] often do not cease to affirm the countermores. They introduce whatever open criticism of the institution the

censors will permit; they add to this by means of oblique or veiled writing, or pointed cartoons ... Inmate use of the official staff language and staff philosophy in discussing or publishing gripes is a mixed blessing for the staff. Inmates can manipulate the staff's own rationalization of the institution and through this threaten the social distance between the two groupings.[107]

Under this pressure, some editors simply resigned their posts, but even this decision came under fire: "Nothing can possibly be achieved by doing this. Penal magazine editors are bound to tread on people's toes once in a while, and they must be willing to accept the ridicule, censure and intolerance no end."[108] Many editors spent a lot of time justifying their approach:

The original staff, with amazing wisdom and foresight, decided that the only way the magazine could command the respect of both the inmate body and the public was to be an independent organ. They would curry no favour with the authorities and grind no axes for the inmates. The staff decided that the criterion against which all submitted material should be judged, would include: are the facts cited true? does the argument advanced further the interests of all inmates? does it stimulate public interest? does it clarify erroneous impressions of prison life and foster a better understanding of the inmate's problems in the civilian mind? The present editorial board cherishes that criterion. They, too, prize the policy of independence. They are proudly aware of Transition's increasing prestige. They are conscious of the responsibility inherent in such public acceptance. No material will ever be published which will in any way alienate that hard won approval.[109]

It is clear that members of the penal press circuit censured one another. Several publications ran penal press exchange columns to highlight what was, or was not, happening elsewhere, and they used these pages to hold their convict counterparts accountable. Most often they offered praise for particular publications on the whole or for particular articles, but on occasion they were blunt in their criticism of tone, or content, or both:

The petty fault-findings that have of lately marred the pages of the junior publication from Ontario [C.B. Diamond] imply a superiority which even the most superficial study of its pages will reveal to be sheer presumption. Fawning, pandering, sniveling and unseemly flag-waving are other Diamond flaws discernible without the aid of a jeweler's glass.[110]

The tension over content was ably captured by Bill Blair in his first essay in the penal press:

> It appears to me that the penal press is produced for a most unsympathetic audience: – the inmate body, apparently under a strong compulsion to totally disagree with the text of all articles which do not directly attack some item of the status quo; – the subscribers, who usually being related to an inmate are consequently not objective to article context when scanning the magazine; – the administration, technically interested in the subject material chosen by the editor, do in effect ignore the calibre of the prose and poetry. Since the publication is produced under the regulatory eyes of the censors and with close appreciation of printing costs, I am always mildly surprised when an issue is released for delivery.[111]

Conclusion

There is no doubt that the initial years of the penal press were difficult. Prisoners and administrators struggled to figure out the logistics of operating these publications and argued over content. Also, despite the commissioner's unequivocal support, not all administrators looked favourably on the presence of the press:

> Our prison magazines are entitled to much more than "tolerance" from the administration. So long as the articles that deal with administrative matters are factually accurate and are constructive in their comments and criticism there is no reason to object to their publication even though they may not represent official policy or be possible of immediate implementation. With this proviso, the prison magazines are entitled to the *active support and encouragement* [italics added] of the administration.[112]

Prisoners did not always agree with one another on the direction and tone of the press. They quarrelled over how writers portrayed the convict population and the New Deal reforms. Still, despite the almost total neglect of the penal press in Canadian literature, it remains one of the most visible, lasting, and controversial of the New Deal initiatives. The early penal press expressed prisoners' views effectively, opened a dialogue among convicts, and facilitated communication with the Penitentiary Service administration and the general public. As Robert Gaucher noted, "in the outside-directed publication, one can trace prisoners' views on the whole post World War II program of prison reform and expansion, on changes in social control legislation and its implementation, and on the major problems and concerns that dominate their lives while in prison and after release."[113]

In other ways, the penal press was not so successful. Optimism waned. Gaucher contended that "by the late 1950s, the effectiveness of the new reformative and increasingly rehabilitative (i.e., treatment oriented) penology was being questioned."[114] Clearly, though, this critique had begun earlier. So had the conflicts. Regardless of the starting point, the first decade of the penal press in Canada was turbulent; it was also plagued by technical problems of publication, administrative censure, and censorship (discussed at length in chapter 6). In its struggles, the penal press mirrored the larger conundrums that politicians, prison administrators, and staff faced as they tried to revamp the penal apparatus:

> The story of PEN-O-RAMA is the story of the new deal, the new penology, for inmates. The new deal gave it birth, and ever since the offspring has been doing everything in its power to give a true picture of the new penology's progress, and to evaluate and point out as intelligently as possible other steps to make the treatment of errant men more humane and equitable . . . In these five hectic years PEN-O-RAMA has endeavored to bring about a better understanding between the citizen of the outside world and the men behind the walls. It has tried to show that PRISONERS ARE PEOPLE.[115]

In the end, the penal press never achieved its full purpose – something that could be said of the New Deal more generally. For example, the two-way conduit for conversation in the press never manifested itself. Yet even though that communication was largely absent from the press, the magazines did generate conversations of various kinds: administrators discussed prisoners' writing among themselves, in correspondence and at wardens' conferences; wardens worked with censorship boards to determine what was fit to print; and censorship itself constituted a dialogue between the prisoners and the administration; so too did editors' resignations. Sadly, we know little about the types of materials to which administrators objected. The administrative files are overflowing with memoranda about controversial articles and editorials, but strangely, few of the original copies have been preserved. Nor is there any information on the content of those issues that were destroyed in their entirety.

We would be remiss if we failed to mention that the penal press was also used to surveil and control prisoners. At one level, the penal press extended the reach of the panoptic. While writers and editors in the penal press were aware that their material was available to the administration and the public, they revealed a great deal about themselves, their values, and their beliefs. We know that administrators kept a close eye on the penal press. By reading his prison's magazine, an administrator acquired a greater sense of what was happening among prisoners in his institution, their pleasures, pains, "beefs," and aspirations. All of that information could be valuable in running the penitentiary and regulating its population. At a second level, as we have seen, prisoners used the penal press to regulate one another. As the next chapter will show, they also used the press to send clear messages that those who failed to uphold certain standards of behaviour would face a form of justice administered by their peers. That is why, as Gaucher makes clear, the press "constitute[d] an exceedingly rich ethnographic source of prisoner experience and prison life in Canada during the post-war period of prison reform and change."[116] The following chapters mine the press for evidence of prisoners' efforts to expose and improve their daily living conditions and to lobby for better release options. First, though, we think it appropriate to allow the final words of this chapter to come from the penal press describing itself. The following excerpts from a lengthy piece titled "The Sharp and Bright Sword" are taken from an article that first appeared in the August 1954 issue of *C.B. Diamond* and was reprinted the following year. It begins:

I am the Penal Press ... that unpretentious, sometimes unpolished and untidy but nevertheless purposeful implement, homespun ambassador of good will and silent promoter of cordial relations. I attempt to speak to the masses on behalf of the man and the youth locked up in prison. I am their appointed agent. I am their messenger. I am the Penal Press.

It might be that, if one were to read into, between and beyond the lines of my working parts and chassis, one could detect a story of pluck and firm resolve. It might just be. For, even in a segregated and unavoidable environment of degradation, punishment, bitter hates, friction, deterioration, and curtailment, I have managed, somehow, to survive and to hold sway. Even despite these frustrations.

In undertones and in overtones, abstractly, absurdly, satirically, clumsily, dexterously, and brusquely, I exude shortcomings, weaknesses, inconsistencies and censorship. Still and all, I continue, you see, to serve my people, and I arise and shake myself scornfully, each quarter, each month, or each week and remain steadfastly forceful, grim, elementary, laughable, abridged, enlarged, pitiable, modified, better, or insipid. But I am there. I am in there pitching ... all the way.

I grant that a little, some, the lion's share, or all of my contents, during the preparatory stages, could have been dissected, adjusted, or vetted, to suit the dictates of custom, eloquence, nicety, or euphony. This I grant.

I admit it ... for what would be the use of denying it? ... even supposing it were permissible, I might not always consider it practicable nor wholesome to record the plane [sic] truth attending the scabby rigours and the festering perplexities of imprisonment. In defence of my policy, I offer this alibi: One does not tell one's wife or mother, stricken with inoperative and incurable carcinoma of the cervix, that she will die, agonizingly, of cancer, does one? I admit this.

But let no uncertainty linger, on one particular score, in any of my reader's minds. There is a reasonable degree, or, shall I say, a type or form of acceptable and unchallenged, bedrock truth coursing through my veins. Certainly there is.[117]

The author then notes that his piece was inspired by a conversation with the *C.B. Diamond* staff about the difficulty editors had getting sufficient copy. He continued:

I think of the heroic contribution being made to the cause of the prisoner by all of my friends in the Penal Press Circuit. I see here a simple, mimeographed relative from a boys' industrial school in a southern state of the U.S.A. And I spy with my beady eye, a colourful cover from far-off Hawaii. And I admire the great literary achievement from an American penitentiary. And I examine a story in photographs from two prisons for adults – one for males and the other for females. And I scan the staid dignity of a Canadian brother. And I see lots of others. And I think the whole business is a pretty heroic contribution.

I am dedicated, you see. I am working for the prisoner. I am produced in a battle with time and against all sorts of odds and barriers. I am waging a strenuous paper war. As I have said, I am dedicated.

I am progressing, too. I am softening resistance. I am slightly, partially, or wholly convincing the man in the street that prisoners are people. Hear that? That prisoners are people. That they are human beings. I am harmoniously conjoined with my fellows, in a sense, against the inroads of ugly, ignoble, ruthless misrepresentation by radio, moving pictures, pulp magazines, crime comics, shoddy fiction, and the daily press. I'm glad that I am progressive.

And I am eager. And I am succeeding, more or less. I am reaching out. I am overcoming and overthrowing arbitrary bias. I am seeking and asking for friends, encouragement, and patronage. I am slowly but surely succeeding.[118]

Later in the editorial, the author provides a neat summary of the role of prison magazines:

> I am the Penal Press, and it is my duty to percolate, to infiltrate, to exhort, to improve, to impart, and to deprecate. I am the servant of the prisoner. I am his mouthpiece.[119]

4 The New Deal – Same as the Old Deal?

Much changed in Canada between 1935 and 1960. The Great Depression came to an end; a generation of Canadian soldiers fought in the Second World War; and after the war, prosperity contributed to unprecedented marriage and fertility rates. Meanwhile, the Cold War, the Korean conflict, and the proliferation of nuclear weapons threatened to undermine postwar stability and fostered political polarization. The country also witnessed significant political changes: a new province entered Confederation in 1949, a new monarch took the throne in 1952, and a new Conservative prime minister took office in 1957. Despite the upheavals, uncertainties, and political developments of the era, penal reform was still on the minds of politicians, prisoners, and the public. As discussed in chapter 2, various prewar reports had criticized the federal prisons as being at best outdated and at worst barbaric. Fortunately, a blueprint for reform (known as the New Deal) was at the ready. The government planned to follow the recommendations contained in the 1938 *Royal Commission Report on Penal Reform in Canada* (more commonly known as the Archambault Report), as summarized by Commissioner Ralph Gibson in 1947 (see chapter 2), to create a better correctional environment that would return even the most "hardened criminals" back to the street as productive members of society. Yet those were policy *intentions*. Prisoners' writing reveals a different picture, in that many reforms were undermined, neglected, or unfinished.

In 1949, Commissioner Gibson emphasized that the purpose of prison was not simply custody, but rehabilitation: "[We are working to] train, uplift and educate ... inmates for better and future citizenship . . . Greater attention to the basic needs of the individual prisoner, more sympathetic concern for the needs and problems of the inmate – better facilities for readjustment on discharge – these are all evidences of a concern for a prisoner as a human being."[1]

Such thinking was epitomized in the catchwords Gibson and McCulley repeated on numerous occasions in the 1950s: "Prisoners Are People."[2] In his 1951 annual report, Gibson made it clear that the Penitentiary Service was making "every effort ... within the present [financial] limitations to introduce new and progressive concepts of modern penology into our total programme."[3] The financial limitations he was alluding to were severe. In 1951, Louis St Laurent's Liberal government had embarked on a $5 billion rearmament plan. By 1953 it was consuming 42 per cent of the federal budget, thus limiting the government's capacity to deliver many promised reforms.[4]

Like the penal reforms that had preceded it earlier in the century, the New Deal was meant to create good citizens and a better country.[5] As noted earlier, the pressure to implement these reforms was sustained throughout the war years and the government remained committed to them (see chapter 2). Indeed, Commissioner Gibson filled his annual reports with descriptions of significant progress in penal reform, which he argued utilized the best practices of modern penology. In May 1952, Minister of Justice Stuart Garson updated the House of Commons on the progress of the New Deal: "We have gradually been replacing outworn and obsolete machinery and equipment in the penitentiary shops ... We have made every reasonable effort to improve personnel employed in the penitentiaries, and the major attention has been focused on the treatment of inmates to bring our practices more into conformity with recognized modern correctional procedure."[6] Meanwhile, reform fever spread beyond the House of Commons. Even prisoners writing in the penal press caught the bug. James P. Carleton wrote upon his admission to Kingston Penitentiary in 1952 that his "first impression of prison and the Tele-Scope [prisoner's newsletter] gives me hope."[7]

By then, Gibson was enjoying widespread acclaim for the reforms he had introduced. He was selected president of the American Prison Association in 1953, and the association held its annual meeting in Toronto that year. In his keynote address, Gibson referred to a wave of riots in American prisons.[8] He arrogantly advised that self-examination was in order and implied that the solutions to problems in US prisons might be gleaned from the reforms being undertaken in Canada:

> During this present year, there has been a wave of unrest in our penal and correctional institutions that has resulted in riots and disturbances in a number of them. I suggest that this presents a challenge to the members of this association, whether or not their own institutions have been involved in these disturbances, to analyse the reasons for these incidents, to scrutinize our own procedures, and to give such assistance and advice as may

be helpful in combatting these unfortunate outbreaks which can do much harm to the cause of penal progress.[9]

The congress was a shining moment in the early New Deal era. Yet that moment was fleeting. Within a year, prisoners in Canada would riot and Gibson would need to reflect on his own advice (see chapter 6).

Given the evidence of prisoner dissatisfaction, which would come to a head with the riot of 1954, and given the continual demands for prison reform in the penal press throughout the 1950s, we must consider whether the reforms were real or illusory. While the New Deal's "Prisoners Are People" mantra was parroted by politicians, prisoners, administrators, reformers, and the public, there were both indicators and contra-indicators of progress. In considering the reform project, we need to be mindful that wholesale change of the penal scheme was never the goal of the New Deal in corrections; improvement was the order of the day, and given the different agencies, bureaucracies, and ideologies involved, change would be complicated. Implementing the New Deal within the penitentiary system would require a multi-pronged and coordinated approach. To this end, the reforms directed their attention not only to prisoners and facilities but also to the staff who contained and supervised them. The New Deal also focused on the public, who made the reforms possible (see chapter 2), and on the media, which would convey the message to the masses.

This chapter incorporates the voices of prisoners, via the penal press, to assess the impact of the specific practices implemented in the New Deal. These materials allow us to build upon the administrative history, which was largely framed in progressive terms, to highlight the era's achievements *and* failures. The chapter begins by considering the influence of shifts in classification and segregation and the tentacular ways in which these changes influenced daily life and control of the prison. It then reviews the efforts made to improve the prisoners' daily lives and to prepare them for their eventual return to the community. The chapter concludes by appraising whether these reforms altered the prison system in a meaningful way.

Classification and Segregation

Stanley Cohen wrote that "the impulse to classify, separate, segregate and exclude" is rooted in the social order and imitated in the prison.[10] Foucault in his genealogy of prisons contended that classification was one of the "fundamental principles of the prison."[11] He goes on to say that convicts are "isolated or at least distributed according to the penal gravity of their act, but above all, according to age, mental attitude, the technique of correction to be used, [and] the stages of their transformation."[12] The Archambault Commission recommended an improved system of classification and segregation. This recommendation should be no surprise: "In prisons, the magic wand of classification has long been held out as the key to a successful system," wrote Stanley Cohen. "If only those who mess up the regime could be weeded out (sent to special prison units or isolation centres) the system could go ahead with its business."[13] Commissioner Gibson bought into the classification-as-panacea paradigm: in his address to the penal congress in Toronto, he claimed that the *"proper classification* of prisoners is an *essential* part of a good correctional system, if a programme of *individual treatment* [emphases added] is to be carried out."[14] In his words, the shifting tide of classification is in evidence. No longer would it be sufficient to house all prisoners together, as was done in the early history of prisons. For the New Deal to succeed, the personalized classification of each prisoner would be necessary. Indeed, classification was all the more urgent now that the silent system had been abandoned and "incorrigibles" could now (so it was thought) contaminate the general prisoner population.[15] To better understand how classification comes to serve as an instrument of power,[16] it is useful to consider the main purposes for which it was used in the Canadian penal apparatus. In their review of Canadian prison reform, Gamberg and Thomson argued that the classification system had three distinct functions: to assist in the rehabilitation of the prisoner, who was seen to be "undersocialized or inadequate, as having failed to develop certain normative characteristics"; to ensure security and efficient operations of the prison by assessing the riskiness of each prisoner; and to provide a mechanism for reducing prisoners' idleness.[17]

Using Classification to Achieve a Rehabilitated Subject

One impetus for the appointment of a commission to study prisons in Canada was the impression that individuals were being made worse by their imprisonment. The narrative depicted young, impressionable prisoners being housed with hardened, unreformable, career criminals. The insane were housed with the sane. Murderers did time alongside thieves. Because of this lack of separation, prisons were seen as a corrupting influence on those who might otherwise become good citizens. This tale led the government to believe that something had to be done to separate the incorrigibles from the reformables. In this way, the administration could also constrain the ability of prisoners to build community. In the proposed regime of classification, new arrivals would no longer be co-housed with the bearers of prisoners' culture of solidarity and resistance.

The first step was to hire staff to do the work. For classification and instructional staff, the Penitentiary Service sought university-educated people with experience in social work and occupational counselling who could foster the rehabilitative ideals espoused in the New Deal.[18] This amounted to the "professionalization of deviancy control" by credentialled workers who could "claim esoteric knowledge, effective technique and the right to treat."[19] For guards, by contrast, an elementary school education was seen as sufficient; it is possible that this requirement was not raised because the government already found it difficult to recruit guards. In his autobiography, former prisoner Frank Anderson noted that at Saskatchewan Penitentiary there was an "exodus of guards" during the war years and "replacements were hard to find because penitentiary wages were skimpy and few valued the security of a government position above higher money elsewhere."[20] As a result, they could hardly serve as the Borstal-style mentors envisioned by Archambault, who were to be "men of educated minds and sound character,"[21] and whom Commissioner Gibson hoped would be better attuned to the "reformative aspect of penitentiary work."[22] By 1947 a new classification staff had been "specially chosen" to interview new prisoners in order to gain information on their "educational, social and economic backgrounds."[23]

In 1949, Gibson reported that classification officers had conducted more than 10,000 interviews that year and written more than 3,000 reports.[24] While these interviews were meant to help individuals better use their time in prison to rectify perceived deficits, the main priority was in fact segregation. The main concern was to keep impressionable and reformable young people away from the "old lags."[25] The government began using two of the extant prisons – the Collins Bay Institution and Saint-Vincent-de-Paul's Federal Training Centre – to house young and supposedly pliable prisoners. Officials acknowledged that in the other penitentiaries, they could only guarantee the separation of "worthy" prisoners from others while they were in their "living quarters."[26] Participation in work, recreation, and other activities would involve intermingling the various classes of prisoners, since there were no specialized reception centres. Despite Gibson's plan, no designated institutions for the incorrigible and intractable were established in the first half of the 1950s.[27]

The segregation of youth received both praise and criticism from writers in the penal press. Many writers agreed, in principle at least, that youth should be treated differently than adults in the system, and

Image 4.1. Prisoner being interviewed by Mr Chabot, Classification Officer. *C.B. Diamond*, March 1956. Gaucher/Munn penal press collection.

some advocated a more radical solution – not sending youth to adult penitentiaries at all.[28] Others felt that the issue of "reformability" was more complex than the simple young/old dichotomy suggested. Ian Macleod, writing in *C.B. Diamond*, highlighted the absurd and arbitrary nature of the many possible choices for segregating the population: "How to segregate? The young from the not-so-young? The first offender from the repeater? Those guilty of an offense against property from those guilty of offenses against persons? The educated from the illiterate? The industrious from the indolent? Long-termers from short-termers? By attitude towards, and adaptability to prison routine? By profession or vocation? In accordance with other influencing factors?"[29]

Social scientists of the era argued that they were employing scientific methods to make their assessments. Some researchers contend that decisions were being made based only on the convicted person's age, sentence length, and criminal history,[30] when in fact classification officers believed they were employing a new technique – behavioural modification – that had been "developed during the Second World War in an attempt to enhance the motivation of American soldiers to fight."[31] With the goal of building on these new "therapeutic" techniques, throughout the late 1940s and early 1950s[32] Gibson and Deputy Commissioner Dr L.P. Gendreau directed the Penitentiary Service to hire more doctors, psychiatrists, and psychologists.[33] As the commissioner explained in 1957, "reformation, which is the ultimate aim of incarceration, stands to succeed best when the deficiencies and needs of the inmates are known."[34] Yet the focus on mental therapies involved more than simply efforts to identify and address prisoners' problems. It was rooted in a particular understanding of criminality that can be linked to what Cohen identifies as "the rise of the therapeutic" wherein "interest was transferred from the body to the mind."[35] The commissioner quoted an unnamed expert in his 1956 report who contended that "criminality is without exception symptomatic of abnormal mental states and is an expression of them."[36] Using the tools rooted in this belief, local classification boards were to determine a course of treatment for each prisoner.[37] Subsequently, newly hired classification officers were to use this information to advise prisoners about available opportunities, provide counselling, and develop pre-release plans with prisoners and prisoners' aid societies.[38] As we will see later in this chapter, the dearth of spaces in educational, vocational, and therapeutic programs made it unlikely that the majority of prisoners' treatment plans were actually followed.

The Penitentiary Service did introduce limited new treatment programs, including group and electroshock therapy (see Image 4.2 of a prisoner being "treated" with a machine at Kingston Penitentiary).[39] Ostensibly, electroshock was used for therapeutic purposes, but it was also part of a poorly documented program of experimentation on Canadian prisoners.[40] The Nuremburg Code (1947), which governed medical experimentation, had been developed in response to Nazi experiments in the Second World War. It required the legal consent of test subjects; however, Canada's minister of justice did not think it applied within penitentiaries. Prison doctors were concerned enough about the ethics surrounding treatment without consent to demand clarification from the department; the minister decided in 1949 that consent from prisoners was unnecessary for electroshock treatment.[41] And they used it extensively. The machine arrived at Kingston Penitentiary in March 1949, and "over the next several years, as many as 117 shock treatments a month would take place at the jail and were credited with ending

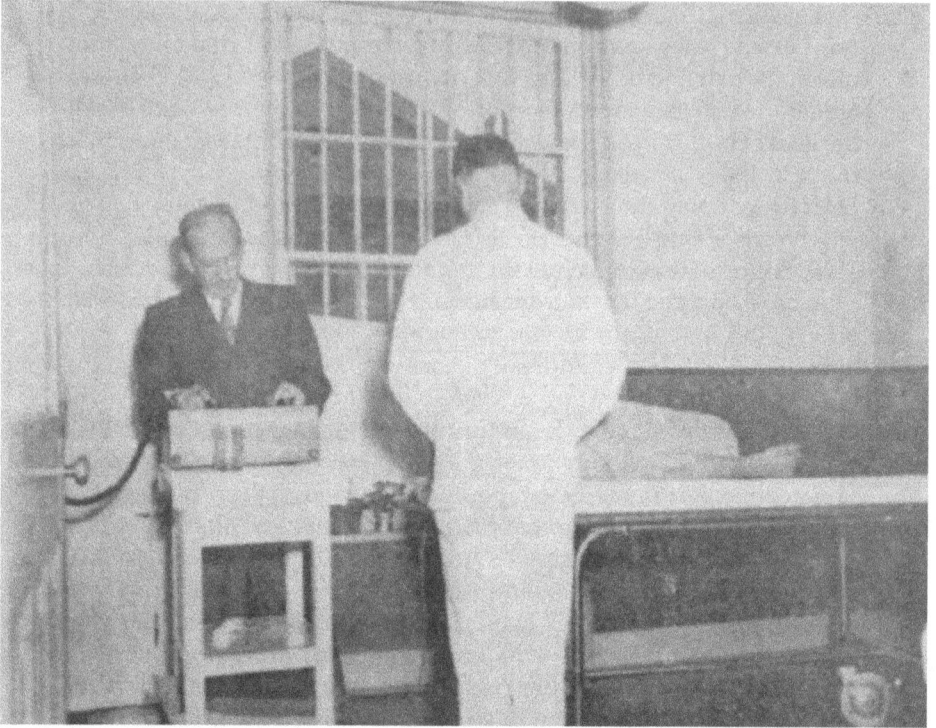

Image 4.2. Dr O'Connor and Mr Sellars treating a patient using electroshock therapy at Kingston Penitentiary. *Tele-Scope*, June 1953. Gaucher/Munn penal press collection.

everything from facial rashes, suicide attempts, hallucinations, incontinence and depression."[42]

The commissioner and deputy commissioners knew that to achieve the goals of rehabilitation and reform, it would not be enough to have classification staff and more psychiatrists at the ready; current and newly hired front-line staff would need to "buy in" to the new direction.[43] Put another way, the Penitentiary Service would need to "rehabilitate and reform" its present front-line staff. To attract a better calibre of personnel throughout the service, the government raised pay scales; to retain and reward them, it created new positions into which they could be promoted; and to introduce them to New Deal principles, it commenced in-service training at each institution. A six-week officer training course run by the RCMP had been launched in Ottawa in 1948,[44] but

Penitentiary Service officials quickly realized that this generic training was inadequate, so they set out to develop their own instructional program, as the Archamault Report had recommended. A training college for penitentiary staff was opened in Kingston in 1952. The minister of justice noted that "the establishment of this institution on a permanent basis is a recognition of the vital importance of continued training of penitentiary officers for their difficult and valuable work."[45] Driving home the importance of the training program, Deputy Commissioner Joseph McCulley told the *Daily Colonist* in October 1950 that "the old evil of uneducated guards was being corrected."[46] The training was six weeks long, and W.F. Johnstone, the superintendent of the Penitentiary Staff College, was explicit about the intent: "Training Courses have as their objective an interpretation of the Commissioner's philosophy underlying our total programme – the belief that 'prisoners are people.' On the Courses we study the social forces which influence us all for better or worse today. Other phases of training present a sound insight into the roles that psychology and psychiatry play in our adjustment to reality and social living."[47]

According to Commissioner Gibson, the response to this new education program was generally positive:

> The response and interest of our officers in these training courses, many of them with ten, twenty and even thirty years' service, has been most heartening. The present courses are for the purpose of orienting our officers to the principles of sound modern penology, to increase their knowledge and to raise their standards in terms of their awareness of the factors that influence human behaviour, their knowledge of social problems and the causes of crime, their efficiency in their own specific responsibilities, their own physical fitness, and their general interest in prison work as a career.[48]

Progressive Conservative MP Gordon Churchill (Winnipeg South Centre) claimed that staff training "has been a most useful program indeed, and possibly has done more than anything else to make the administration of the penitentiaries more efficient than was the case in the past."[49] Writers and editors in the penal press also lauded the new training program, and some participated in it. In July 1952 the editors of *Tele-Scope* attended the college to meet with the guards, give their input, and educate them about the penal press.[50] Afterwards, they dedicated space in their publication for the head of the program to outline what he hoped to achieve.[51]

But training all the guards would take time, and not all would be receptive. The Archambault commissioners had foreseen the latter problem. "Several officers," they wrote, "should immediately be retired from the service."[52] There is no evidence that this was ever done. Guard retraining did take place at a modest pace in the postwar years and tended to be reserved for long-term staff. Wardens reported that the training produced a marked improvement among officers who attended it; however, prison employees included significant numbers of more "transient," short-term staff, among whom turnover was high and exposure to the new ideals was minimal.[53] Gibson admitted as much when he wrote in the May 1954 issue of *Tele-Scope* that only half the staff at Kingston penitentiary had attended the training.[54] Some prison-based writers worried that when progressive administrators like Gibson left, the system would regress.[55] In the meantime, newly trained/indoctrinated guards worked shoulder-to-shoulder with the literal old guard, who were likely to be, as Erving Goffman explains, "the long-term employees and hence the tradition carriers."[56]

Mirroring the concerns that led to the classification system for convicts, one prisoner worried about the corrupting influence of the senior officers: "the dead hand of tradition lies heavy upon their minds, so that they take no notice of changing conditions, and do not progress in their methods, even in an age when rapidly changing values and methods are likely to leave them far behind – no – has left them far behind."[57] Perhaps Justice Archambault was correct when he wrote "there are few officers in the service who have either the capacity or the training to exert any reformative influence on the prisoners. They are 'guards' and nothing more."[58] Archambault's imagery may suggest that these guards were simply tired – "dead wood" in the Penitentiary Service; yet they were also the senior officers, and in a hierarchical system staffed largely by former military men, their influence over new recruits was considerable.[59] Archambault identified a case of this nature at Saskatchewan Penitentiary, where the warden, Lt-Col W.H. Cooper, was described as "arrogant," "overbearing," and "inefficient," with a management style that carried "petty militarism to the extreme." The commissioners wrote that Cooper was unable "to command the respect of either the officers or the prisoners."[60] The negative influence of senior administrators like Cooper could be long-lasting. The success of the New Deal would depend on minimizing their influence and changing the values of the entire staff. This would be difficult to do. Indeed, it may have been easier to separate the "incorrigibles" from the "reformables" *behind* the prison bars.

Both the administrative and prisoner-generated records indicate that recalcitrant guards paid only lip service to reforms. In *Concerning .... Rehabilitation Deterrents*, Jack Vandermyn, a prisoner at Collins

Bay, argued that guards complied with the new initiatives because they feared losing their jobs if they did not. He concluded that "their [guards] feet dragging and subtle sabotage of otherwise worthwhile programs [*sic*] cause untold damage."[61] Clearly, agreement with the new reforms was not total. Having staff who believed in the initiatives was vital. Getting prisoners to buy into the New Deal was also essential – and difficult.

Achieving Security and Efficiency through
Classification and Segregation

The primary concern of any prison is security, and while not explicitly stated in either Archambault's report or Gibson's plan for implementation, classification and segregation offered possibilities for improving control within the prison.[62] In their study of Canadian prison reform, Gamberg and Thomson noted that classification was a means to determine the security risk a prisoner posed and thus could be used by the administration to ensure prisoners' compliance. An individual's degree of incorrigibility[63] could determine the supervision they received as well as the privileges they could access: "Both the threat of increasing the grade of risk, and the possibility of relaxing it, serve as potent control measures for the running of the prison. It is used to punish unacceptable behavior and induce compliance."[64] The administrators surmised that by isolating new prisoners from more experienced ones, they could instil greater compliance. The degree to which such practices were implemented is unclear: while spectacularly detailed on other subjects, the commissioners' annual reports during the 1950s and early 1960s do not discuss the use of segregation. However, by 1955, according to prisoners, segregation was being introduced in some prisons as a means to transition an individual from freedom to captivity and to adjust him to penitentiary life. In some penitentiaries – those in which new prisoners had once been subject to a thirty-day isolation period on arrival – under the new "humane approach to penology," first-time prisoners were now to be placed on a range and on a work crew with "suitable others." After they had gone through the classification process, they would be integrated gradually into the general prison population.[65] Clearly, all of this was meant to ensure that their preliminary contacts were with those who complied with the established order. The state wanted the prisoners to understand, participate in, and agree to the conditions of their confinement. That being said, the evidence on implementation is weak, and it is unclear whether the proposed segregation procedures were ever applied.

In an attempt to change the narrative, convicts suggested that the segregation system be expanded and used for different purposes. In June 1952, Communist Party of Canada organizer Sam Carr, a prisoner at Kingston Penitentiary, lobbied for a pre-release segregation unit that would mirror, as closely as possible, the conditions "prevailing in the world at large."[66] Within these non-cellular communal units, prisoners would be able to use regular cutlery and dishes, wear street clothing in the evenings, enjoy more liberal visitation privileges, and go on occasional trips into the community. In at least one institution, this idea was implemented: just five months after Carr made his suggestion, a pre-release unit was established at nearby Collins Bay Institution. The men there applauded this initiative as "something constructive."[67]

Reducing Idleness through Classification

While there can be no doubt that significant changes occurred post-Archambault, prisons remained dreary, dreadful places to live. In *Pen-O-Rama*, Al Parsons vividly described his cell at Saint-Vincent-de-Paul Penitentiary and the commonality of his experience:

> [My cell is] 9 feet long, five wide and 9 feet high. I can pace the length in two steps and a short one. I can reach the walls without stretching. The only thing that's out of reach is the ceiling. This cubicle with its 30 inch thick walls and its network of bars at the front is where I spend something like 18 hours every day. It serves as boudoir, living room, dining room and bathroom. It has three shelves, a table, a chair, a toilet bowl and the wash basin, a cot that hinges and hooks on the wall. And it has something else ... Something I didn't notice much at first ... The concrete floor is worn. Even the plainly visible crushed rock that went into the cement is worn. Not just a little, in some spot [*sic*] almost an inch. Did you ever go to a circus or zoo and watch a caged animal pacing back and forth, back and forth, with quick short, nervous steps? Did you know that they do that hour after hour? Did you know that, stupid and futile as it is, men do it too? That even you would do it if you are caged long enough? ... The floor in my cell tells a tale ... A tale of a man who walked for years without going anywhere ... A tale of feet which wore away the cement and stone while their owner's hearts beat with hope, smothered with frustration, or maybe broke with pain ... All the cells in prison have this one thing in common, the floors are worn, worn by feet, by the hearts and brains and souls of men who pay their debt to society in a coin which is of no earthly use to anyone.[68]

As Parsons's eloquent description makes clear, the Archambault Commission's report was not the "death knell of the failures and archaic treatment used in Canadian penal institutions."[69] In fact, at some prisons, conditions were deteriorating. The prison population doubled between 1947 and 1960, from 3,362 to 6,344. As a result, men lived in closer quarters than ever before (see chapter 6 for more on the impact of overcrowding on implementation of the New Deal).[70]

According to both contemporaries and academics, the dream of the reformed prison was naive, given the nature of these facilities. Sociologist Erving Goffman characterized prisons as "total institutions," concerned as they were not with living conditions but rather with strictly and methodically organizing the daily lives of their inhabitants to meet the institution's own needs.[71] Nearly twenty years earlier, during a parliamentary debate, Progressive Conservative MP Walter Dinsdale (Brandon) anticipated Goffman's analysis when he stated that "the usual prison program is really designated not to rehabilitate the prisoner but rather to prevent trouble within the prison."[72] So then, how could the New Deal's reforms be realized? Some scholars, such as Thomas Mathiesen, contend that prison reforms are not implemented in a simple and straightforward manner. Rather, the positive aspects of reforms are often absorbed into the extant system, transformed to fit into "the prevailing structure without threatening it," and ultimately strengthen the existing order.[73] In this way, "fresh ideas and initiatives" are neutralized, thus revealing the system's inherent power dynamics.[74] In this vein, Gamberg and Thomson argued that the new classification system and the new focus on rehabilitation during the New Deal were being used to more efficiently manage the prison population:

> One of the perennial problems associated with imprisonment was idleness. Of course, in the ideology of the early prison, idleness was in itself a bad thing, while working was a positive value. But when the crucial question is not a concern for the well-being of the prisoner but rather the orderly running of the institution, idleness – that idleness in the specific context of incarceration – seemed to be linked causally with rebellious attitudes and activities on the part of the convicts. In this sense the diversification of staff to run programmes served potentially to defuse the atmosphere and provided activities which could be justified on rehabilitative grounds. This was particularly true of the programmes designed to fill the prisoners' leisure time.[75]

If Gamberg and Thomson are correct, prison administrators could rhetorically frame the investment in anti-idleness activities in terms of the New Deal even while reaffirming extant operational structures. Thus, the rhetoric around the New Deal's implementation is important. In his June 1949 address to the Canadian Penal Congress, Commissioner Gibson declared that the confinement and reformation of prisoners was paramount and that "the prisoner [would] be treated humanely, fairly and permitted such privileges as may reasonably be allowed with due regard to disciplinary and administrative requirements."[76] The lexicon itself was problematic for prisoners and for some sympathetic administrators. For example, two years after Gibson's address, Deputy Commissioner Joseph McCulley noted that he disliked the framing of education, recreation, increased visitation, and vocational training as "privileges"; he saw them as basic needs rather than dispensations to be extended or revoked based on behaviour.[77] McCulley argued that if privileges were removed arbitrarily or frequently, prisoners would see the New Deal as "sheer hypocrisy."[78]

Setting aside the debate over rights versus privileges, the Penitentiary Service did make changes that improved the lot of prisoners in terms of alleviating their boredom and perhaps even improving their chances for post-carceral success. These reforms included more sports, recreation, entertainment, and in-cell activities; increased access to media; expanded educational and vocational opportunities; and the introduction of a pay and canteen system.

"MAN DOES NOT LIVE BY BREAD ALONE":
SPORTS AND RECREATION IN PRISON

The Archambault Commission called for recreation programs to reduce the amount of time prisoners spent in their cells. In late 1948, during a tour of several American prisons, Commissioner Gibson saw prisoners at Alcatraz playing softball.[79] After consulting with the wardens, the Penitentiary Service introduced organized sports in 1949.[80] Softball proved to be the most popular, but prisoners also boxed, played basketball, hockey, and soccer, and participated in other, less physically demanding games like horseshoes, shuffleboard, and hand tennis. The program was a significant break with past practice, and the commissioner felt compelled to justify it in his annual reports. Citing Archambault's statement that "a properly planned programme of recreation should be regarded not as entertainment, but as part of the treatment necessary to strengthen soul, mind and body," Gibson emphasized that the program was intended to fulfil prisoners' "basic psychological needs" and create an institutional climate conducive to reformation.[81] Prisoners agreed. Vic Ashton wrote in *Transition* that "the crushing pressure of incarceration alone leaves little room for levity. On the contrary,

Image 4.3. Prisoners watch a boxing match at Saint-Vincent-de-Paul Penitentiary, c. 1958. Special Edition of *Pen-O-Rama: Le Penitencier par Images*. Gaucher/Munn penal press collection.

the fears, longings and frustrations, the repression of natural emotions, and worries concerning those left outside, induce conflicting tensions which, without some recreation or diversion, can result in the sullen bitterness and revengeful attitudes produced under the old regime."[82]

In *Pen-O-Rama*, Fernand Dallaire even suggested that a sports program was "the greatest of all opportunities given to us by the New Deal."[83] To support his position, in an article titled "Sports & Rehabilitation," he contended that the entire population benefited in a way that supported the rehabilitation agenda. Players learned to "recognize qualities in others and to discover qualities in themselves which they hardly knew they possessed." For spectators, sporting events broke the monotony of prison life and provided "a topic of conversation which often [led] to constructive ends." Officials may have benefited the most. Dallaire wrote that they gained "an opportunity which has been lacking in the Penal System" – the opportunity to organize and lead prisoner activities.[84] Erving Goffman noted that such activities also served to frame the institution as benevolent rather than simply controlling. "In exchange for being allowed to demonstrate ... [good qualities] about themselves," Goffman writes, "inmates through their intermural team convey [good] things about the institution ... demonstrat[ing] to outsiders and observing inmates that the staff, in this setting at least, are not tyrannical."[85]

Sports programs were organized and run largely by the prisoners themselves.[86] This was viewed positively by administrators, who framed their efforts as promoting responsibility and skill-building. These organizing bodies eventually expanded beyond their original function, with the result that inmate committees became a mainstay in prisons. Gibson encouraged this development, explaining that the experience of serving on inmate committees tended to make prisoners "much more sympathetic to the problems of the administration."[87] In his 1950 report, he was very clear about the impact of this initiative:

> The [sports] programme is in charge of inmate committees who arrange the teams and schedules, provide umpires and arbitrate in all disputed decisions. Furthermore, these inmate committees have taken a large measure of responsibility for the behaviour of the inmate population which is permitted to watch the games as spectators. These committees have proven to be a valuable liaison between the inmates and the authorities. Quite apart from the purely physical benefit resulting from such a programme there are other intangible but extremely valuable results. Inmates are learning – and a very necessary lesson it is – to control their affairs, to abide by rules and regulations which are established for the benefit of all and to accept defeat in a sportsmanlike spirit. These are all fundamental to the development of a sounder ethical attitude and cannot help but have a personal value in regard to future behaviour patterns.[88]

Clearly, officials were learning that sports encouraged self-regulation and surveillance.[89] Prisoners, fearful of losing access to sports, were careful to keep one another in check. Sometimes they used the penal press to remind one another of the benefits of obedience. The following excerpt from *Sports Bulletin* points to how prisoners took on the disciplinary role:

> When the boys begin abusing privileges instead of helping their committee protect them, it becomes impossible for the committee to ask for more privileges. We said it before, and we'll say it again: – ABUSE OF

PRIVILEGES WILL PREVENT YOUR COMMITTEE FROM ASKING FOR
MORE ... In the future, when we catch anybody who is deliberately abus-
ing a privilege, to the detriment of his fellow inmates, we will publish
his number, name, and offense. It will be understood with the authorities
that no disciplinary action will be taken against him because the Committee has laid down the policy of not going to the authorities against the
inmates.[90]

Further complicating the disciplined/disciplining binary, prisoners were rewarded when they complied, and their own newsletters countenanced the change: "For the first time in the history of
Canadian Penitentiaries, the authorities gave a banquet for inmates
[to honour the Senators for their winning season] ... as a gesture
of appreciation of the good sportsmanship and the ability to accept
self-discipline."[91]

It would be a mistake to think that only the efforts of the players and incarcerated spectators mattered. Both the penal press and
the administrative records acknowledged staff, administrative, and
public support for sports in prison. For example, the personnel at
Saint-Vincent-de-Paul Penitentiary donated money to purchase new
sports sweaters for the players,[92] and the John Howard Society provided boxing gloves. Even private businesses showed their support:
the Coca-Cola Company, for example, donated a new scoreboard
to Collins Bay Institution.[93] Members of the public expressed their
endorsement of sports in prison by attending games and/or competing against the prison-based teams. Wardens took advantage of their
presence to portray themselves, and the New Deal, in a particularly
positive way. Goffman noted that events like these have a ceremonial
quality, complete with invited dignitaries and family and friends in
attendance:

A high-ranking officer attends as a symbol of management and (it is
hoped) of the whole establishment. He dresses well, is moved by the
occasion, and gives smiles, speeches, and handshakes. He dedicates new
buildings on the grounds, gives his blessing to new equipment, judges
contests, and hands out awards. When acting in this capacity, his interac-
tion with inmates will take a special benign form; inmates are likely to
show embarrassment and respect, and he is likely to display an avuncular
interest in them."[94]

On occasion, the prisoners amplified the jovial nature of events by providing refreshments to the guests. For outsiders, this simple act had

the effect of humanizing the men, as is evident in the following excerpt from *Tele-Scope*:

> Enjoying the sports and refreshments [at Kingston Penitentiary] were many guests of Warden Allan. They were pleasantly surprised by the polite and friendly courtesy shown them by the inmates who serve their refreshments ... As a matter of fact, when it was explained to them that the refreshments were paid for by the inmates from their own welfare fund, the visitors gallantly dipped into their purses and wallets and gave the fund quite a boost.[95]

As early as 1950, outside softball teams began coming inside the walls for games.[96] Professional players also visited the prisoners. In 1951, the NHL all-star team played softball against the K.P. Saints.[97] Two years later, Armand Savoie, the Canadian lightweight boxing champion, and his trainer, Guy Soucy, came into Saint-Vincent-de-Paul Penitentiary to watch the matches being put on there.[98] The appearance of these celebrities undoubtedly raised prisoners' morale and helped them feel less forgotten. Appearances by community teams and sport celebrities served a different function – they focused mainstream press attention on the New Deal reforms.

The media sent journalists to games inside penitentiaries, and articles on sports programs appeared in papers across the country. Andy O'Brien of the *Montreal Standard* was such a frequent visitor and vocal supporter of the sports program that the prisoners at Kingston Penitentiary saw him as an ally in their struggle to gain more privileges.[99] Editorials were generally favourable, with the *Toronto Daily Star* even commenting that it was "encouraging to find such an intelligent penitentiary policy at last."[100] As Goffman noted, the sports program served to give the public a sense that progress was being made in the prisons.

ENTERTAINMENT, LEISURE, AND HOBBYCRAFT

Entertainment in prison was, like the sports program, thought to have multiple purposes. As the commissioner noted, it was a diversion from the mind-numbing conditions of incarceration:

> As a further means of relieving the monotony of life over those week-ends in which statutory holidays occur on Monday, film showings were made available in all institutions on statutory holidays except during the mid-summer months. Previously the long holiday week-end during which time the prison has been closed was somewhat of a nightmare and tension, a

degree of which is understandably always present, increased on such occasions.[101]

As the following excerpt from *Pen-O-Rama* reveals, this reform generated a strong sense of gratitude toward the administration, among prisoners who were obviously very well-versed in the New Deal:

> Under the new system that is gradually taking over from the old one, we enjoy a vaudeville show now and again, put on by pretty entertainers who always give their best. They donate their talent and their only compensation is the happy smiles and cheers from an audience made up of society's discard, who might well be redeemed by the psychological effect of being entertained like ordinary human beings ... This new rehabilitation program began in 1948, when Major-General R.B. Gibson, Commissioner of Penitentiaries, and his able assistant, Mr. J. McCulley, dug the Archambault Report out of the dustbin. Being human, as well as intelligent persons, they fortified themselves with scientific data on modern penology and reached the conclusion that prisoners are people. They evolved a system that has gradually given Canadian penitentiaries a much-needed face-lifting, which has paid off, mainly in less internal friction and better morale.[102]

Entertainment initiatives in prisons varied both within and between institutions. In his 1954 annual report the commissioner indicated that in some prisons, radio systems had been upgraded to provide access to two channels and headsets, "replacing the blare of the one-programme loudspeaker which some inmates found so disturbing to their study, their reading, and often to their rest."[103] In other facilities, prisoners were permitted to program radio shows for outside audiences.[104] In a few institutions, prisoners formed orchestras,[105] some of which went on to win awards.[106] Interestingly, while the Penitentiary Service claimed that this entertainment was part of their reforms, and the penal press supported those claims, at various institutions the events were organized and partly financed by prisoner-run Recreation and Entertainment Committees and depended on performers donating their time.[107]

Performances by outside entertainers had another benefit that was often commented on in the penal press: prisoners got the opportunity to see women in person (i.e., not in the confines of visitation).[108] Many of these singers and dancers left pin-up pictures, which were subsequently run in the prison newspapers (see Image 4.5).

Prisoners sometimes used their entertainment skills to raise funds for charities. For example, in 1952, prisoners at Saskatchewan Penitentiary

Image 4.4. Prisoners at Kingston Penitentiary watch a performance of the Billy O'Connor–Ben Silverton Show. *Tele-Scope*, c. 1954.

sponsored an amateur hour on the local radio station. Minister of Justice Garson took these efforts as evidence that the New Deal was creating civic-minded prisoners: "Donations were received over the telephone during the course of the evening," the minister enthused, "and over $1,000 was realized for the work of the anti-tuberculosis league."[109]

Image 4.5. Our Own Pin-Up Gallery: Lovely Hélène Aimèe was a featured singer in our last show. *Pen-O-Rama*, January 1953. Gaucher/Munn penal press collection.

In addition to organized sports and outdoor recreation, a wider range of communal and in-cell activities were made available to prisoners in the late 1940s and early 1950s. In 1949, a hobbycraft program was introduced that allowed prisoners to use their cell time for painting, drawing, leatherwork, woodwork, knitting, and petit point (see Images 4.6 and 4.7).

The commissioner defended the program in his reports, referring to the difficulties of confinement and arguing that "retention of reason dictates that the inmate do more than vegetate while confined to his cell."[110] He also made the link to institutional security clear: he saw hobbycraft as an incentive to compliance because participation was

Image 4.6. Carved wooden trucks made by a prisoner as part of hobbycraft program. *Pen-O-Rama*, September 1956. Gaucher/Munn penal press collection.

"dependent upon the good behaviour and regular work habits of the inmate concerned."[111]

Prisoners were quick to sign up for hobbycraft. The commissioner noted in his annual report that 259 prisoners had been approved for this privilege by March 1950. He bragged that of these, only twelve "had the privilege cancelled for some abuse and in the great majority of cases the violation was a minor or technical contravention of the regulations laid down and in all cases suspension of privilege was only for a limited period."[112] By the following year, more than eight hundred prisoners were engaged in hobbycraft and institutional libraries were offering "how-to" books. Some incarcerated artisans took up handicraft production to fill the idle hours. In doing so, they helped meet the security needs of the institution: a busy prisoner would be using his time productively. Other convicts sent their crafts home to family, thus using their art to maintain relationships with the outside world.

The two biggest problems with the hobbycraft initiative were both related to funding. The most pressing matter for both the prisoners and the administrators was unequal access. Prisoners had to cover the

Image 4.7. Prisoner making a rug in his cell as part of hobbycraft program. *Pen-O-Rama*, September 1956. Gaucher/Munn penal press collection.

costs of materials, and some of them lacked sufficient means. Out of sympathy, staff members at one penitentiary took up a collection "to provide such materials for a limited number of convicts for whom it appeared the pursuit of a hobby would have a good effect."[113] Once the penal press became profitable, it lent financial support to the hobbycraft initiative. Profits from newsletter subscriptions were injected into each institution's Inmate Welfare Fund, and prisoners could apply for a hobbycraft starter loan.[114] This model would be used in other instances as well. For example, in 1951, inmate funds were drawn upon to ensure that indigent and friendless prisoners received Christmas parcels.[115]

The second difficulty was finding a market for the handicrafts.[116] Prisoners were sometimes allowed to sell their products to staff, the public, or prisoners nearing release. In many cases, 10 per cent of the sale price went to the Inmate Welfare Fund, thus supporting recreation and entertainment activities for *all* prisoners.[117] Various organizations – the Rotary Club, the Elizabeth Fry Society, the John Howard Society – offered sales support. CCF MP Harold E. Winch (Vancouver East) argued that since hobbycraft was part of the new reforms, the government needed to be more proactive in marketing the products: "I should like the minister to give consideration to giving greater assistance to inmates in the marketing of their hobby products. I think it would give them a great deal of encouragement. It would enable them to have more money at the time of their release and to a great extent might provide them with trades which they could enter on being released."[118]

There is no indication that the minister or the administrators beneath him took up this challenge. In fact, it seems that the commissioner was reluctant to play too active a part in the marketing and sales of these products. In August 1954 the assistant editor of *Pathfinder* wrote to Gibson to request permission to advertise particular hobbycraft items for sale in the magazine's pages, with 10 per cent of the proceeds going to the Inmate Welfare Fund.[119] Gibson responded by informing the warden of Saskatchewan Penitentiary that the request was denied because, among other reasons, the penitentiary should not be in the "mail order business."[120]

Reading had long been a popular way for prisoners to pass the time. Under the New Deal, uncensored daily newspapers were allowed into the prisons for the first time, and prison library collections grew.[121] Prior to this change, prisoners got their news "spoon-fed to [them] on Sunday at the end of church services ... News magazines such as Time, Newsweek and Macleans, [were] each carefully censored to exclude any reference to Canadian crime or prisons."[122] Not surprisingly, editorials appeared in major daily papers commending the government for its decision to grant prisoners access to uncensored newspapers, which they saw as reflecting "the progressive approach to prison administration."[123] Wardens, on the other hand, were not as comfortable with the change. The opinions of penitentiary staff and wardens varied between institutions. Memoranda to and from Deputy Commissioner McCulley reveal that one of the main sources of tension was the uneven application of censorship; simply put, prisoners in one penitentiary could read what others housed elsewhere could not.[124] Some wanted to continue to censor the news to keep prisoners from getting ideas about committing new crimes and to prevent them from learning what offences others had committed. Writers in the penal press countered that prisoners already had access to this kind of information via radio and (in a limited number of prisons by the late 1950s) television.[125] The prisoners wanted to stay connected, and the minister of justice supported this:

> Another extremely interesting innovation of the past year was the authorization of inmate subscription to daily newspapers, without censorship. If it is hoped that prisoners will sooner or later return to the outside world, it is obviously necessary that they should not lose complete contact with

what is going on in that outside world. In any case news sooner or later penetrates prison walls, and almost invariably in a perverted form. It seems to us much wiser to permit inmates to receive the news in the same way any other citizen may, and that he should also have the benefit of other material contained in the daily newspapers which will keep him in touch with the currents of thought and activity in the world to which he will return. This privilege has been much appreciated by the inmates and so far has presented no serious problems.[126]

In addition, the New Deal encouraged the mainstream media to cover prison life, for the press could help educate the public and secure their endorsement of the reforms. This view found support at all levels of government. Senator David A. Croll stated that "for years the problems of penology have been buried behind the thick stone walls of our penitentiaries. It is more than time that we pulled them out into the sunlight and have a good look at them."[127]

Staying Connected: Visitation and Correspondence in Prison

The tedium of prison was also alleviated by letters from home and by occasional visits. When the Archambault Commission began its work, prisoners could write one letter home per month and receive one visit every other month. In 1936 the regulations were relaxed slightly: prisoners could now write two letters and receive one visit each month. If a prisoner did not receive a visitor, he was permitted an additional letter.[128] The Archambault commissioners plainly recognized the need for prisoners to maintain contact with their loved ones:

> Probably nothing can exert a more wholesome influence on the conduct of a prisoner then the receipt of visits or letters from members of his family. Such communications should be encouraged, and the regulations concerning them should be made as elastic and reasonable as the circumstances will permit. After observing the operation of the present system in Canadian penitentiaries, your Commissioners have reached the conclusion that the regulations governing such communications are altogether too stringent and that too often they are carried out in a manner antagonistic to the prisoner and his family.[129]

Prisoners contended that the rules around visitation were outdated and that there was "no reasonable reason for not changing a visiting and correspondence code that was conceived of when the 'silent' system was an integral part of the punitive policy in all institutions."[130] They further argued that prisoners had proved themselves by cooperating with the implementation of other reforms; in their view, more leniency in correspondence and visitation policies would be a logical extension and recognition of that cooperation.[131] Someone in the commissioner's office was reading and considering their pleas for reform. In a hand-written note in the margins of a letter the commissioner received from a warden, the author refers to the November 1953 edition of *Pathfinder*, writing: "This article is also one of the penal press references which I have picked out for study in conjunction with my current work on correspondence and visiting regulations."[132] But as we will see, despite the Archambault Commission's strong recommendations, and the reasoned pleas of prisoners for changes to visitation procedures, meaningful reform in this area was not implemented as part of the New Deal.

VISITATION

The first comment the Archambault commissioners made on visitation was that the visits were too short. Prisoners were granted thirty minutes once a month, with a possible maximum of six hours a year. In most cases, it took longer for the visitor to travel to the prison than the time allotted for visitation. Over and over, inmate committees and writers in the penal press lobbied for change. Prisoners wanted the time increased to a minimum of one hour per visit. They also wanted special time allotments for those who had travelled considerable distances. Specifically, some proposed that in addition to a minimum one-hour block, they should be granted one minute for every five miles travelled, up to a three-hour maximum.[133] Where the distances were too great or expenses too high to permit travel, prisoners suggested that they be allowed a telephone call in lieu of the visit.[134] These suggestions were ignored, and the duration of visits and telephone calls did not change.

The Archambault Report also suggested that new visiting rooms be constructed in penitentiaries that would permit prisoners to visit without the use of a cage, except when necessary in the interests of security. In November 1953, Acting Warden Crofton of Saskatchewan Penitentiary argued against changes to visitation areas: "All precautions have to be taken that no inmate is given the opportunity of passing out information which might be detrimental to the security of the institution," he wrote. "[This] could easily happen if a glass partition were placed between a censor and visitors."[135] Prisoners, for their part, agreed with Archambault's recommendations, arguing that renovated visiting facilities were necessary because the current visitation conditions were demoralizing.[136] Writers in the penal press pointed out that visitation spaces varied among institutions, and they used this fact to lobby for improvements. Even when attempts were made to modify or construct friendlier spaces, these efforts were often thwarted, with the official explanation often taking the shape of what Thomas Mathiesen called the "impossible to implement" neutralization technique. Jack Grady, who was serving time at Kingston Penitentiary, challenged this administrative foot-dragging in *Tele-Scope*:

> Almost two years have gone by since the plan of remodeling the visiting room was proposed. According to the plan, the cages were to be ripped out and tables installed so that the inmate and his visitor might actually see each other and be able to converse in a normal tone of voice. This, of course, would have been a big improvement, both from the point of view of the inmate and from that of his visitor. The time, moreover, was to be lengthened out. Why was the project shelved? For a while the avowed reason was that there weren't enough officers available. That can no longer be a valid reason, for there is no apparent shortage of officers now. Perhaps reasons of "security" are responsible, since the visiting arrangements in an institution are likely to be the cause of much concern among officials. But this need not alarm security minded officials if they'd take the required precautions.[137]

Another criticism the Archambault Commission levelled against the visitation program related to the strict limits on who qualified to be a visitor. They suggested that Regulation 101, which listed those permitted to visit, be amended. The regulation permitted convicts "whose conduct and industry [were] satisfactory" to receive visits from their spouses, children and their spouses, parents and spouses' parents, siblings, and grandparents.[138] Archambault proposed that the list be expanded to include uncles, stepfathers, stepmothers, half-siblings, step-siblings, and cousins, at the discretion of the warden. Again, the prisoners supported this change but advanced the idea that an even broader social support network would be appropriate. In *Transition*, one contributor pointed out that the restrictions had a negative impact on a prisoner's future release: "Most inmates are not permitted to write or receive money for visits from friends, nor allowed to contact anyone who is not an immediate relative. Because of such restrictions, about 25% of Canada's penitentiary population never write or receive letters or have visits during the whole of their sentences."[139]

Again, change did not come with the New Deal. The same pattern would emerge in terms of the regulations governing correspondence.

CORRESPONDENCE

The Archambault Commission's recommendations regarding changes to correspondence regulations mirrored those for visitations. Essentially, the commissioners felt that the rules were too severe and wanted to relax the censorship of letters, expand the categories of correspondents, and permit more respect for the privacy and integrity of prisoners. In the 1950s, outgoing letters were strictly regulated in terms of length (two handwritten pages), and each person was allowed to send only two letters per month to immediate family members. This policy seemed to contravene the Standard Minimum Rules for the Treatment of Prisoners, which stated that "prisoners should have the opportunity of communicating with their relations and respectable friends, under necessary supervision."[140] Some writers in the penal press attempted to persuade the administration to broaden the types of people who could correspond with prisoners by drawing on the rhetoric of the New Deal:

> The long-held objection that a convict's former friends are not the fitting subjects of correspondence is insufficiently confirmed to warrant the continuance of the present restrictions. The convict's ties to crime are to be found in the next cell and not in the literary efforts of persons of dubious character ... The rule that creates this condition is archaic and unnecessarily restrictive. Such an outmoded and intolerant regulation has no place in a progressive penal program.[141]

Even members of Parliament viewed these limits as overly restrictive, especially since all letters to and from prisoners were read by staff to ensure their "suitability."[142] Obviously, this was a slow and tedious process, which likely accounts for the authorities' desire to maintain restrictions on the quantity of correspondence. Administrative documents also indicate that administrators were concerned about "the greater prevalence in recent months of correspondence" being sent into and out of the prison that had been written with "invisible ink" made from urine or the juice of potatoes, limes, lemon, and so on.[143] So great were their concerns about this that the administration consulted the RCMP, hired experts to assess the possibility, and subsequently purchased ultraviolet lights to detect the presence of these secret messages.[144] Yet when Deputy Commissioner Gendreau inquired as to whether the new technology "had been found to be of any particular use," he was informed in vague terms that the device was "very useful, and is used as and when there is suspicion of letter contents." Tellingly, his correspondent cited no cases of actual detection.[145]

Prisoners in Dorchester Penitentiary met with the warden to discuss an expansion of correspondence privileges and reported in *Beacon* that "nothing can be done at this time. You now receive one extra letter in lieu of your monthly visits, and can receive extra letters in case of emergency but, with only two men handling both incoming and outgoing mail – to say nothing of many extra tasks – it is doubtful that the letter issues could be increased without additions being made to the Censorial Staff."[146]

Between the 1930s and 1960, only minor modifications were made to visitation structures and the regulations surrounding correspondence. Reflecting on the lack of progress on these issues, John Brown, a prisoner at Kingston Penitentiary in 1954, despondently concluded that "the Old Deal ... flourishes as vigorously as ever."[147] The ideas of the New Deal, to borrow Thomas Mathiesen's terminology, were being effectively neutralized.

Education and Vocational Training

Classification officers, following their interview with a prisoner, recommended ways to ameliorate his educational and vocational deficits with the goal of returning him to the community as a "good citizen." In an article written for *Canadian Welfare* and reprinted in *Tele-Scope*, Commissioner Gibson called for both vocational and liberal education for prisoners:

> If those willing to benefit could be given an opportunity of learning thoroughly a skilled trade in demand in the outside world, their chances of successful re-establishment would be greatly enhanced ... Education, or perhaps re-education in its broadest sense, is an integral part of the treatment process. An education program should be designed not merely to bring those who are illiterate up to a minimum standard but should be sufficiently broad in scope to influence the basic attitudes of those who participate and to open to them new means of occupying constructively the leisure time at their disposal.[148]

Good citizens needed to be thoughtful and productive. To that end, the penal reforms implemented between 1935 and 1960 emphasized giving convicts work skills, improving their literacy, and, in some cases, improving their general knowledge.

EDUCATIONAL OPPORTUNITIES

That prisoners wanted more educational opportunities is not surprising. While official data were not collected nationwide, piecemeal evidence indicates that the literacy rate among prisoners was lower than among the general public. This led to some discussion in the House of Commons when the Commissioner's Report for 1949–50 was released. Specifically, Progressive Conservative MP Gordon Churchill (Winnipeg South Centre) considered the correlation between educational attainment and criminal behaviour and wondered if it "would be wiser to spend more money on education and eliminate the illiterates rather than keep them in penitentiaries for years at heavy expense and then try to educate them."[149] In 1949, Commissioner Gibson wrote that prison regulations required that the penitentiaries provide an education to teachable illiterates who had not completed compulsory public schooling; those deemed "unteachable" or having a "low mentality" were exempted. That year, 412 eligible prisoners received "two or three half-days of classes per week between September and June."[150] In 1951, the commissioner lamented that "the actual number of inmates served in this way is ... comparatively small."[151] His subsequent annual reports would focus on infrastructure and omit any mention of attendance.

While prisoners in some provinces were able to access correspondence courses – through the Department of Veterans Affairs, provincial governments, Queen's University, and various private agencies[152] – others could not, or found it difficult to complete these courses during their in-cell time. In his 1950 annual report, Gibson acknowledged the challenge of completing these courses within the peculiar prison environment:

> It should once again be noted that while it may be casually assumed by an outsider that prison inmates have a good deal of time on their hands available for such purposes, serious study cannot be pursued quite as easily as might be imagined. Radio broadcasts which are heard in most of the ranges interfere and would present a real difficulty even to students who had a much larger ability to concentrate. There is also the ever-present chatter between cells and ranges which interferes with any student desiring to do serious study. The fact that so many inmates have achieved satisfactory standings is therefore a tribute to their serious interest. In a few cases it has been possible to provide quiet ranges, but the nature of the architecture of most of our institutions and the generally crowded conditions have not rendered this a feasible solution in most cases.[153]

To remedy this problem, some in the penal press called for students to be allowed out of their cells for three hours after the conclusion of the workday to attend classes.[154] Others argued that the entire prison population should receive compulsory education up to grade twelve.[155] We know too that the penal press emphasized the importance of education. To that end, it offered vocabulary-building articles and other educational materials and encouraged participation in classes when they were available. *Mountain Echoes* even dedicated space in its publication to a "school column."[156]

Teaching the 3 R's in the classroom was the main priority. In addition, prisoners and administrators attempted to extend the educational experience. To that end, they organized activities like educational film viewings and special interest courses. Some prisoners, depending on where they were serving their time, had access, on an ad hoc basis, to evening discussion groups on philosophy, courses on prospecting or mineralogy, or even the chance to participate in a Dale Carnegie course to improve their communication, problem-solving, and leadership skills. Access to education remained a problem, however. It was expensive to hire instructors and provide supplies and equipment; also, there was a lack of available learning space, and the sheer size of the prison population further limited access to educational opportunities. As clinical psychologist Dale E. Smith noted, regardless of individual ambition, "goals become more difficult to achieve as more individuals must compete for the same amount of resources." Regarding the strain that crowding places on individuals, he added that "it is in this sense that limitations imposed by increased populations pose a threat to the individual's well-being."[157]

VOCATIONAL TRAINING

Prison labour had long been in place in federal prisons.[158] In 1947, a formal vocational training program was introduced at two Canadian penitentiaries, Collins Bay Institution and Saint-Vincent-de-Paul's Federal Training Centre (see Images 4.11–4.13).[159] By 1954 the program had expanded into three more institutions. This training was designed to give the participants sufficient skills to be employed as journeymen. D.J. Halfhide, the Penitentiary Service's chief vocational officer, identified the aims of the training program as follows:

(a) To assist in rehabilitation through trade training, so that upon release many will be able to find employment in a trade of his own choice.
(b) To give technical training equivalent to that received by apprentices in the trades, as required by apprenticeship regulations.
(c) To provide actual work experience into the trades.
(d) To develop work habits acceptable to employers of labour.[160]

The vocational courses offered pathways to several trades, including machining, masonry, sheet metal work, motor mechanics, carpentry,

156. The courses indicated in the table below were conducted during the fiscal year:

—	Dorchester	Federal Training Centre	Collin's Bay	Saskatchewan	British Columbia
Automobile		X	X		X
Diesel Mechanics					X
Draughting					X
Carpentry	X	X	X		X
Sheet Metal		X	X		X
Commercial					X
Barbering	(Part-time)	X	X	(Part-time)	
Brickmasoury	X	X	X		
Electrical		X	X		
Machine Shop		X	X		
Machine Shop (Basic)		X			
Plumbing	X	X	X	X	
Rural Repair				2	
Painting and Decorating				X	
Cabinet-Making		X			
Plastering		X			
Elementary Training		X			
Upholstery	X				
	4	12	8	4	6

Image 4.8. Table of available vocational opportunities. *Report of the Commissioner of Penitentiaries*, 1956–57.

and plumbing and steam fitting. In his 1956–57 *Annual Report*, Commissioner Gibson included a table to emphasize the availability of training options (see Image 4.8).

However, a close inspection of the table reveals omissions that skew its significance. The three penitentiaries that offered no vocational training at all are not included on the chart, which makes it seem that more training opportunities existed than actually did. So, in effect, full-time vocational training was available to only a small group of prisoners. In an average year, well over 4,600 of 5,000 prisoners were *not* involved in vocational training. Even at Collins Bay, where vocational training for young and "reformable" prisoners was a priority, the numbers enrolled in vocational courses fluctuated between 13 and 18 per cent in 1955.[161] In 1960, the commissioner "reported 333 inmates enrolled in training-courses, out of a total prison population of 6, 344."[162] In the early 1950s, Gibson reported that the creation of spaces in the vocational training program was hindered by a lack of shop space and, at small institutions, by demand for prisoners to serve in the prison operations, maintenance, and construction departments. Reflecting the observations of Erving Goffman and Thomas Mathiesen, priority was being given to the orderly operation, maintenance, and financial concerns of the institutions.[163] Moreover, many prisoners were ineligible for vocational training. The programs required at least a grade eight education, which meant that many prisoners had to attend upgrading classes before taking a program or during the early part of it.[164] To rectify this, in 1957–58, an experimental program was introduced at Saskatchewan Penitentiary that allowed prisoners to attend school full-time over a four-month period in order to raise their grade level so that they could access vocational training; the commissioner bragged with uncharacteristic vagueness in his annual report that "the project was successful with a significant number of candidates."[165] This program, however, did not solve the problem for recidivists and prisoners over the age of thirty, who were barred from vocational programs, a situation that did not change until the late 1950s.[166] In addition, since most prisoners served sentences of less than four years, even those who were eligible stood a poor chance of being admitted to and completing a vocational course.[167] As the commissioner explained in his 1955 report, "there is no room or opportunity for training during the average sentence, which is disappointing to the inmate, to his parents and to those responsible for the vocational programme."[168]

Prisoners were selected for vocational training by a committee that prioritized the "reformable" prisoner and thus chose mostly young prisoners and/or first timers (see Image 4.9). And even some prisoners who met the criteria could not receive training, as Jack H., a writer in *Tele-Scope*, makes clear:

> If an inmate is deemed re-formable he is sent to Collins Bay penitentiary to learn a trade. However, not all re-formable youths, and first-offenders are sent there, regardless of whether they wish to learn a trade or not. Yet everyone, except the inmates, seems to be under the impression that all inmates have equal opportunity to learn a trade and thus lay the basis for their rehabilitation. Under existing conditions here, anyone wanting to learn a trade must look around for someone who knows a little and glue himself to him in order to pick up odds and ends.[169]

Image 4.9. An inmate being interviewed by the Treatment Board. *C.B. Diamond,* March 1956. Gaucher/Munn penal press collection.

Prisoners suggested that shorter or more generic courses be offered (blueprint reading, layout work, etc.) so that more of them could take part.[170] To be sure, there was a general show of support for the new program, and most of the suggestions in the penal press around vocational training were directed at expanding its reach.[171] In the House of Commons, Progressive Conservative MP Walter Dinsdale (Brandon) suggested that "perhaps the emphasis might be placed upon broader vocational training rather than training in a specialized category, and that the net results would be more beneficial."[172] It seems that everyone agreed that vocational training programs for prisoners had merit. However, prisoner Sam Carr, writing in *Tele-Scope,* pointed out that even if they had acquired skills in prison, ex-convicts would encounter "prejudice and rank discrimination" in their quest for employment.[173]

TRADES, INDUSTRIES

AND SERVICES

Tailor Shop

This photo shows a part of the tailor shop, where all the officer's uniforms are manufactured with the aid of modern machinery that does not appear above. It is placed along the wall in the opposite corner of the shop.

Image 4.10. Through the Shops: The Tailor Shop. *Pen-O-Rama*, February 1953. Gaucher/Munn penal press collection.

TRADES, INDUSTRIES AND SERVICES

This photo shows a corner of the Carpenter Shop where all types of furniture and other incidental articles are made. The men are in the process of putting the finishing touches on a piece that was made specially for the Sacristy of the Roman Catholic Chapel, at the Federal Training Centre,

Image 4.11. Through the Shops: The Carpenter Shop. *Pen-O-Rama*, April 1953. Gaucher/Munn penal press collection.

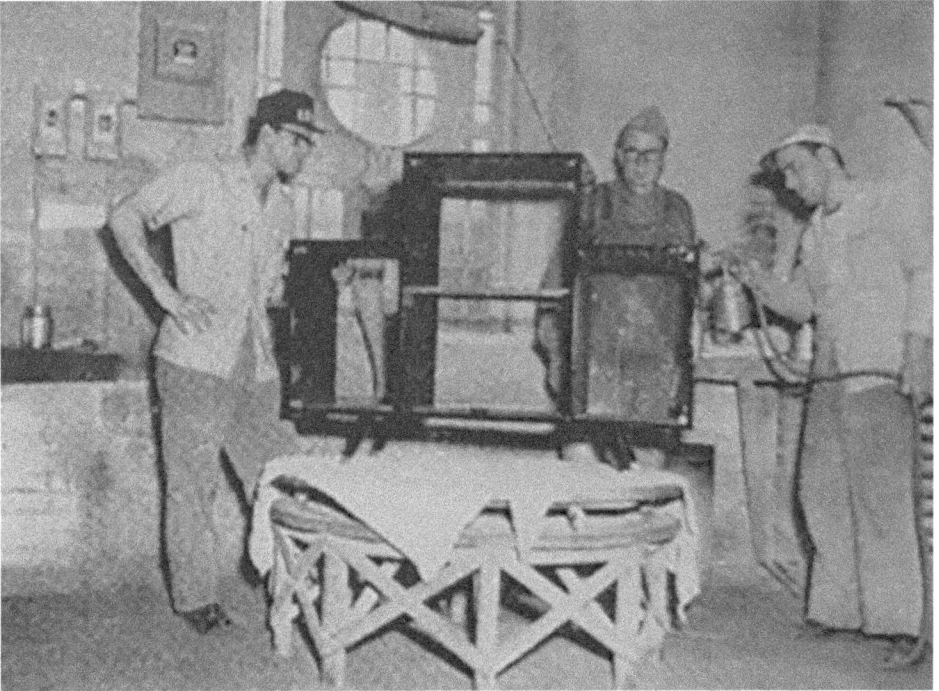

Image 4.12. Through the Shops: The Painter Shop. *Pen-O-Rama*, June 1953.
Gaucher/Munn penal press collection.

Work and Industry

The Archambault commissioners had called for "work ... and ... plenty
of it,"[174] and in the postwar years the prison bureaucracy responded. In
part, their efforts reflected the Archambault commissioners' tendency to
conceive of prison labour in terms of the Protestant work ethic ("Idleness
in Canadian prisons cannot be tolerated. It is destructive to the physical
and moral fabric of the prisoners"),[175] but importantly, work was, as a
by-product of classification, also a mechanism of control. In acknowl-
edging the importance of prison industries, Commissioner Gibson cited
James Bennett, director of the US Federal Bureau of Prisons, who wrote
that "no single phase of life within prison walls is more important to
the public or to the inmate, than efficient industrial operation and the
intelligent utilization of the labor of prisoners. Prison industry is of vital
significance in the economic aspect of correctional administration; is an
invaluable aid in lessening the problems of discipline and security and

Image 4.13. The Motor Vehicle Repair Course. *C.B. Diamond*, March/April 1956. Gaucher/Munn penal press collection.

is inseparably connected with any sound program of rehabilitation."[176] Bennett simultaneously advocated the use of prison labour to secure the prison and to reintegrate prisoners into the liberal-capitalist order. Obviously, Gibson shared these views.

According to the official record, prison shops were modernized and expanded. To make more rational use of local resources and achieve economies of scale, efforts were made to consolidate specific industries in particular prisons. For example, in his 1953 report, Commissioner Gibson stated that "the establishment of inter-penitentiary manufacture has permitted a greater volume of work to be assigned to the individual shops in quantities sufficient to establish continual operation ... In the shoe and tailoring industries ... this is being accomplished to a considerable extent by pooling our service requirements into one or two shops."[177]

As an incentive to labour and rehabilitation, and to provide prisoners with a modest amount of spending money and a potential source of savings for release, a graduated pay scale for prisoners was introduced.[178]

According to André Dion, one of the first editors of *Pen-O-Rama*, the most revolutionary of the New Deal changes was the implementation of a graduated prison pay system on 1 October 1951. Prior to that, prisoners were paid 5 cents per day for work inside the prison.[179] Under the new system, the base rate doubled immediately to 10 cents per day and prisoners could earn up to 20 cents based on "their work efficiency [and] on their general conduct and attitudes."[180]

A few months after the new remuneration plan was introduced, small canteens were opened in the penitentiaries where the prisoners were able to spend some of their increased, but still meagre, earnings. Almost immediately, individuals on both sides of the bars, convicts and administrators, expressed financial concerns. The incarcerated expressed dissatisfaction with the distribution of profits. According to André Dion, one of the early problems with canteens was that the proceeds from sales were not remitted to the Inmate Welfare Fund, which, as we saw earlier in this chapter, benefited prisoners in need. He suspected that the money was being used for the guards' activities.[181] While there is no evidence to support Dion's assertion as to where the money was going, if other prisoners believed this to be true, it may have been a source of tension. Indeed, Dion's belief was so common among prisoners that Deputy Commissioner Gendreau spoke to it at the 1955 Warden's Conference: "In some cases the inmates went so far as to tell me that the officers ate up the profit, they threw banquets, parties and enjoyed themselves. In other instances they went so far as to tell me that these funds were being used to pay insurance for officer's quarters." He dismissed these claims as "silly ideas" spread by "trouble-makers."[182] It is unclear how the profits were distributed in each prison, but we know that as late as 1953, writers in the penal press were advocating for their fair share of canteen profits[183] and lobbying the commissioner on this matter, with some success.[184]

On the other side of the bars, administrators worried that prisoners would spend all their earnings in the canteens. Under the wage system, spending all their remaining earnings would have been easy to do. Concerned that prisoners be released with more cash in their pockets, the wardens and administrators decided that "a portion of the daily remuneration must be saved against the day of release; the balance may be spent for the purchase of small amenities such as chocolate bars, chewing gum, toilet supplies, etc."[185] Even after a forced savings regime was introduced, some wardens worried that prisoners would have too much money to spend at the canteen: "A Grade 3 man going to Canteen every two weeks has $1.80 to spend if he works 12 days and earn 15 cents per day. Presumably will spend 56 cents for tobacco and that leave [*sic*] $1.24. Some Penitentiaries feel this is a lot."[186] While administrators implemented a forced-savings regime, some prisoners, like Arnold Abrahams, of *Transition*, suggested that an improved pay scale would be a better solution:[187]

> A man earning 10¢ a day must work six days a week in order to have 14¢ to spend each week in the commissary. This year there will be 10 official holidays. Since approximately 50% of the men, give or take a man or two, are earning 10¢, that means that for 10 weeks this year half the men will derive no benefit at all from the commissary. The biggest drawback to the present pay system is the disparity between 10 and 20¢ brackets. After the regulation issue of tobacco and the compulsory saving deduction a 20¢ man has not double but almost five times the buying power at the commissary of the 10¢ man. We suggest that it would be more equitable to either abandon the 10¢ category completely or at least start everyone at 15¢.[188]

A raise in pay was not just on the prisoners' minds.[189] Organizations like the Western Pulp and Paper Workers argued that prisoners' remuneration was insufficient and that they should be unionized, granted a forty-hour work week, and paid full wages; this was not a position that the government entertained.[190]

Some in the penal press, in prisoners' aid societies, and in Parliament thought that prisoners should qualify for unemployment insurance benefits on release, though there were different views on how this would be achieved. In the House of Commons, CCF MP Harold Winch (Vancouver East) suggested that part of the prisoner's earnings be automatically docked for this insurance to aid in his successful reintegration into a difficult economic climate:

> I can assure you that one of the biggest problems that this country faces is the fact that the government spends a great deal of money first of all on incarcerating these people because they have broken the laws of society. Then, after we have them in custody we try to rehabilitate them by training so that they will become useful members of society. Then, when their term of imprisonment is up and they are released they come up against the situation which we have had for far too long namely the serious unemployment situation where the socially responsible unemployed cannot get jobs.[191]

Despite the recession that began in 1957, the government did not pursue Winch's suggestion that prisoners qualify for unemployment insurance.[192] Indeed, aftercare, on the whole, was not within the purview of the New Deal; in keeping with the recommendations of the Archambault Report, the Penitentiary Service left such services in the hands of private organizations. This policy was justified on the grounds that voluntary agencies could provide services over a greater geographic range and that prisoners could use their services without feeling as though they were "being directed or supervised by a law enforcement or government agency" after discharge.[193] Even so, the Penitentiary Service did institute a new relationship with aftercare associations and employment agencies, assisting in the organization of local societies, organizing several conferences to bring together prisoners' aid societies from across the country, and providing increasingly large funding grants to assist them with their work.[194]

Mollycoddling and the Defence of the New Deal

Except for the death penalty, the deprivation of liberty was the most severe penalty available to the courts. Yet that people were sent to prison *as* punishment was not enough for some members of the public: they wanted people sent to prison *for* punishment. And this was perhaps the reason for the greatest sustained opposition to the New Deal. The government and the commissioner may have wanted the public to embrace the mantra that "prisoners are people," but many saw them only as "bad people," as undeserving people, as people upon whom the "rod" was not to be spared. Garfinkel contends that a prisoner's identity is spoiled through a series of status degradation ceremonies designed to replace any previous identity markers with a new, stigmatized status: convict.[195] Many members of the public embraced the principles of revenge and retribution rather than the ideals of rehabilitation and reformation. They found support in some of Canada's major newspapers, which ran articles and editorials decrying the new, "softer" initiatives. Letters to the editor implied that prisons were being run like country clubs.[196] Unable to see the conditions of incarceration firsthand, the public drew its conclusions largely from the images created in the press, some of which highlighted the new sports and entertainment happenings.[197] But the pushback did not just come from radical right nonprogressives. The following speech by Progressive Conservative MP James M. Macdonnell (Greenwood) shows that even moderates sympathetic to the reforms were challenged by the extent of the changes:

> Though we all sympathize fully with the aims of the penitentiary administration, particularly since we received the recommendations of the Archambault report, I think we all feel that the old idea that it was nothing but punishment and protecting society by shutting up people behind walls has now gone, and we recognize that what we are trying to do is not only protect society but turn the offenders into better citizens. At the same

time, I think we must not get to the stage where we talk about it as if being there was a reward for meritorious service ... I think we should keep the thought clear in our minds that this is a serious matter and that these men are there because of the things they have done against society."[198]

Macdonnell's concluding remarks lend support to Rusche and Kirchheimer's claim that "no reform program has been willing to abandon the principle that the living standard of the prisoner must be depressed in order to retain the deterrent effects of punishment."[199]

The early writers in the penal press argued for the New Deal reforms to have a "thorough trial."[200] By the mid-1950s, however, they sensed that a significant shift in public perceptions had occurred. While it is difficult to assess the level of public dissatisfaction with the reforms, prisoners felt they had to defend them. One prisoner lamented that the public was more concerned about conditions at the local dog pound than at the local prison.[201] Another writer in *Transition* empathized with the public's pessimism: "The coolness, of course, is understandable: a society plagued with record breaking crime-waves casts a jaundiced eye at those who have been caught."[202] This writer's sentiment notwithstanding, a punitive response was not the only possibility. Indeed, one impetus for the reform project had been the juvenile delinquency scare during the Second World War (see chapter 2).

Writers like Tony Anthony of *Mountain Echoes* tried to convince readers (and possibly those like Macdonnell) of the need for change by appealing to their basic sense of decency: "Is it coddling to throw out the barbaric and bring in the humane?"[203] Others tried to draw on crime prevention discourses: "Modern penology has discovered, through trial and error, that to increase the standard of living in penitentiaries is to decrease recidivism."[204] Still other prisoners claimed that under the "McCulley-Gibson system," they were "making every effort to straighten up ... because the way was pointed out to them by a humane, decent prison system."[205] One prisoner took a more highbrow, albeit somewhat aggressive, approach:

> Here is the answer to those who oppose change in the attitude taken towards those offenders against the law; the answer to those who are anxious to maintain a punitive rather than a redemptive system of correction. Demosthenes recognized that imprisonment and deprivation of his natural rights, far from creating in the mind of an offender, a state of repentance, was much more likely to arouse his hatred of society and compel him to impose upon it the only form of retaliation available to him, namely, a repetition of the offenses for which he had already been deprived of his liberty.[206]

While some prisoners were taking a defensive stance, former Deputy Commissioner McCulley, who had resigned in 1952,[207] maintained his optimism and downplayed the significance of those who did not support the reforms:

> I am, however, convinced of this fact: that the general public will not much longer tolerate correctional institutions which will carry anywhere in their programme the signs or symptoms of the intolerance, the stupidity or the ignorance which marked the prisons of an earlier era. I make no apology ... it is my present satisfaction to endeavour in some small way to develop in the minds of our present staffs and of the public at large an awareness that prison work is primarily an educational task and that only as such can it ultimately justify itself.[208]

McCulley pressed the idea that Canada's federal prisons were modern and fundamentally different from before, but his analysis missed one crucial point: a prison, no matter how it is dressed up, is always a prison, and the fundamental conditions of confinement had not changed. In 1953, prisoners at Saskatchewan Penitentiary attempted to convey this sentiment to the public by using *Pathfinder* to publish a picture of a "prison cell interior with an accompanying article designed to remind our outside readers that penitentiary life is not all peaches and cream."[209] The author of the letter, editor James Clark, ended by noting that "permission for this has been refused."[210] Four years later, *Pen-O-Rama* attempted to create an "anniversary album" depicting life at Saint-Vincent-de-Paul, to be called "The Penitentiary in Pictures." Administrators were initially supportive but later withdrew their support when confronted with the associated costs.[211] Later that year, the editors of *Tele-Scope* would have more success drawing attention to the realities of prison life; in 1957, prisoners at Kingston Penitentiary used the pages of *Tele-Scope* to offer readers a multi-page visual of where they spent their time (see Images 4.14–4.18). While some of this tedium had been broken by the introduction of the New Deal, Ben Jauvin, incarcerated in Quebec, took the time to calculate what this really meant for a prisoner:

> Allow me, if I may, to use the following statistics to make a point. On a ten year sentence, an inmate must serve seven years, seven months eleven days. This is providing that there is no ticket of leave granted him. The following is the break-down:
>
> TIME SPENT AT WORK – 11,700 hours
> MOVIES, STAGE SHOWS, EXT. [*sic*] – 413 hours
> SPORTS, REGULAR EXERCISE PERIODS, ETC. 3000 hours.
> RELIGIOUS SEVICES [*sic*] – 600 hours
> TIME SPENT IN CELL – 50, 511 hours
> TOTAL – 66, 224
> SUMMARY – As is evident an approximate 75 percent of an inmates [*sic*] sentence time is done in his cell.[212]

Image 4.14. Prisoners show their outside view at the penitentiary. *Tele-Scope,* December 1956–January 1957.

Or he can look through the bars. But if he cells on a bottom range, the view is not exactly aesthetic.

Image 4.15. Prisoners show their inside view at the penitentiary. *Tele-Scope*, December 1956–January 1957.

And if the prisoner gets restless, he can hook his bed against the wall and pace the length of his cell.

Image 4.16. Prisoners show a cell at the penitentiary. *Tele-Scope*, December 1956–January 1957.

This will be his home for years to come.

Image 4.17. Prisoner looks into the prison cell. *Tele-Scope*, December 1956–January 1957.

Image 4.18. Image of cell with door closed. *Tele-Scope*, December 1956–
January 1957.

More existentially, prisoners like Bill Martin tried to describe the feeling
of imprisonment:

It's loneliness that etches deeply. It's frustration that stifles ambition. It's
monotony that corrodes personality, leaving many dull and apathetic. It
is quiet desperation for some and violent outburst for others less able to
endure. Yes, prison is all this and more, and underlying it all, perhaps, is
the sense of futility.[213]

The New Deal ... Same as the Old Deal?

The New Deal cannot be reduced to a simple success/failure dichotomy. Prisoners felt both optimistic ("This is 1953, and I fear no contradiction when I say that there has been more penal progress in the last seven years in Canada than in the previous century"),[214] and dejected ("The year that just ended, 1953, was 365 days of unmitigated monotony and mental misery. We know that the year before us is the identical twin of the one in the past").[215] Through their words, we can surmise that while prisoners did benefit from the reforms in meaningful and sustained ways, many aspects of their confinement remained the same. More than sixty years after his release from prison, André Dion recalled the importance of the gains made during the early 1950s. He remembered the visceral impact of the prison and the moments when he felt treated like a person instead of a number. He, like other prison writers, also elaborated on his frustration with the unexpected implications of the changes and the slow pace of reform. For those living in the prisons at that time, and for some progressive politicians, administrators, and staff in corrections, that pace seemed glacial or non-existent. In 1954, a prisoner at BC Penitentiary offered his thoughts:

> Almost 20 years ago a Royal Commission was set up to investigate the prison system and make recommendations for improvements. Many improvements have been made, but the inmates are a more disillusioned band than ever. The changes hoped for did not materialize. There has been no real improvement in the ticket-of-leave system, the much talked about parole board has not materialized, nothing has been done to abolish the ignominious visiting and letter writing facilities, men are still locked up for 18 hours a day.[216]

Of course they were disillusioned. Prisoner James Carleton, who had been so hopeful on his admission to Kingston Penitentiary, had changed his mind by the time of his release two years later. In *Tele-Scope*, he wrote: "I have learned that the term rehabilitation is a meaningless word and that recidivism is the natural result of prison." He concluded: "There is a long way to travel by sincere thinking people who want to make rehabilitation a reality, and not a hollow word in Canadian Penology."[217] The following chapters examine the administrative efforts to fulfil the unaddressed aspects of the New Deal and the consequences of prisoner frustration – demonstrated through riots and conflicts over the content of the penal press.

5 Time Off: Clemency, Remission, and Parole

A man deprived of his freedom will become preoccupied with its return. It is no wonder then that the penal press devoted considerable space to exploring how to minimize time served in prison. But short of escape, getting out of prison has never been quick. From his cell at BC Penitentiary, Vic Ashton penned the following poem:

Incentive
Not so very long ago
In the Big-house by the sea,
A transition long awaited
Finally came to be.
And throughout the institution
Drastic changes made debut;
The old Regime was cast aside
To make way for the new.

The Minister of Justice
Had approved of many plans;
Earphones, sports and picture shows,
Newspapers for the fans.
Razors, Mirror, shaving soap,
A commissary for the boys.
Hobbies. Music, Christmas gifts
Were added to the joys.

Then all the guards were cautioned
To offer kindness where they could.
To replace curses with psychology
As do the cons some good.

Now all these changes help a lot
And I'm glad of their commission,
But MAN! How reformed I could be
For a little more remission!"[1]

It was not only the incarcerated who concerned themselves with early release. The possibility of earning time off was important to people at all levels of the system. For administrators and correctional workers, such a mechanism might be used to encourage compliant behaviour in prisoners.[2] Prison reformers felt that a parole system or an improved remission service would help bring about a more progressive penal system, one that reflected the New Deal for prisoners. Indeed, the Archambault Commission, which in 1938 drew the blueprint for the reforms that would be followed in subsequent decades, had been critical of the way that prisoners earned early release. Their concerns were many, ranging from a lack of proper record-keeping, to discrepancies between provinces, to political interference in deciding who received parole. As shown in previous chapters and in Ashton's poem, many of the penal reforms suggested by the commissioners were adopted during and immediately after the war. Yet on the matter of early release from prison, change came more slowly.

There were many reasons for the delay. Differing views on the purpose of imprisonment combined with archaic penal holdovers to produce a confusing and sometimes dysfunctional system. At the same time, systemic drag and multiple and sometimes competing governmental and bureaucratic interests inhibited change. For example, the Archambault commissioners wanted "the administration of the Ticket-of-Leave Act [to] be brought under the direction of the Prison Commission" that they had recommended to oversee a prison system unified under federal control;[3] however, for that to occur, provincial authorities would have to cede jurisdiction. Given that these federal–provincial issues of jurisdiction had not been addressed (and never would be), General R.B. Gibson was specifically forbidden from dealing with "matters referred to in sub-section two of section five of the Penitentiary Act, 1939. (i.e., Exercise of Royal Prerogative of Mercy and the Remission Service)" in his report on the implementation of the Archambault Commission's recommendations.[4] It was not until 11 December 1953 that an "informal committee [was] established to investigate and report upon the principles and procedures followed in the Remission Service of the Department of Justice in connection with the exercise of clemency and to recommend what changes, if any, should be made in those principles and procedures."[5] Despite the limited scope of their mandate, the committee did not submit a report to the minister of justice until 30 April 1956. Response to their report (commonly known as the Fauteux Report) was tepid. The committee members believed that the public had little interest in the issue and blamed the slow course of penal reform on public indifference: "Improvements in correctional facilities in Canada have lagged far behind those in the other social sciences. *It appears to us that the factor chiefly responsible for this state of affairs has been a continuing lack of public interest in the subject which ... has amounted almost to apathy* [italics added]."[6] Yet, it seems equally likely that their delay in submitting their findings played a role dampening that public interest. Prisoners and reformers had been waiting almost two decades to see change and had high hopes. Prisoners doing time between 1935 and 1959 showed, through their writing, that they both understood the problems in the current system and had ideas for making it more workable. Unfortunately, once the report was released, they realized that while their solutions occasionally aligned with official state goals, they more often diverged.

We begin this chapter by considering the remission system in place when the penal press came into being (1949). We then examine the process applied by the Remission Branch (which, despite its name, supervised clemency and other acts of grace, but not remission), how this was experienced by incarcerated men and women, and the changes proposed by the prisoners and by the members of the Fauteux Committee. After that, we consider how the queen's coronation provided prisoners with a moment of respite from their frustrations with the lack of change. Finally, we review how prisoners envisioned a reformed parole system and the degree of alignment between that vision and the Fauteux Report's recommendations. We end by looking at the path to and implementation of the Act to Provide for the Conditional Liberation of Persons Undergoing Sentences of Imprisonment (the Parole Act).

Good Time

In 1949, a prisoner could not be faulted for being uncertain of his release date. There were too many factors involved in this calculation for an inexperienced convict to achieve any kind of easy clarity. Had they received a determinate sentence or an indeterminate one? Were they being held in a provincial facility awaiting transfer to the federal system? Had they earned all their "good time" credit in the first year, or had they missed out on the full seventy-two days? To help the reader understand this complexity, Image 5.1 provides a fictitious scenario involving four men: three (Bill, Larry, and Jim) have been sentenced to

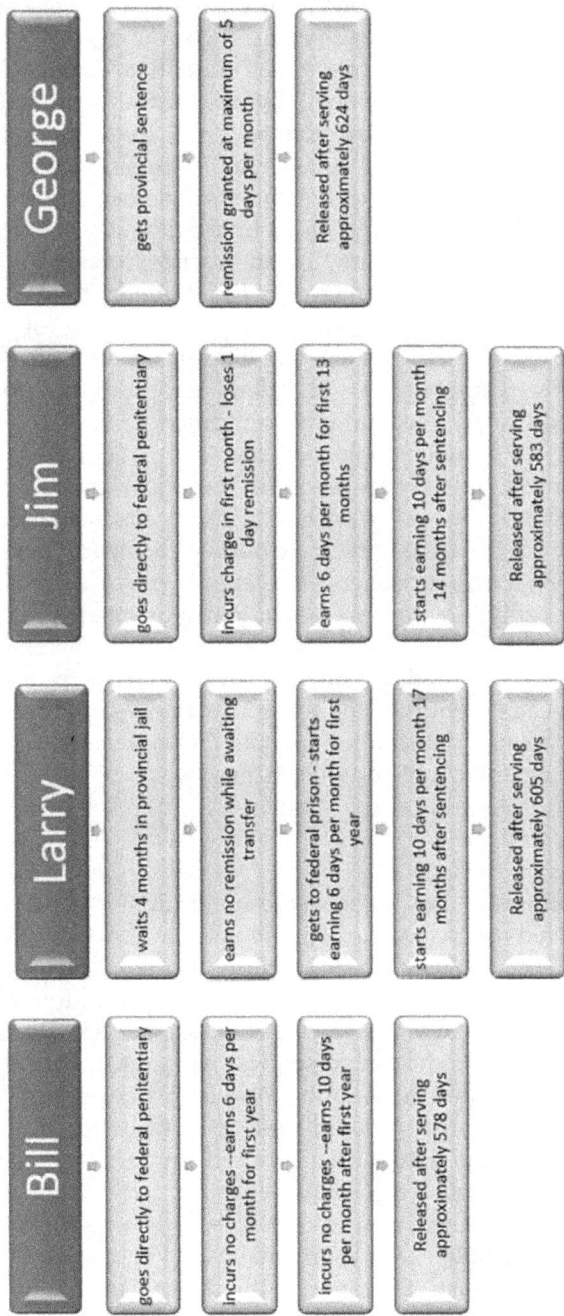

Image 5.1. Scenario of possible good time calculations.

two years of federal time, and one (George) has been sentenced to two years less one day, a provincial sentence.

Under the remission provisions of the Penitentiary Act (1906), a prisoner could earn time off his sentence by demonstrating good conduct, diligence, and industry. In common parlance, these days deducted from the sentence were called "good time." Remission was clearly a reward, and records were kept of a prisoner's daily behaviour so that he could be assigned up to five days' good time per month.[7] At first blush, the idea seemed straightforward, but in practice, remission relied on many structural and individual factors. For example, the Prisons and Reformatories Act (1868) authorized statutory remission for prisoners in "improved" provincial prisons, but the rate of remission differed between provinces and between the federal and provincial prison systems.[8] In an odd twist, a federal prisoner sentenced to two years (like Bill) was likely to be released sooner than a provincial prisoner (like George) sentenced to two years less a day.[9] For those sentenced prior to 15 August 1938, no remission was granted during the first six months of their sentence.[10] During the immediate post-Archambault period (after 16 August 1938), federal prisoners could expect to receive six days each month until seventy-two days were acquired; a prisoner earning all his remission days (like Bill) could expect to reach this number in one year. After hitting this threshold, the rate improved to allow the prisoner to earn ten days each month for the remainder of his sentence.[11] But the calculations were not that simple, and both the Fauteux Report and the prisoners pointed out problems with them.

The First-Year Problem

The first problem was that prisoners did not begin to receive remission until they arrived at the federal institution. In the above graphic, Larry had been sentenced, but while detained in a local or provincial facility pending transfer to a federal penitentiary, he received no remission credit. Such transfer delays might occur, for example, when space was not available or when the convicted person was needed to testify at another court case.[12] This created an inequity between prisoners who immediately entered the federal system (Bill) and those who did not (Larry); in some cases, it also created disparities between co-convicted persons. The Fauteux Committee argued that statutory remission legislation should be "carefully reviewed" with a view to creating a "more uniform and practical system ... that would eliminate anomalies and inequities."[13]

Prisoners also argued that it was illogical to give a prisoner a lesser rate of accumulation during the "first year and hardest year of incarceration."[14] Jon Bennett wrote in *Tele-Scope* that failure to gain remission in this early period created a situation where the individual (like Jim) was "doubly penalized by the fact that [the period] when he can gain the full ten days for every 30 done, is postponed,"[15] as happened to Larry in the example above. Bennett's complaint was echoed in the Fauteux Report, which did the same calculations and noted that prisoners who forfeited remission earned during their first year were excessively penalized, since it would take them longer to reach the better rate trigger.[16]

The Earned/Lost Problem

After reviewing the remission systems in Spain, Cuba, England, and parts of the United States, Tony Ricardo, editor of *Beacon*, concluded that Canada's process took "a back seat" to those of the more "penologically progressive countries of the world."[17] He contended that even if the total amount of remission was earned, it was too little:

> As we see it, an ideal "good time" system, geared to this modern day and age, would be an increase to a full one-third reduction of sentences for general good behaviour and industry, and a further five days a month "merit time" for outstanding efforts in self-improvement. This type of system would be the most likely to succeed in the dual role of maintaining both a high degree of discipline and morale, and of utilizing the reformative incentive of "good time" to its utmost.[18]

Other writers in the penal press argued for radical change. Some advocated the British system, in which all remission was granted at the start of a sentence and then lost, rather than earned.[19] A writer in *Sports Bulletin* suggested that this could be achieved by basing remission on the sentence handed down by the court.[20] As Tommy Nickols wrote in *Tele-Scope* in 1951, this approach would have made the determination of a release day more calculable: "An inmate will be informed, on being admitted, as to what his sentence is, and the total amount of remission gainable will be deducted." He continued: "Any loss of remission in Warden's Court will then be added to the 'short way' sentence and none of it will be open to be regained."[21] Perhaps this approach would also have addressed the above-noted differences across jurisdictions, with some remitting differently or not at all.

In practice, however, it seems that a hybrid system was already in place. Both the Fauteux Report and prisoners spoke of both earning and losing remission. Fauteux explained it this way:

The system of computing statutory remission is cumbersome and difficult to explain. Undoubtedly it was intended that at the end of each month an inmate would be credited with a number of days' remission, depending upon the quality of his conduct and industry. Presumably the grant was intended to range from nothing to the maximum authorized by law, depending upon the circumstances of each case. In practice, however, it is rarely possible to grant remission on this basis. The usual practice is to grant the maximum amount authorized, and no remission is lost unless the inmate is charged with a breach of discipline and an order of forfeiture of remission is made by the warden.[22]

In an article aptly titled "The Mathematics of Remission," the author noted that individuals earned one day for every three days per month served, and lost one day for every five days that they spent in solitary confinement, but did not lose remission in hospital unless they spent a full month in the infirmary, in which case they lost a day.[23] If brought before the Warden's Court on institutional charges of misconduct, prisoners could not easily predict the amount of remission they would lose for an offence. One prisoner at Prince Albert lost five days of remission when a cell search revealed that he had penned, but not yet sent, "love letters" to a fellow prisoner.[24] This type of convoluted practice was precisely why the prisoners wanted a new system. But change to remission would not come quickly. As of the end of 1959, three years after the Fauteux Committee released its report, the system remained the same.[25] In the meantime, prisoners found hope in a certain type of divine intervention.

Acts of Grace

In the mid-twentieth century, Canada was still deeply attached to its colonial roots. In 1938, when the Archambault Commission submitted its report, the head of state was King George VI. His daughter, Elizabeth, commenced her reign following his death in 1953 and was on the throne to receive the Fauteux Report in 1956. While their role could be seen as merely symbolic, it would be a mistake to overlook its real impact on the lives of prisoners and the hope for early release that it represented. As we will see, most of the work that resulted in prisoners serving reduced time was done by bureaucrats; but there was a moment when the regent used her authority to directly benefit *all* Canadian prisoners. We start our examination of "Acts of Grace"[26] with the coronation amnesty; after that, we will consider how the Remission Branch intervened in all the other forms of amnesty.

Amnesty

For prisoners, Queen Elizabeth II's coronation was not simply pomp and circumstance. With her ascension to the throne, Canada's incarcerated men and women caught "Amnesty Fever,"[27] and with good reason. To mark King George VI's Silver Jubilee in 1935, every prisoner had been granted two months of amnesty for every year of their sentence.[28] If tradition was followed, some sort of amnesty would be granted to prisoners to mark Elizabeth's coronation.

Members of Parliament wondered about this precedent and made inquiries in the House of Commons about a possible amnesty.[29] The mainstream press supported the principle: "There is something to be said in favour of an observance of this old custom. It would give an accession to reward co-operative behaviour, to give some who show promise of using it wisely an opportunity of a fresh start in life with the same hopeful expectation with which others of us look to the new reign."[30] The editor of *Tele-Scope* made it clear how important hope was at that moment:

> With the total absence of a parole system, the administration of the Ticket-of-Leave Act [see below] has not changed for the better. Of the over eight hundred men in this prison, ONE, only one was granted "Xmas clemency" after he had served 21 years. Of the same number of men, ONE, only one, has been granted "Easter clemency" after serving all but four months of his sentence. Is it to be wondered that thousands of penitentiary inmates, many staggering under inhumanely burdensome sentences, fervently pin their hopes for actual survival on the AMNESTY at a coronation!"[31]

To the prisoners' delight, tradition was followed. On 9 April 1953, the governor general announced an amnesty of thirty days per year of sentence.[32] *Pen-O-Rama* was the first penal press publication to offer its thanks to the queen for her "act of clemency."[33] *Tele-Scope* followed, wishing the queen a long reign and thanking the "Governor-General and the Cabinet for the amnesty granted to inmates of Canadian prisons and penitentiaries"; the editors added that "this amnesty has given some courage to men carrying heavy burdens and it is our fervent hope that it marks another step to a more enlightened and effective system of handling offenders in Canada."[34] Beyond the morale boost it created, the amnesty (which applied only to time served after 1949) led to an immediate surge in the number of releases from prison. The Commissioner of Penitentiaries noted in his annual report that "owing to the amnesty, the total number of releases by expiration of sentence in May 1953 was 386 against 105 in April and 159 in June of the same year."[35]

Image 5.2. *Pen-O-Rama* celebrates the coronation, May–June 1953.

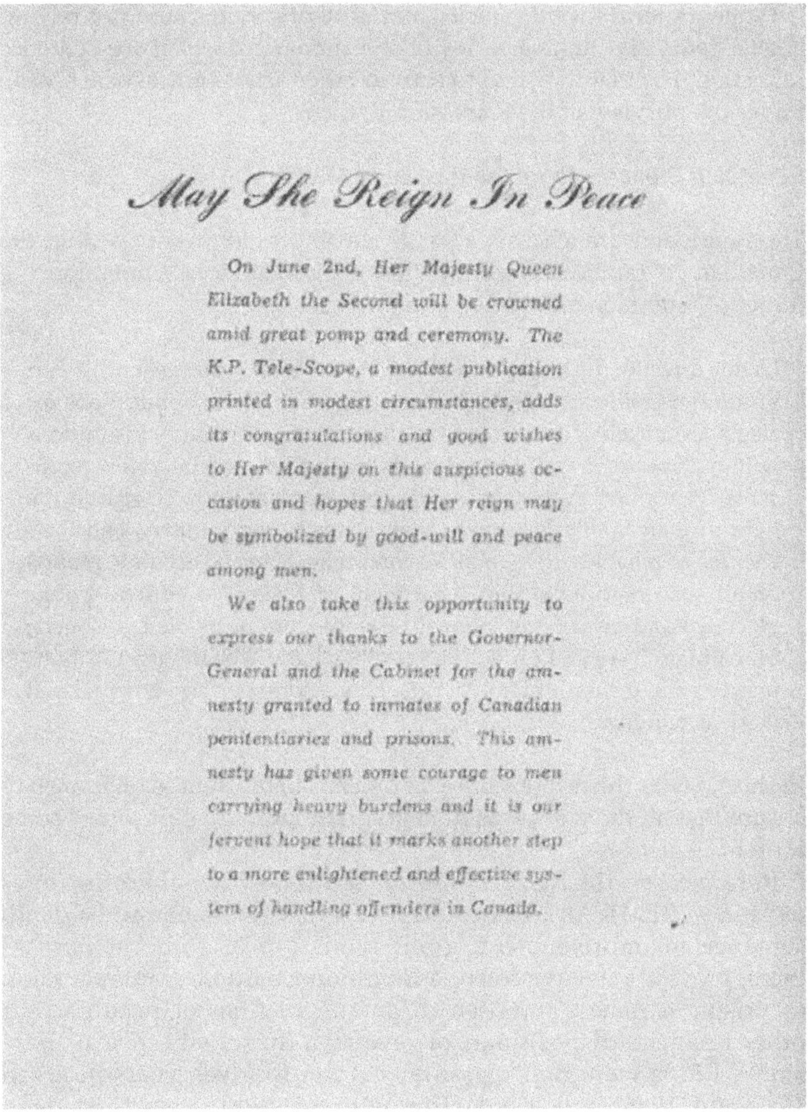

May She Reign In Peace

On June 2nd, Her Majesty Queen Elizabeth the Second will be crowned amid great pomp and ceremony. The K.P. Tele-Scope, a modest publication printed in modest circumstances, adds its congratulations and good wishes to Her Majesty on this auspicious occasion and hopes that Her reign may be symbolized by good-will and peace among men.

We also take this opportunity to express our thanks to the Governor-General and the Cabinet for the amnesty granted to inmates of Canadian penitentiaries and prisons. This amnesty has given some courage to men carrying heavy burdens and it is our fervent hope that it marks another step to a more enlightened and effective system of handling offenders in Canada.

Image 5.3. *Tele-Scope* marks the coronation, June 1953, back cover.

While grateful for the general amnesty, prisoners could not rely on new regents and anniversaries of the monarch to plan for sentence reduction. For that they had to turn to other acts of grace, which were under the purview of the Remission Branch.

Remission Branch – Royal Prerogative of Mercy

The Remission Branch was a small but important agency within the Canadian government. According to the Civil Service Commission, the duties of remission officers were as follows:

> Under direction of headquarters at Ottawa, to exercise general super-vision over all local aspects of the work arising from applications for clemency on behalf of prisoners in all penal or reformatory institutions within a specified area; to visit such institutions and interview appli-cants for clemency; to appraise their determination to reform in the light of their family history, of their conduct and industry, and their chances of rehabilitation; to make comprehensive and accurate reports on all such matters to the Department of Justice; to address public meetings and arouse the interest of employers in paroled prisoners; to maintain co-operation with semi-official and welfare organizations interested in the reformation of prisoners; and to perform other related work as required.[36]

In short, it was the responsibility of officials in the Remission Branch to ensure that all the work was done to grant individual prisoners some form of clemency.

In rare cases, the Remission Branch pursued Royal Prerogatives of Mercy (RPM). An RPM could be exercised to commute a death sentence to imprisonment, grant remission of corporal punish-ment, provide a free pardon or a conditional pardon, grant remission of prison sentences imposed in default of fines or pecuniary or other financial dispositions, or reverse a driver's licence suspen-sion.[37] RPMs were rarely granted: in the fourteen years between 1941 and 1955, only seven free pardons (which acknowledged innocence) and sixteen ordinary pardons (acts of mercy)[38] were granted.[39] Between 1934 and 1955, twenty-four prisoners were granted remission of corporal punishment.[40] In 1955, there were only twenty-nine cases in which remission was granted for a fine or pecuniary penalties.[41] Obviously, few prisoners utilized this mechanism.[42]

Remission Branch – Ticket-of-Leave

Without question, most of the Remission Branch's time was consumed by applications for a Ticket-of-Leave. An Act to Provide for the Conditional Liberation of Convicts (more commonly known as The Ticket of Leave Act) was passed in 1899. Under this legislation, federal and provincial prisoners (the latter were serving less than two years) could be granted licence to be at-large under specific conditions. In all cases, conditions required the licensee to report monthly to the local police, to notify the police of his place of residence and of any intent to relocate, to carry the licence and present it to a magistrate or police officer upon request, and to avoid associating with "notorious" individuals or engaging in acts of vagrancy.[43] Through this mechanism, a prisoner could serve the remaining portion of his sentence in the community. The freedom thus granted was tenuous. The licence was subject to revocation if its holder violated the imposed conditions or if he committed a new indictable offence. In either instance, he would be returned to prison to serve out the balance of the sentence that remained *at the time the licence was originally granted*.[44] Time served in the community did not count once the clock was reset by revocation.

That ticket-of-leave applications consumed most of the Remission Branch's time is not surprising. Many prisoners applied: between 1946 and 1955, 44,569 new cases were opened, and each required investigation.[45] The process was tedious and time-consuming (see Image 5.4 for a visual representation of the process triggered by an application), and as Frank Anderson notes, waiting for the process to unfold was stressful:

> The usual time frame for a negative response from the Remission Service was two months and notification, known as a "bump" would arrive as a printed form which was placed on the bars of your cell for you to find upon returning from work. When the time came for it to appear and nothing happened, anxiety and depression set in and my nightmares returned, seeming more vivid and threatening.[46]

Application for a ticket-of-leave was not necessarily made by the prisoner. Sometimes relatives, friends, lawyers, community groups, or religious leaders applied on behalf of the prisoner. In 1955, the Penitentiary Service began to allow wardens to recommend prisoners for ticket-of-leave, even if the individuals themselves did not apply. While it would be tempting to see this change as a product of New Deal idealism, it seems more likely that the main reason was to address the overcrowding problem that had resulted from a doubling of the prison population between

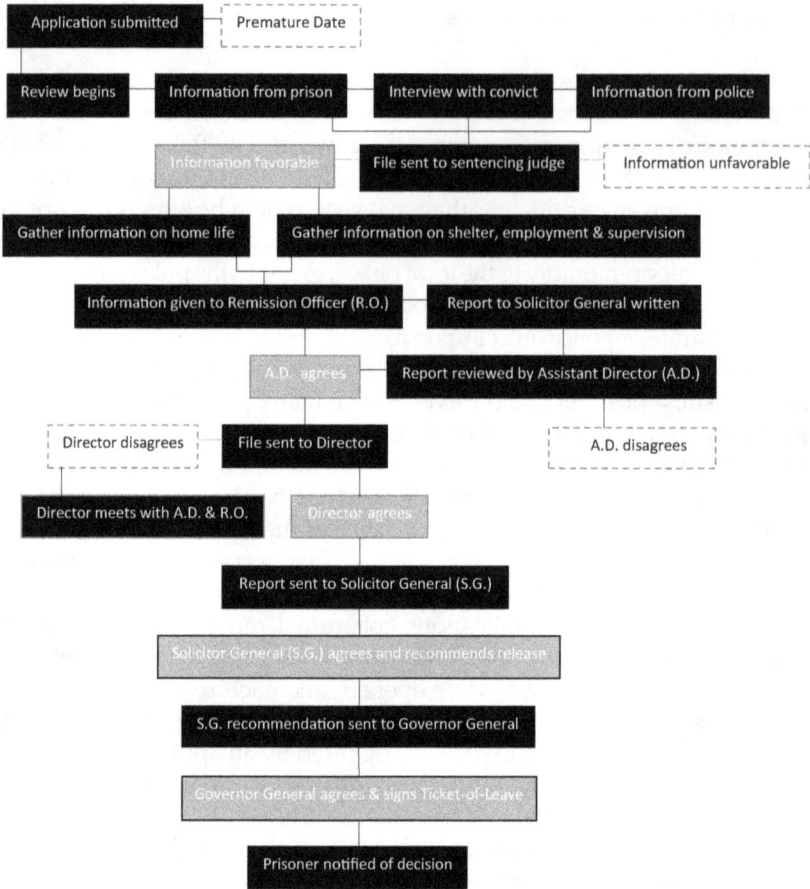

Image 5.4. Flowchart of ticket-of-leave process.

Table 5.1. Number of admissions to federal penitentiaries

Year	Total admissions*	Total population
1947–48	1,802	3,777
1948–49	2,320	4,138
1949–50	2,396	4,650
1950–51	2,245	4,712
1951–52	2,091	4,562
1952–53	3,025	4,829
1953–54	3,194	5,025
1954–55	3,026	5,412
1955–56	3,038	5,426
1956–57	2,907	5,347
1957–58	3,836	5,682
1958–59	3,799	6,181
1959–60	4,417	6,219

*includes transfers

Source: CDOJ, *Annual Reports: 1948*, 91; *1949*, 113; *1950*, 103; *1951*, 119; *1952*, 133; *1953*, 143; *1954*, 144; *1955*, 142; *1956*, 142; *1957*, 156; *1958*, 187; *1959*, 191; *1960*, 193.

Table 5.2. Federal and provincial ticket-of-leave applications and grants, 1951–1955

Year	Number of new cases opened	Number of ticket-of-leave granted	Grant rate (%)
1951	3,887	818	21
1952	4,162	792	19
1953	3,804	857	23
1954	4,215	906	22
1955	4,281	1,343	31

Source: Fauteux Report, Appendix A.

1947 and 1960.[47] As Table 5.1 shows, and as the commissioner's report noted, there had been "an unprecedented rise in penitentiary population"[48] – there was simply a need to make room in the prisons.[49] As A.J. MacLeod of the Remission Service put it, "[I'm] a little unhappy we cannot let more out – trying to operate with limited [aftercare] facilities."[50]

The commissioner stated that the change in submission procedures had generated a surge in ticket-of-leave applications.[51] However, the data in the Fauteux Report do not support that claim.[52] Table 5.2 shows

Table 5.3. Releases and tickets-of-leave from Canadian penitentiaries, 1954–55

Institution	Total releases	Number of ticket-of-leaves	Rate of release by ticket-of-leave (%)
Dorchester	296	80	27
St. Vincent de Paul	414	110	27
Kingston	411	16	4
Collin's Bay	163	40	25
Manitoba	160	15	9
Saskatchewan	229	46	20
BC	229	29	13

Source: Fauteux, Appendix.

the number of new cases opened between 1951 and 1955 and that there was no significant change across those years. However, the involvement of the wardens in submitting applications may have carried weight with the Remission Branch, as a significant increase in grant rates is evident in 1955 (see Table 5.2).

The prisoners kept track of the ticket-of-leave statistics and used the press to disseminate that information. Images 5.5 through 5.7 indicate the priority given to these prison censuses by *Tele-Scope*, *Beacon*, and *Mountain Echoes*. In these three publications, the "con-census" is part of the front material; BC Penitentiary's *Transition*'s Pen-istics (Image 5.8) is featured in the body of the publication.

The information these statistics imparted to prisoners did not always foster hope. One writer in the press noted that "even the slowest thinkers among our many long timers can look at our monthly statistics, on the index page, and deduce their probable fate. Those statistics usually read: pardons, 0; tickets, 0. These fellows are aware, then, that even if they sprouted halos a foot high the only way they are going to get out of here is to serve their time, or die."[53]

The release data led prisoners at some institutions to conclude that the "local" rate of ticket-of-leave releases was ridiculously low. For example, Harvey Blackstock noted in *Tele-Scope* that only 1 per cent of the prisoners in Kingston Penitentiary were granted ticket-of-leave in any given month.[54] Indeed, Table 5.3 indicates that when actual release data for each penitentiary are considered, the men and women at Kingston did have very poor odds of gaining a ticket-of-leave. This low grant rate may have been related to the "type" of prisoner incarcerated there.

THE K.P. TELESCOPE

Printed and Published monthly by the men of Kingston Penitentiary, Kingston, Ontario.

Authorized as Second Class Mail by the Post Office Department, Ottawa, Canada 1951. Subscription Rates: One Dollar per year. Send all Remittances for Subscriptions c/o The Warden, Box 22, Kingston Ontario.

Vol. V   No. VI   *AUGUST 1955*

CONTENTS

CENSUS
JUNE

TOTAL POPULATION	1041	DISCHARGED	30
HIGH NUMBER	3398	TICKETS-OF-LEAVE	1
MALE POPULATION	947	PARDONED	0
FEMALE POPULATION	76	ESCAPED	0
RECEIVED	57	DEATHS	1

TRANSFERS TO COLLIN'S BAY 24

Image 5.5. Census, *Tele-Scope*, August 1955.

CONTENTS

—— ILLUSTRATIONS BY JIMMY COOKE & ANDRE BAHL ——

Image 5.6. Con-Census, *Beacon*, November–December 1959. Gaucher/Munn penal press collection.

ADMINISTRATION

C.E. DesRosiers	Warden
J. Wickey	Deputy Warden
A.E. Steele	Chief Keeper
N. Orlesky	Principal Keeper
H.H. Stevens	Chief Engineer
U. Belanger	Classification Officer
J.D. Weir	Teacher-Librarian
W.J. Hancock	P.T.I.
R. Howard	Hobby Officer
Rev. G.W. McNeill	Prot. Chaplain
Rev. H.J. Bedford	R.C. Chaplain
W. Aikenhead	Chief Steward

MOUNTAIN ECHOES is published by the inmates of the Manitoba Penitentiary with the kind permission of Major-General R. B. Gibson, Commissioner of Penitentiaries. It is designed to provide inmates with an opportunity for self-expression and a medium for discussion of public problems, and in the interest of promoting useful thought and action within the institution.

No articles of a scurrilous or defamatory nature or in any way detrimental to the administration of justice will be published. The views expressed herein are not necessarily those of the administration or editorial staff.

CENSUS
February 1 to March 1

Population	466
High Number	7879
Received	32
Discharged	28
Tickets-Of-Leave	1
Pardons	0
Escapes	0
Deaths	0
Transfers-Out	3
Transfers-In	3
Deported	0

Image 5.7. Census. *Mountain Echoes*, March 1959. Gaucher/Munn penal press collection.

```
*****************************PENISTICS*****************************
*                                                                 *
*      January 22, 1953 to March 26, 1953 inclusive.              *
*Main Prison        521        Tickets of Leave          3        *
*Doukhobours         17        Douks. Discharged          0        *
*Total Population   538        Douks. Ticket of Leave    10        *
*Admitted  .         60        Deaths                     0        *
*Discharged          16        High Number             7700        *
*                                                                 *
******************************************************************
```

9

Image 5.8. Pen-istics. *Transition*, April 1953. Gaucher/Munn penal press collection.

Under the "Rules of Practise" for ticket-of-leave, prisoners who were "confirmed recidivists or an instinctive criminal," those convicted of drug offences, and those "previously convicted of one major crime, or two intermediate, or several minor offences," were not eligible. Furthermore, prisoners who had previously received clemency or who were under treatment for syphilis were excluded from consideration.[55] Given that many first-time and younger prisoners in Ontario were sent to Collins Bay, there may well have been a disproportionate population of ineligibles at Kingston Penitentiary.

While rules for non-interference with sentences were noted, in practice they served more as guidelines or taboos. For example, the Fauteux Committee noted that those who had a previous record were still considered but with "greater prudence in the evaluation of each case."[56] A prisoner who was undergoing medical treatment (including for syphilis) could also be considered if treatment in the community would be "as good or better than he is receiving in the institution."[57]

As with grants of remission, the timelines for a ticket-of-leave were not always precise.[58] According to Minister of Justice Stuart Garson, an application for a ticket-of-leave was not usually filed until at least half of a sentence of imprisonment had been served, although he conceded that "6 to 12 per cent of all paroles are granted before the inmates concerned have served half of their sentences."[59] Garson went on to indicate that this half-time standard was essential to the prisoners, to the institution, and to the public:

> The rule is designed primarily, in the cases where it applies, to ensure some degree of equality of treatment as between inmates. In the cases where it is applicable it does remove uncertainty from the mind of the inmate concerning the time when he may expect to be considered for release on parole and thus helps him to accept the reality of his sentence. If no such rule existed an inmate might during the early part of his sentence continually

build false hopes for early release only to have those hopes dashed when he was not released as soon as he expected to be. Such a state of affairs would impede rather than promote his reform and rehabilitation. Moreover, the rule makes possible a minimum period during which the officers in the institution can plan and carry out a proper program of treatment and training for the inmate. Again, it furnishes to the courts and law enforcement authorities generally some assurance that a reasonable proportion of the sentence imposed by the court will be served by the convicted person and that, thereby, the deterrent value of the sentence will be preserved.[60]

When the Remission Branch received an application, an officer examined the case and conducted an investigation, which could include obtaining police reports, character references, and offers of employment. That officer expected the institution to report on the prisoner's physical and mental condition, his behaviour while in prison, his education and vocational prospects, and his suitability for rehabilitation. An application took at least six to eight weeks to process, and this effectively eliminated the possibility that short-termers, serving six months or less, would receive a ticket.[61] This finding was especially relevant in the federal system, given the large number of individuals serving four years or less (see Table 5.4).

Remission officers did visit the institutions and meet with prisoners, but there were only nine officers in the entire country to do all this work.[62] Officer C.A.M. Edwards made "two visits in each year to Kingston Penitentiary and Collin's Bay Penitentiary and the larger provincial prisons in Ontario, as well as Dorchester Penitentiary and the larger provincial prisons in the Maritime provinces and Newfoundland."[63] Meetings with prisoners, then, were both rare and brief. Frank Anderson's description of his moments with the remission service representative in 1945 highlights the speed of the proceeding: "The Man opened my file and instantly recognized my case ... Without a question or second glance, he closed my file firmly. 'Don't bother coming back to see me for another five years!' he snapped. I was stunned. So much for trying to better myself."[64] Penny McCormick noted in *Tele-Scope* that the women at Kingston Penitentiary were allotted up to fifteen minutes to meet with the remission officer and that, even if they succeeded with their application for leave, it occurred too close to full release (a few weeks or months) to act as a real incentive.[65]

As shown in Image 5.4, once completed, each report was submitted to the head of the Remission Branch, who made the final decision. This process left prisoners feeling that "one man has the power to determine whether an inmate is to be given the opportunity for parole."[66]

Table 5.4. Number of admissions and length of sentence

Year	Total admissions*	Length of sentence 4 years or Less
1947–48	1,547	1,235
1948–49	1,843	1,498
1949–50	1,966	1,632
1950–51	1,951	1,619
1951–52	1,806	1,382
1952–53	2,101	1,603
1953–54	2,418	1,869
1954–55	2,328	1,793
1955–56	2,363	1,840
1956–57	2,266	1,857
1957–58	2,992	2,300
1958–59	2,975	2,348
1959–60	3,332	2,636

*excluding transfers
Source: CDOJ, *Annual Reports: 1948*, 91, 94; *1949*, 113, 116; *1950*, 103, 106; *1951*, 119, 122; *1952*, 133, 136; *1953*, 143, 146; *1954*, 144, 146; *1955*, 142, 144; *1956*, 142, 144; *1957*, 156, 158; *1958*, 187, 190; *1959*, 191, 194; *1960*, 193, 196.

According to Dave Nolan of *Tele-Scope*, the major flaw in the system was that it was not possible for "one man to be familiar with the parole qualifications of the inmates of all seven Canadian penitentiaries."[67] Change was needed. As Liberal MP Lucien Cardin (Richelieu-Verchères) noted in Parliament, "the Ticket of Leave Act passed in 1899 is, of course, completely inadequate and out of date, and it cannot cope with circumstances and conditions which have been brought about by our modern society and by our social psychology, if you wish to call it that, which inmates carry with them into the remotest corners of our penal institutions."[68]

Politicians, experts, prisoners, and civil servants agreed on that point. But no consensus developed over what changes to make. Those who were languishing in prison held some hope that the Fauteux Committee, which had been struck to examine the "principles and procedures followed in the Remission Service of the Department of Justice," would be the impetus for change.[69] Politicians felt that the committee showed promise but became frustrated by the length of time its members took to table its report. As Progressive Conservative MP James M. Macdonnell (Greenwood) explained in the House of Commons in 1956, a committee was appointed in 1953, which was more than two years ago. I do not want the minister to tell us that there were busy men on that committee. Of course they were busy and that was a matter he had to take into consideration when he appointed them ... All I know is that they have had two years, twenty-four months, with more and more unnecessary expenditure of money and more and more waste of human material, which is even worse ... I would further hope that at the present time he [the minister of justice] is trying very hard to speed up this matter.[70]

Prisoners kept their expectations in check even after the report was submitted on 30 April 1956, because, they argued, "for some unknown or obscure reason, it is inevitably the fate of such reports that they are paralysed at their origin by over-procrastinating governments at least where penal affairs are considered."[71] In this case, however, the prisoners were wrong. The committee members (Gerald Fauteux, William B. Common, J. Alex Edmison, and Joseph McCulley) had managed to get the proverbial ball rolling,[72] and the newly elected Progressive Conservative government committed itself to developing a full system of parole.

Parole

The Fauteux Report was clear – the committee members wanted an autonomous five-member National Parole Board to be established. This would require amendments to, or the repeal of, the Penitentiary Act, the Ticket-of-Leave Act, and the Prison and Reformatories Act. They called for substantial change that would reflect the New Deal in corrections, achieve equitable national standards, and ensure each case submitted received due consideration. On 12 May 1958, a mere six weeks after receiving the committee's report, the government, in its Speech from the Throne, served notice that it intended to enact the needed legislative changes; three months later, it did so. On 11 August of that year, it introduced Bill C-49 to create a new parole system in Canada. That the government was certain the bill would pass is evident in the following statement from Minister of Justice Davie Fulton:

I appreciate very much indeed the attitude of the committee towards this resolution, which I think illustrates the striking degree of unanimity in principle on the general approach to this problem. There may be details with respect to administration and so on about which we will differ, but I do think it is quite an interesting illustration of the extent to which there is in this house and in Canada generally agreement that our system does require overhaul in this respect.[73]

While some prisoners believed that public attitudes toward penal reform had changed by the late 1950s (see chapter 4), Fulton's statement indicates that, at least in Parliament, support for a parole system remained strong. A reading of various documents and reports makes clear that politicians, reformers, prisoners, commissioners, and administrators saw the merits of releasing individuals early and supervising them while they were transitioning back into the community. It was hoped that providing oversight and guidance to parolees would reduce recidivism rates.

Autonomy

Autonomy was key. A parole board needed to be a "quasi judicial body rather than…. a Minister of the Crown acting in an exclusively administrative capacity."[74] Both the government and the prisoners wanted members to make decisions based solely on a case's merits and not on extraneous variables such as re-election. Bill Martin, writing from Kingston Penitentiary, echoed this sentiment when he argued that a functional parole system needed to be "free of politics and all improper influences."[75] If the principles of the New Deal were to be upheld, freedom in decision-making was essential. Prisoners agreed with the Fauteux Report that rehabilitation should take precedence over retribution and that the new parole board would need to be responsive to the uniqueness of each individual and his circumstances. In fact, writers in the penal press had long been arguing that too much time spent in prison was counterproductive:

> In dealing with parole risks, modern paroling agencies no longer place the emphasis on what the offender has done in the past. Retribution contributes nothing to his rehabilitation. The stress is now only on the man's behavior, his attitude and his general ability to adjust to a law-abiding life upon release. With this guiding principle, a modern parole board becomes a means whereby the offender can be released under supervision at a time WHEN IT IS THOUGHT HE IS MOST LIKELY TO ADJUST HIMSELF IN SOCIETY."[76]

Board Composition

Who exactly would be making these decisions about a prisoner's liberty was a bit more contentious. The Fauteux Committee felt that the initial board should be composed of the following five types of individuals: a senior member of the judiciary (granted leave for this purpose); a senior member of the existing Remission Service; a senior administrator from one of the adult men's prisons; an individual familiar with the administrative aspects of police work; and, finally, a person with "noninstitutional correctional work" experience.[77] Once these positions were vacated, the committee members envisioned dispensing with specific occupational and experience-based criteria, so long as the appointees were educated, understood "the problems with which the offender is most often confronted," and had sufficient "integrity, intelligence and good judgment as to command the confidence of the public."[78]

Not all prisoners agreed with the recommendation regarding the board's initial composition. Bill Martin contended that the members should be college graduates with a background in the social sciences but not law enforcement.[79] He added that appointing a member from the former Remission Service would be a mistake because that person would "bring old attitudes and habits with them"[80] – a concern previously discussed in relation to "old lag" guards (see chapter 4). It was not just current prisoners who highlighted the need to select board members carefully. In Parliament, former prisoner and current parliamentarian Frank Howard (CCF, Skeena) made the following cautionary observation: "I know the minister himself would be the first to say that the attitudes, the education background and the philosophy of these individuals must be given paramount consideration, for certainly the parole authority could make or break what is an excellent piece of legislation."[81] Another MP, Liberal Raymond Eudes (Hochelaga), was concerned about gender representation on the board and argued that a woman should be appointed so that female prisoners would receive adequate consideration.[82] His suggestion did not seem to gain traction – there was no further debate on this matter, and no woman was appointed to the inaugural board.

In the penal press, W. Lake, a prisoner at Manitoba Penitentiary, contended that a national board was not needed at all. He suggested that the prison staff should be responsible for determining parole: "It doesn't take an expert in psychiatry or sociology to know within reasonable limits what a man is like and what his probable chances are of going straight upon his release. Make the keeper responsible for his handiwork. It is up to him to teach his charges, encourage them to live right, do better and aim higher."[83]

In the end, when the first National Parole Board was established on 1 January 1959, it did not follow the Fauteux Report's recommendations regarding initial appointments. J. Alex Edmison, a member of the committee, benefited from his own recommendation when he was appointed to the board along with two other lawyers (T. George Street, chairperson, and Edouard Dion). Also appointed was the former Assistant Director of the Remission Branch, Frank P. Miller. Benoit Godbout was appointed board secretary. There was no judge, no police representation, and no senior prison administrator.

Interim Progress: Automatic Review

The work of appointing an inaugural board was important, but the civil service did not wait for all the i's to be dotted and the t's to be crossed before implementing some of the suggested reforms. For example, as had been noted in the parliamentary exchange of 11 August 1958 (see above), legislative changes would be required to implement the new parole system. Yet more than six months earlier, when questioned in the House of Commons about the progress of implementation, Minister Fulton had been eager to demonstrate that changes were already being made:

> Another recommendation was that as soon as possible a system of automatic parole review should be instituted for Canada ... It was recommended that this automatic parole review should be instituted thereby dispensing with the system for requiring application for parole. A system of automatic parole review *has been started in three out of eight Canadian penitentiaries*. The system of automatic parole procedure that has been developed in respect of the inmates at these three institutions will, as quickly as circumstances permit be extended to the remaining penitentiaries. [Emphasis added][84]

Indeed, by June of that year, Fulton had told the House that "the remission service has instituted a system of automatic parole review which is 40 per cent completed."[85] It was unclear, though, when exactly in a prisoner's sentence this review was to occur:

> At the present time there is a rule of thumb that an inmate must have served half his sentence before his file is closely examined for parole. I have discussed this matter with Mr. Streets [sic], the chairman of the new parole board, and have asked him to take a look at this rule of thumb and to keep it in mind. I am not satisfied that a rule of thumb is the kind of rule you want when you are dealing with human factors.[86]

Not until the parole regulations came into effect on 15 February 1959 would prisoners be able to calculate the date on which they would become eligible for release. All federally sentenced prisoners had to

Table 5.5. Proportion of time served when paroled (Canada), 1949–1962 (%)

	≥35	35–50	50–70	≤70
1949	3	12	64	21
1953	1.5	8.5	78	12
1957	3	17	64	16
1959	1	13	61	25
1960	5	22	55	18
1961	8.8	14.3	55	20.7
1962	9.0	15.6	56.6	18.8

Source: National Parole Board Annual Report, 1962

serve at least one year. After that, a one-third rule was in place. This meant that, except for those serving a life sentence, prisoners serving more than three years had to serve one-third or four years (whichever was less) before being eligible for parole. Those serving life were eligible after seven years (or after ten, if serving a commuted death sentence). On paper, this represented a change from "rule of thumb," but in practice, most prisoners still realized they had to serve at least half their sentence before any hope of release. Table 5.5 shows how remarkably consistent paroling practices had been under the Ticket-of-Leave Act (1949–57) and the early Parole Act (1959–1962).

Prisoners feared that change was illusory; the more optimistic felt that it was merely slow to manifest itself. Whichever the case, they had other points of discontent on which to focus: lack of contact, rate of denial, and the characterization of a certain group of prisoners.

*Disappointment: Prisoners Are People but We Don't
Need to Meet Them*

Perhaps the prisoners' biggest disappointment with the new parole system, which might have been addressed had they been consulted by the Fauteux Committee, was the lack of direct input from prisoners. They had hoped to meet with the parole board. They wanted an opportunity to speak on their own behalf so that decisions would not be made based solely on their files, which were written by workers who may or may not have supported the New Deal. In a system designed to strip the individual of his individuality through status degradation ceremonies,[87] it is not surprising that the prisoners sought this repersonalization opportunity. And there was precedent: as the Fauteux Report acknowledged, other parole boards did meet with prisoners. However, the board opined that this process "does not serve a sufficiently useful function ... to justify the expenditure of time and money that would be necessary to enable in a country as large as Canada, members of the Board to travel to all institutions for parole interviews with inmates."[88] Once again, we hear Mathiesen's argument that financial concerns will always supercede rehabilitative goals. On the whole, this section of the Fauteux Report seems at odds with most other parts of the report and certainly with the ideals of the New Deal. Instead of implementing a process that exemplified the "prisoners are people" mantra, the committee had recommended that all parts of the process be in writing.

In contrast to what prisoners wanted, the Fauteux Report recommended that a "regional representative of the board"[89] interview prisoners and gather all relevant material for the board's consideration.[90] The government agreed, and the position was created. These representatives were tasked with gathering enough information for the board to decide whether a person had derived "maximum benefit from imprisonment" and would not pose an undue risk to the public, and whether "reform and rehabilitation" would be aided by gradual release into the community.[91] The regional representatives were kept very busy. In the first year, "Regional Officers interviewed 4,518 inmates and made 687 visits to institutions. On these visits, they held an average of six interviews a day."[92] Based on this preliminary work, and in what would later become known as a "paper decision," the board would declare a parole verdict, which would be communicated to the prisoner. That verdict would be final, conclusive, and non-appealable. In what became a very controversial point in subsequent years, the reasons for the decision were not to be provided to the prisoner. A lot rested on what was written in the file.

Disappointment: Denial of Parole

Most prisoners would be disappointed with the board's decision as most applications under the Parole Act were denied. Of the 5,120 cases submitted to the board in 1959, 2,790 resulted in parole not being granted. It would be a mistake, however, to see this as indicative of a reproduction of the status quo. Table 5.6 indicates clearly that the rate of successful applications had increased across the country between 1959 and 1962, with dramatic improvements at the institutions that had experienced very low grant rates under the ticket-of-leave system. Simply put, in the period immediately after implementation, the odds of getting an early release had improved considerably. The same, though, could not be said of the general trend in subsequent years. Looking at the data for the first four years, it appears that after the initial spike in grant rates, a downward trend was evident in every penitentiary.

Table 5.6. Parole decisions from Canadian penitentiaries, 1959–1962

Institution	1959		1960		1961		1962	
Dorchester	Denied	134	Denied	238	Denied	295	Denied	345
	Granted	186	Granted	144	Granted	131	Granted	80
	%	58	%	61	%	44	%	23
St. Vincent de Paul	Denied	330	Denied	526	Denied	478	Denied	351
	Granted	165	Granted	209	Granted	95	Granted	81
	%	33	%	40	%	20	%	23
Kingston	Denied	129	Denied	235	Denied	383	Denied	349
	Granted	83	Granted	131	Granted	125	Granted	110
	%	39	%	56	%	33	%	32
Collin's Bay	Denied	127	Denied	153	Denied	214	Denied	288
	Granted	87	Granted	113	Granted	107	Granted	84
	%	41	%	74	%	50	%	29
Manitoba	Denied	97	Denied	117	Denied	178	Denied	239
	Granted	38	Granted	58	Granted	57	Granted	60
	%	28%	%	50	%	32	%	25
Saskatchewan	Denied	102	Denied	155	Denied	83*	Denied	317
	Granted	78	Granted	96	Granted	85	Granted	56
	%	4 3	%	62	%	102	%	18
BC	Denied	106	Denied	200	Denied	296	Denied	331
	Granted	93	Granted	85	Granted	63	Granted	60
	%	47	%	43	%	21	%	18

Notes: *No automatic reviews held this year.
Source: National Parole Board Reports, 1959–62

Some writers in the penal press bought into the self-management mantra employed by the parole board. For example, a December 1960 piece in *C.B. Diamond* placed a great deal of the onus on the individual prisoner's attitude:

Your attitude toward both staff and fellow inmates is of prime importance. If, for instance, you are one of those rough, tough, bitter, I-don't-give-a-damn guys, the odds are you can paint your cell with every confidence that you will be inhabiting it for the balance of your sentence. And if you are in the habit of throwing temper tantrums – changing jobs, quitting courses, causing trouble – over little things, then you, too, may ask for a paint brush. The Board, it seems, is not interested in unstable types and/or children. Reasonable enough?[93]

Prisoners who were refused parole could apply again later, but this was tricky. Because prisoners were not given details as to why their parole had been refused, it was difficult for them to know where change was needed. The handbook produced by the parole board, and distributed to prisoners, said that parole was assessed according to the following nine factors:

1. Type and seriousness of original offence
2. Past behaviour
3. "Type of person" and likelihood to reoffend
4. Risk to society
5. Educational, vocational, and "habitual" improvements made during incarceration
6. Family circumstances before and after prison
7. Soundness of parole plan
8. Employment possibilities after release
9. Self-awareness and self-control[94]

Clearly, some of the above considerations were ones over which individuals had some sway, whereas others, such as offence type and past circumstances, were set in stone. Because they had not been informed of the grounds for the decision, prisoners had to guess. The board's position was clear and not encouraging: "There is not much use applying again unless you have reason to think we have some reports about you which indicate you have improved since your last application was considered. If you have not changed, you cannot expect the decision of the Board to be changed."[95]

In a twenty-three-point letter to the National Parole Service, prisoners at Dorchester Penitentiary sought clarity on the reasons a person might be denied parole. In that letter, the prisoners contended that not knowing the reason for a negative decision was poor form. This argument was rejected by R.G. Rowcliffe, regional representative of National Parole Service:

[Question from prisoners] Since it is considered improper to punish someone without giving a valid reason, why does the national parole board insist on not giving a reason for a turn down? [Response] The National Parole Board does not divulge reasons for rendering a favorable decision either. There are many circumstances in everyday living in which questions receive negative answers without an accompanying explanation. An adverse decision by the national parole board is not punishment. The sentence of the court is in no way increased or modified.[96]

Rowcliffe also contended that individual applicants already knew their shortcomings and that if they did not, many people inside the prison were available to point them out![97] The *C.B. Diamond* writers informed prisoners that their classification officer would know the reason for denial and could share that with the individual if asked.[98] It is unclear whether that officer actually would have done so. In the first years after the inception of parole, prisoners writing in the penal press continued to press for change on this issue.

Disappointment: Drug Addicts and Alcoholics

Prisoners also expressed disappointment in the stance the Fauteux Committee took on "drug addicts." While the report did not suggest that they be excluded from consideration, it was not progressive in its thinking on this matter. A prisoner at BC Penitentiary criticized the report for adopting the "popular attitude of hopelessness" in relation to this "large percentage of Canada's walled-in population."[99] The committee used phrases like "no reasonable expectancy of reform"[100] in relation to incarcerated drug users. The parole handbook was slightly more encouraging: "Drug offenders can also be granted parole but naturally because there is such a serious problem involved in the use of drugs, we must be more careful than usual but if it seems that you sincerely intend and seem able to stay away from drugs in the future, we want to help you do so."[101]

Interestingly, the language applied to drug users was considerably different from what was used to describe alcoholics. The latter group were framed in terms of having a "problem" they could "overcome" if they tried. The committee praised those who attended Alcoholics Anonymous and commented on how well they had adjusted to "civil life."[102] In contrast, the psychology-based language of addiction was applied to drug addicts,[103] which made it more difficult for prisoners so-labelled to establish that drugs were something they consumed and not a reflection of their character.

Prisoner-critics of the Fauteaux Report would eventually find some vindication: their concerns over both the parole process and the framing of drug addicts would be addressed. In 1969, the chairman of the Parole Board, George Street, convinced the solicitor general to grant prisoners the right to appear before the board and receive the reasons for any decision. In 1977 these changes were incorporated into the Parole Act.[104] Meanwhile, increased knowledge of drug use, in part prompted by the social movements of the 1960s and 1970s, led to a greater understanding of addiction issues, with the result that those who used illicit drugs were generally treated the same as those who used alcohol. But that was in the years to come. In the late 1950s, the public still needed to be convinced of the merits of the New Deal and, more specifically, the need for a new parole system.

Getting the Public On-Side

While the new parole system did not have unanimous public support, the principles of parole continued to be advanced by those in the know. Prisoners had used the penal press to advocate for change in ticket-of-leave practices, to praise the creation of automatic parole, and to press for further improvements. But the readership of the penal press was not broad enough to reach the public. Nor was it the prisoners' responsibility to inform those masses. The Fauteux Report had, in its first recommendation, implored the three levels of government "to acquaint the public with the purpose of a sound system of corrections and the benefits derived from it."[105]

The government could not rely on a simple economic argument to persuade the masses. It was easy to argue that parole was less costly than imprisonment, but that was not the public's sole concern. Many did not want their convicts mollycoddled, and, more importantly, they did not want them to commit further crimes after release (see chapter 4). Those who studied penology and criminology argued that parole would not increase the risk to society; indeed, they argued that it would *improve* safety. The United Nations contended that a system of parole had many advantages for society and for the convicted individual. Those benefits included

1. giving a prisoner the opportunity to demonstrate their rehabilitation in the community;
2. minimizing the "impact of the process of deterioration produced by imprisonment";
3. encouraging prisoners to maintain outside contact;
4. offering support to the released prisoner during his reacclimation;
5. keeping the prisoner aware of his obligations as a citizen who would one day return to society;
6. encouraging the prisoner to "derive maximum benefit from the facilities provided by the prison"; and
7. encouraging prisoner to have good conduct while in the penitentiary.[106]

But these documents were read only by a select, interested group. As the lessons following the receipt of the Archambault Report and the coverage of the 1934 riot made clear, the government knew it was critical to get the public on-side (see chapter 2). The minister of justice and members of the board engaged the media, the public, and interested bodies extensively, as Minister of Justice Fulton explained in the Commons:

> The honorable member from Saskatoon asked about the steps which are being taken to, I think he used the phrase, educate the public as to the purpose and advantages of parole, and I would like to draw his attention to the activities of the board members which have been carried on since they assumed their function on February 15 last year. There have been 26 television and radio interviews, four magazine articles and numerous press releases. Members of the board also had 35 meetings with prison inmate committees and made 37 speeches to magistrates' associations, to aftercare agencies, university students, service clubs, and general public meetings in Canada. That was up till December 31 of last year. Since January 1 of this year addresses have been made on 26 separate occasions. There have been 15 television appearances, ten radio talks and further numerous press releases. Certainly I would judge, on the basis of the press comments which I have seen, that the efforts of the board, guided by its chairman in this respect, have been very successful indeed in creating a public acceptance of the work and objectives of the board, and also a public acceptance of the results of that work.[107]

Writers in the penal press applauded the efforts of both politicians and parole board members for their efforts to sell the merits of parole and convince the mainstream audience of its social and economic benefits. It was not uncommon for columnists in prison publications to let readers know the nature and type of public relations work being done.[108] There was reason to celebrate. In 1960, men and women were being successfully released from prison in record numbers; of course, they were also being incarcerated in record numbers.

Early Progress Reports

The board trumpeted its early successes through statistical data. The government, the board, and the prisoners were anxious to have more men and women released from prison, and this was happening. The board's first ever annual report recorded that paroles had increased by 106 per cent in 1959 over 1958. The minister of justice took time to brag about this:

> When honourable members stop to think that that means there were 3,044 paroles granted less 214 failures, or in other words 2,830[109] inmates would

otherwise still be incarcerated who are now out on parole and successfully observing the conditions of their parole, thus better enabled to return to society as useful and law abiding members thereof – that is 2,830 people now in society as the result of these paroles within one year – then I think the decision of the government supported by parliament to set up a national parole board under the national parole act has been entirely vindicated.[110]

Though it lacked sufficient longitudinal data to make claims about recidivism, the National Parole Board was keen to be seen as successful and contended that the rate for the first year was "exceptionally low."[111] *C.B. Diamond* took care to point out that recidivism rates of parolees (7%) were far less than the general rate for released convicts (70%).[112] Prisoners even cautioned their incarcerated brethren not to take the return to prison of parolees as indicative of the system's failure; one editor advised prisoners not to assign too much credibility to those who complained about their parole supervision prior to reincarceration:

> The prospective parolee should remember that those who have been returned are not liable to be kindly disposed to the Board and will certainly have a tendency to find fault with the system. And there are faults. There will always be faults in any system that depends on human beings for its efficiency. The Board are, in my opinion, honestly trying to set a good policy for the future and any conditions imposed on a man are for the purpose of assisting him to make the transition from prison to the street. The conditions are tailored to fit the parolee and are not imposed dogmatically as they were in the Province of Ontario's parole system.[113]

While Mathiesen indicated that reforms were often blocked by institutional requirements, in this case, the goals of the two meshed.[114] Those involved knew it was not a perfect system, but it was doing what it had set out to do: it had mitigated prison overcrowding to some degree,[115] saved the government money, and helped convicts transition back into society. All of these points were iterated by Gordy Thompson, editor of *Transition*, in June 1960. Following a visit and interview with the western supervisor of the National Parole Board, Alex Edmison wrote that in 1959 double the number of paroles had been granted federally and at his institution (BC Penitentiary) and that the paroles were longer than those granted by the remission system. Thompson added that

> these figures become startling when one is acquainted with the economic, preventive, and rehabilitative aspects of parole. Economically, the savings

is tremendous. The average cost of imprisoning a man for one year in a penitentiary is twenty-two hundred dollars … To keep two thousand men imprisoned for that length of time would cost nearly four and a half million dollars … On the other hand, a man may be supervised on parole for amounts varying from fifty to one hundred dollars annually. As important as the savings may be, of greater value are the preventive and rehabilitative features of early release. Most crimes are committed as a last resort, the offender's affairs having been allowed to reach such pass that he finds himself in a semi-desperate situation. On parole, however, he is not allowed to reach such straits. He must at all times, live as normal a life as is possible for him to do … After a man has worked and played under the conditions of control for two or three years, the benefits derived from normal living offer excellent inducement for lasting rehabilitation."[116]

Reason for Optimism?

Supporters of the New Deal for prisoners had some reason to celebrate. Progress had been made. In keeping with the reform ideals, every person housed in a penitentiary in Canada gained some relief because of these parole interventions. The calculation of "good time" remission had not changed; even so, prisoners in this era did benefit from a general clemency to mark the queen's coronation, and the antiquated Ticket-of-Leave Act had been replaced with a new system of parole. All of this meant that more women and men were being released from prison, conditionally or otherwise, although parole rates would begin a downward trend before too long.

The official record documents enthusiasm as well as early implementation and success; the prisoners' accounts offer a more complicated picture. When the two are read together, it is evident that the dominant ideology guiding the New Deal was butting against the weight of traditions, practices, social beliefs, and political systems. Indeed, the reform impulse was being corrupted by "deposits of power" and "social deposits" left behind from previous eras.[117] Long-standing beliefs about drug use meant that convicts labelled "drug addicts" fared less well than those labelled "reformable," despite the ideal that each incarcerated person should be treated as an individual rather than as part of an aggregate. This chapter also suggests that the benefits derived by prisoners were unevenly distributed: some found themselves in privileged positions. Prisoners with strong outside support were able to add that to their parole file, while those who had lost the support of family and friends because of lengthy incarcerations, or who lacked that support to begin with, were disadvantaged.

Furthermore, the prisoners' accounts illuminate some of the inherent contradictions between the espoused ideology and the actual practices of those who operated the system. While the mantra held that prisoners were people first, many actions of the state and its representatives undermined this sentiment. The Fauteux Committee never sought input from prisoners about changes to the Remission Service despite their considered expertise on the matter and their frequent writings in the penal press. Reflecting the move toward increased professionalization – but running counter to the ideology – once established, the actions of the parole board depersonalized individual prisoners by relying solely on a file to assess each person's character and potential. Integration of a new philosophy was not complete.

6 New Deal/Old Deal: Discontent and Censorship

Prisoners and administrators often clash over prison conditions and penal reform issues, and this was true in the New Deal era (1935–60). Now, however, their confrontations were playing out in the pages of the penal press. Commissioner Gibson's administration permitted prisoner-editors a certain amount of latitude as long as the criticisms were "constructive." But at certain moments, administrators silenced prisoners' voices. Most often it was individual columns, articles, and editorials that were censored, but on occasion, entire issues of prison magazines were cancelled and destroyed. This chapter examines the struggles between prisoners and administrators using censorship as a point of entry to explore the differences of opinion, the battles over content in the penal press, and the issues that gave rise to the greatest controversies.

As we saw in chapter 3, prisoner-editors were determined, from the very outset, to use the powers of the fourth estate[1] to engage in constructive criticism and to communicate with the administration and the public.[2] The administration, for its part, was set on portraying the regime as progressive. At times, these two objectives could not be reconciled, and when that happened, the more powerful interest usually prevailed, although not without political fallout as well as consequences for the future of the reform project.

As the previous chapters have made clear, improvements were made in Canada's federal prison system in the late 1940s and early 1950s. But there were limits to that progress. Educational and vocational opportunities were available to small groups of prisoners at certain institutions; but outside of working hours, men still spent long periods of time isolated in their cells; and diversions such as hobbycraft, letter-writing, and visitations depended greatly on a prisoner's personal and financial situation. Reform was further complicated by the resource strain caused by a dramatic increase in the prison population over the course of the 1950s. In the words of Warden Cummins at BC Penitentiary, by 1957, overcrowding was "the major problem and it is so important to us that it overshadows every effort that we make."[3] As prison populations rose, the Penitentiary Service's ability to control prisoners diminished, as did its capacity to provide appropriate opportunities for them.

The commissioner wrote in his annual report for 1952–53 that "the deadly dullness and boredom of week-ends [has] disappeared."[4] John Muise, writing in *Tele-Scope*, contested that assessment, describing an unchanging and monotonous routine inside Kingston Penitentiary. In the morning, he walked single file to the kitchen to discard the previous evening's dinner tray, picked up his breakfast, and returned to his cell. After breakfast, he again filed down to the kitchen to drop off the tray before going to work. At lunch, he picked up his meal (tea, beef beans, potatoes, and bread) and returned to his cell. In the afternoon, he went out for exercise for thirty minutes or returned to work. At the end of the afternoon, he picked up his evening meal tray and went back to his cell. The lights would be turned out six hours later, and the same scenario would repeat the next day.[5] This account echoed Oswald Withrow's description of prison life thirty years earlier. And it was well understood by the administration. When Commissioner Gibson submitted an article titled "Treatment of the Offender in Federal Institutions" to *Tele-Scope* in May 1954, he was more circumspect in his assessment of the reforms than he had been in his annual report: "Even with the humane and helpful changes that have been made in the treatment of offenders," he wrote, "imprisonment, with its loss of liberty, its regimentation and discipline, its long hours of cellular confinement, its complete removal of the individual from his family and home ties, still remains as a very real punishment for criminal behaviour."[6]

As should be clear, for Commissioner Gibson, the audience mattered.

The Official Face of Reform

Gibson and the Penitentiary Service administration were committed to communicating a vision of progress to the public. That commitment was captured in the title of Gibson's 1949 address to the Canadian Penal Congress, "The Penitentiaries Move Forward,"[7] and it was reflected in Toronto in 1953 at the congress of the American Prison Association – an organization Gibson led. Gibson's administration took great pride in having introduced the New Deal to Canada's prisons, a progressive commitment so important to them that they brought in Eleanor Roosevelt to serve as the keynote speaker. This gesture was laden with symbolism, given the former First Lady's well-known association with progressive causes and her obvious connection to the original New Deal, which had been introduced by her husband to address the economic problems of the Great Depression in the United States.[8]

As we have seen, in previous eras, administrators' depictions of prison reform had often gone uncontested, save for the occasional, exceptional, and punctuated retort from prisoners and outsiders. In the 1920s and early 1930s, the superintendent and allied prison reformers painted a picture of steady if incomplete progress. Any criticism was directed outward against political leaders and their lack of commitment to funding and realizing the vision. Outside critics appeared only sporadically (and usually as a result of riots) – in prisoners' memoirs like Oswald Withrow's – or in government inquiries, like that of the Archambault Commission.

The Contested View of Reform

As noted in chapter 3, the penal press was one of the most publicly visible manifestations of the New Deal in Canada's prisons. For the administrators who helped create it, the penal press was more than just a publicity ploy. Allowing prisoners a voice emphasized their humanity – a goal underscored by the mantra "prisoners are people" – as well as the Christian humanism of their benevolent keepers. The penal press was intended to build morale among prisoners and to permit them to make constructive suggestions for future reforms. In addition, Commissioner Gibson and his subordinates believed that it was important to build connections between prisoners and their communities in order to maintain public support for prison reform. The penal press was one of several initiatives that contributed to that end. But the penal press also introduced a new multivocality to the public discourse around prison reform. The writers and editors of the penal press advanced new analyses and focused on new targets. The introduction of the penal press unleashed a new, more immediate, and continuous barrage of criticism from prisoners.

Prisoners' criticisms disrupted the administrative narrative and threatened to undermine administrators' agendas. The Penitentiary Service's depiction of the unfolding reforms – and indeed, its own competence – was open to challenge; so was its ability to control the public's understanding of pivotal events. This helps explain the commissioner's more cautious assessment of reform and its limits in his article in *Tele-Scope*. He knew that his audience understood the prison system well and was likely to correct any inaccuracies in his account.

For the first time, the objects of reform were able to contest their treatment and redefine the public's understanding of the prison system. It was a fraught situation that at times, as noted previously, became intolerable to administrators. One of the earliest major controversies over editorial freedom involved a riot at Kingston Penitentiary in 1954. The following paragraphs provide an account of the riot and its origins and then discuss the conflict between administrators and prisoner-editors over how to explain the event.

Situation Critical: The New Deal Riot

In the early afternoon of 13 August 1954, a group of arsonists entered the *Tele-Scope* office in the main cell block at Kingston Penitentiary. The men opened an access door and crawled up into the attic. They had carefully prepared their next steps. The attic was divided by firewalls into four sections. They knocked the locks off of each of the steel firewall doors and transported lumber and paint cans into each section. In each area, the arsonists built pyramids of the flammable materials, which they ignited using copies of *Tele-Scope* as tinder. Within minutes, the roof was ablaze.[9]

Owing to the age of the building and the difficulties of accessing the attic system – the door in the *Tele-Scope* office offered the sole point of entry – Kingston's firefighters faced a difficult challenge. But with the help of prisoners they managed to extinguish the last remnants of the fire by 10:30 p.m. that night.[10] Meanwhile, more than four hundred of the main cell block's residents were removed to shops, where they spent the night. The next day, guards informed these prisoners that the main cell block had been deemed safe and that they would be returning to their cells. The prisoners refused to go, arguing that the building remained unfit for habitation. A scuffle between three of the prisoners and a guard ensued. Other prisoners began to shout, smash windows, and destroy machinery, and the situation threatened to spiral out of control. Under those circumstances, penitentiary officials decided to allow the prisoners to spend a second night in the shops. A fire marshall was scheduled to inspect the building the next day, and that would settle the safety question.[11]

In his report on the events that followed, Commissioner Gibson would contend that the prisoners' temporary accommodations had facilitated communication and organization. In that account, he wrote that several agitators took advantage of the situation to stir up resentment among the prisoners co-housed in the shops.[12] The following morning, during the exercise period, a small group of those agitators claimed that some of their fellow prisoners were still locked up in the shops and needed to be released. The group overpowered a guard, took his keys, and headed for the shops. Once inside, those prisoners destroyed machinery and set fire to the buildings. Other prisoners joined them.[13] All told, some two hundred prisoners – one-fifth of the prison's population – participated in the disturbance.[14] But it was, in some ways, a strange riot. More than one staff member expressed amazement that the prisoners made no attempt to injure or confine their guards or the prison administrators, though they had every opportunity to do so.[15] This was an attack on property, not persons.

With the situation clearly out of hand, prison officials called in the army, as they had done during the 1932 riot. Approximately 150 soldiers made their way to the prison from the nearby army base. The soldiers fixed their bayonets, fired several warning shots, and then drove the rioting prisoners into one corner of the yard. Within a few hours of beginning, the second phase of the disturbance was over and the apparent ringleaders were locked in solitary confinement cells. No prisoners had escaped and no lives were lost, but the property damage was extensive.[16] Several prisoners were punished for participating in the riot. One man was placed in solitary confinement for at least seven months.[17] In his thesis on the Kingston riot, Chadwick Marr has speculated that the riot "likely led to the increased use of shock treatments ... as it allowed the punishment of the instigators to be masked in the rhetoric of treatment for those supposedly suffering psychopathic tendencies."[18] There is some evidence that electroshock treatment was used against an "ardent communist" who had become "disruptive" when his beliefs were challenged.[19] Moreover, in the commissioner's annual report for 1949–50, Gibson admitted that electroshock treatment had previously been used to resolve "conflictual situations ... without further difficulties."[20]

Marr noted that "the really difficult task facing penitentiary officials was explaining the cause of the ruinous behaviour."[21] Gibson feigned perplexity. Though he would admit in his annual report that the prisoners had hoped to gain greater control over recreational activities,[22] he initially claimed in October 1954 that the rioting prisoners had issued no demands and that the prison inmate committee had raised no serious issues in the weeks leading up to the incident. To this, he added that "many privileges to improve the day to day living and working conditions of the inmates had been introduced at Kingston Penitentiary over the past five years."[23] Given the apparent absence of expressed motives among the rioters, and his conviction that the prison system had undergone significant improvements, the commissioner chose to attribute responsibility to a small group of "psychopaths" who, he argued, took advantage of the volatile but temporary situation in the shops.[24] Gibson characterized these men as "hardened and disgruntled criminals, serving long terms, whose resentment against society and against all authority no rehabilitative programme can break down."[25] Apparently, this was the Penitentiary Service's standard interpretation of such events. According to Herbert Gamberg and Anthony Thomson, throughout the 1950s "rebellious prisoners were described as psychopaths and as being mentally disturbed" in official reports.[26] Marr, however, disputed Gibson's analysis, concluding that the prisoners' "actions must be seen as a revolt against the very idea of imprisonment."[27] He contended that they "were lashing out against the prison that they loathed and the entire notion of imprisonment, however reformed and 'scientific.'"[28] That mindset among prisoners is worth considering in detail.

Antecedents to the Riot: Daily Life and Overcrowding

It is important to remember that the level of control and discipline remained constant in the penitentiaries during the 1935–60 period and that even the most trivial aspects of a prisoner's daily existence were strictly regulated. At wardens' conferences in the 1950s, the administrators debated the number of baths per week and whether it was appropriate to allow ablutions twice in a seven-day period.[29] The wattage of lightbulbs in cells (and the length of wire needed to suspend them) was a recurrent topic among administrators – too much wattage was too costly and too little made it difficult for the prisoners to read. Wardens debated the issuance of tobacco to prisoners in solitary confinement and agreed that if a man was left in isolation for more than a month, dispensation would be appropriate.[30] Officials spent as much time discussing the cloth and cut of prisoners' uniforms as they did considering when whipping a prisoner was warranted.[31]

Despondency among prisoners in the 1950s should have been anticipated. The New Deal conceived of prisons as places of reformation where the principles of rehabilitation could be applied; but implementation proved difficult because the prisons were bursting at the seams. As Warden Cummins had emphasized, overcrowding affected everything from prisoner morale to the ability to offer programs. It undermined administrators' most progressive efforts. In 1959, in the House of Commons, Minister of Justice Davie Fulton raised the problem of overcrowding: "I can say that all our federal penitentiaries are overcrowded and the matter is one of real concern. The two worst were at Montreal and British Columbia. Speaking from recollection I would say

Image 6.1. Crowded prisons. *Tele-Scope*, March 1959. Gaucher/Munn penal press collection.

that Dorchester and Prince Albert are about next in order. As I recall it, the situation in Manitoba is about the best."[32] The UN's recommended Standard Minimum Rules for Treatment of Prisoners stated that "if for special reasons, such as temporary overcrowding, it becomes necessary for the central prison administration to make an exception to this rule, it is not desirable to have two prisoners in a cell or room." These rules were not being adhered to.[33]

In the penal press, prisoners described how overcrowding impacted their lives. According to one contributor to *Beacon*, the authorities had created three-man cells by knocking down the partitions between two individual cells; then "one upper and two lower bunks were placed in the resultant double-sized cell."[34] The men were literally tripping over each other, and this made it difficult for them to engage in initiatives like hobbycraft or education. When "renovations" were not possible, beds would be placed in the corridors in front of the cells. As CCF MP Harold Winch (Vancouver East) noted, this "does not make for a happy situation."[35] It was hardly the "more modern manner, as recommended by the Archambault commission."[36] Redressing overcrowding in prisons became a priority.

The government's solution was to build more prisons. Joyceville Institution was built in 1959 to move men out of Kingston Penitentiary. The Federal Training Centre, opened in 1952, was erected "to alleviate the over-crowded conditions at St. Vincent de Paul Penitentiary and to make better provision for the segregation of young and reformable types of offenders."[37] Yet overcrowding persisted, undermining reform efforts. In his 1950 report, the commissioner noted that new, reform-oriented spaces at Saint-Vincent-de-Paul Penitentiary were quickly appropriated:

> The outstanding event was the opening of the new school building at St. Vincent de Paul Penitentiary on October 12, 1949. This building is a thoroughly modern, four classroom structure with suitable offices, conference rooms and other necessary facilities for an adult education programme. Although easy of access, it is unattached to any other prison building, is of pleasing architecture in the modern style and in all ways sets a standard for future development. *Unfortunately, however, the building had only been in use for a short time when some of the additional space thus provided had to be requisitioned for temporary dormitory use owing to the continued increase of the population at this institution. This was a most discouraging but inevitable development.* [Emphasis added][38]

The building of new prisons did not alleviate the "hopelessly outdated and antiquated" conditions of the existing ones.[39] Convicts and politicians alike argued that the facilities were too full and too old to meet the goals of the New Deal. Prisoners predicted that this problem would continue, given that more men were being given longer sentences, thus increasing the number of individuals in prison on any given day.[40] They lamented this trend: "It is unfortunate the situation should prevail at a time when Canadian penitentiaries have just introduced a reform programme."[41] The editors of *Pathfinder* predicted that "any decrease in the harmful effects of imprisonment under the new program [would be] offset by the lengthy sentence imposed by the courts."[42] The governments of the day were aware that the prison population was growing and that they were not preparing adequately.[43]

The harshness and futility of prison life informed many of the New Deal's attempts at reform. Deputy Commissioner McCulley emphasized that "if our inmates are reminded from moment to moment every day of every week of every month for years at a time, not only by the stone and iron bars but by every other facet of prison life, that they are being held under duress, we cannot wonder if sooner or later their resentment wells into open rebellion."[44] He recognized that the Penitentiary Service was not going to create "perfect prisons" but contended that there was "a sincere desire to make our penitentiaries humane, whole and constructive places."[45]

Gibson was well aware of these conditions but remained adamant that prisons were moving forward. He insisted that the riot leaders at Kingston had been "psychopaths" who simply could not be reformed, thus explaining the 1954 disturbance in such a way as to deflect blame away from his approach to implementing reforms. In the months that followed, the commissioner, politicians, and the mainstream newspapers advocated the same solution to the problem: the construction of a dedicated institution for the segregation of "anti-social" and irredeemable prisoners.[46] This had long been part of the postwar reform vision, and in the wake of the riot, Gibson now had an opportunity to press for action. Indeed, prison officials did not wait for the new facility to be built – they took immediate steps, implementing stricter segregation of "psychopathic" prisoners within existing institutions and excluding them from rehabilitation programs.[47] This was not, as some have argued, "a gradual shift away from the rehabilitative ideal."[48] Rather, it was about exerting power and control over those prisoners perceived as the leaders of the convict cohort – a goal not inconsistent with the Archambault Commission's recommendations. After all, the commission had recommended the removal "from the penitentiary population prisoners who may be agitators."[49]

Gibson made his purposes explicit in his 1955 annual report: "A few malcontents sparked a destructive demonstration in hope of influencing the administration to relax its strict control of recreational activity. *Advantage of these events has been taken ... to inaugurate more effective supervision of inmate activity, and to segregate* within each institution those inmates who show a psychopathic tendency to stir up trouble among their better-disposed and more industrious fellow-inmates" (emphasis added).[50]

For prisoners at BC Penitentiary, the events of 1954 seem to have served as a tipping point. They now unleashed a barrage of criticism on their keepers, who felt the blow more than they might have before the Kingston riot. The December 1954 issue of *Transition* included original contributions and reprinted articles that targeted a wide array of penal practices, institutions, and officials. Writers criticized the police, the judiciary, juvenile home administrators, prisoners' aid society officials, and the penitentiary service bureaucracy, accusing them of corruption, incompetence, inefficiency, and indifference.[51] Perhaps most grating for the penal administrators who had trumpeted their triumphs in Toronto the year before were repeated accusations that they were behind the times. One writer asserted that "Canadian penologists ... always seem to be twenty years behind the general trend."[52] *Transition's* editorial column blamed public attitudes and "an archaic penal system that is useless as a medium of rehabilitation" for high rates of recidivism among federal prisoners.[53] Elsewhere, the editors argued that "the barbaric treatment of young girls" in British Columbia's juvenile detention homes was responsible for turning them to a life of crime.[54] Finally, *Transition* editor Al Sieben took issue with the commissioner's suggestion that Canada build a specialized prison to deal with the so-called incorrigible leaders of the Kingston riot. Sieben asked, "How far have we progressed ... [Is the] net result: a Canadian type of Alcatraz? Will this be a monument to progressive penology?" He argued that the actual cause of the riot was prison conditions, pointing out that prisoners were still confined in their cells for eighteen hours a day. He wrote that prisoners were "destroyed by endless days and nights of prison solitude with never a comforting word, never the touch of a loving hand, not even the right to consider [themselves] human being[s]. These are the real men, these are the real prisons."

Sieben concluded: "Today, the movement to build an Alcatraz is indeed a sad foreboding [of] the wisdom and understanding of our authorities. Instead, they should raze the monstrous prisons of today. They should build prisons where so-called incorrigibles can regain their self-respect and human dignity."[55]

The critical tone of *Transition* magazine soon became the subject of serious concern to some in the administration.

Censorship: Controlling the New Deal's Narrative

Later in December, Deputy Commissioner Ralph March, who had taken over after Joseph McCulley's resignation in 1952, raised a series of objections to the prisoners' arguments. The contrast between McCulley – the champion of the penal press – and his successor could not have been drawn more starkly. March wrote that the December 1954 issue of *Transition* was "malicious and destructive, almost from cover to cover," replete with untruths, half-truths, and "destructive criticism."[56] What seemed to bother March most was the prisoners' direct criticism of the authorities and of the administration's interpretation of the Kingston riot. Gibson wrote to the local warden, forwarding March's objections, suggesting that the publication be suspended, and inquiring about the "supervision or check" placed on the material published in *Transition*.[57]

When presented with the deputy commissioner's complaints, Warden Douglass at BC Penitentiary met with the institution's Library Board, which was charged with censoring material submitted for publication in *Transition*. While their discussions were not recorded, the board members (two chaplains and the schoolteacher-librarian) explained in a written report to the warden that most of the material submitted to them was rejected as unsuitable, but that at times, pieces that were "far from ideal" were published after revision, the board choosing this as "the least objectionable [approach to] a very poor situation."[58] In addition, they noted that *Transition*'s editors sometimes published material that had not been submitted for vetting.[59] Part way through the meeting, the warden decided to bring in *Transition*'s editorial staff. This latter part of the meeting did not go well, and in a letter to the commissioner, the warden attributed the breakdown of the meeting to the character of the prisoners. The warden described the staff members in general as "not the best type" and singled out two unidentified prisoners as "anti-social" and "difficult" but also as excellent writers who were indispensable to the operation.[60] He also explained that the editorial staff had been selected by the Inmate Welfare Committee, which he assumed was the practice at all institutions.[61] When Warden Douglass presented *Transition*'s editors with Deputy Commissioner March's criticism, and informed them that their next issue was also unacceptable, they resigned en masse. As they explained, they "felt that unless the paper expressed the wishes of prisoners it would lose it's value [*sic*]."[62] This argument may have rung familiar to the commissioner. Back in 1953, the editor of *Pathfinder* wrote to Gibson stating that "blanket censorship can result only in confusion and frustration. If the editorial content must conform to the opinions and the ideas of one or more officials, the *Pathfinder* will become just a house organ." He continued:

It is the editors wish that the *Pathfinder* be truly an inmate magazine. Toward that end, we respectfully suggest the local administration be freed of all responsibility as far as the magazine's views and policies are concerned, and that we be trusted to present a magazine that will be a credit to the inmates, the Administration, and the Commissioner of Penitentiaries. Failing this, we further suggest the present editorial staff be relieved of their editorial responsibilities.[63]

History was already repeating itself.

In a subsequent letter, which Warden Douglass of BC Penitentiary forwarded to Commissioner Gibson, *Transition*'s editors argued that they had previously asked for clear instructions respecting content, but none had been provided. So they had developed their editorial policy using other penal press magazines as their guide.[64] Publication of *Transition* was suspended following the group's resignation. These events were noteworthy enough to be reported in the *Vancouver Sun*. According to the *Sun*'s reporter, Deputy Warden Cummins alleged that "the six-man staff of the prison magazine ... had 'abused' officials of the Department of Justice and that the staff planned to do 'the same thing again' in the December issue" of *Transition*.[65]

At a warden's conference in January 1955, Deputy Commissioner March expressed his concerns about the changing tone of the penal press. But when he contended that some of the material contained "half-truths" and "false statements" as well as sarcastic attacks on law enforcement authorities – claims he had also made in his memorandum on *Transition* – the wardens took him to task. Warden Johnstone (Kingston Penitentiary) read out the article under scrutiny. While the particular piece is not cited by title or author, the minutes indicate that it was a piece on drug policy published in *Tele-Scope*. Likely the article had been written by Harvey Blackstock, titled "Special Treatment for Drug Addicts." In it, the author comments on the deaths of two women at the Prison for Women. This article was an unabashed indictment of prosecutors who called for longer sentences to be imposed on drug addicts, based on the idea that federal prisons had "special treatment" for them.[66] Blackstock wrote that "the Canada Opium and Narcotic Act, under which both of these women were sentenced, belongs to the middle ages," and that "the *only* 'special treatment for drug addicts in the penitentiary', about which prosecutors talk so glibly, is death either from natural causes or suicide."[67] These critical statements prompted the following exchange between the deputy commissioner and a warden:

> MR. MARCH: That sort of thing has no place in an inmate publication.
> WDN. RICHMOND: It may be true, though.
> MR. MARCH: It may be true, yes.[68]

The minutes of the meeting indicate a "heated exchange." Gibson interjected that he expected prisoners writing for the penal press to frame their criticism "in a dispassionate way."[69] How prisoners, who were daily subjects of the reforms, were to emotionally detach themselves in this way is unstated.

The conversation that followed revealed that some administrators were more concerned about how the material would be read by the public and allied agencies than about the content itself. As Gibson explained, "the Administration will bring upon itself a lot of criticism if we allow this to go on."[70] Two years earlier, he had banned an article written from the perspective of the prison cell that was critical of the New Deal and disparaging of administrators' claims that progress was being made: "With all its changes, the new penal program in my country hasn't affected me too greatly. Confidentially though, I don't care for it. There is always the danger those darned humanitarians may start hollering for changes to be made in me one of these days too. What a dreadful prospect! I have changed but little over the centuries, and my effectiveness never suffered as a result." (For the entire piece, see Appendix B.)[71]

In his 25 August 1953 response to the warden at Saskatchewan Penitentiary, which he intended to be shared with the editor of *Pathfinder*, Gibson wrote: "I hope that inmate CLARK and his editorial staff will appreciate that it is not the desire of the administration to impose censorship on their magazine but to give help and guidance in dealing with articles or statements that might give a wrong impression to the public outside, and so react to the detriment of the inmate body."[72] At the warden's conference, several administrators, including the commissioner, worried that the tone of the press would alienate allies and fellow law enforcement personnel. In one exchange, Deputy Commissioner March responded to his critics. "The [John Howard Society]," he said,

> however good or bad it may be, is trying to do something for inmates. A publication published an article recently which, by inference, kicked the feet off them. It was picked up and reprinted by at least one other institution. It had to do with [the] percentage of [the] Society's income which went for [the] actual benefit of the men. It may be true but are you going to keep [the] goodwill and zeal of [the] JHS or any other society if you kick the feet off them?[73]

March also worried that the tone of the criticism was contagious and might quickly spread from one publication to the next. This was a reasonable concern, given that editors held subscriptions to magazines from other prisons and routinely reprinted noteworthy pieces in their own publications (see the wardens' discussion of these practices during the 1957 warden's conference below). In any case, however heated the discussion, the matter was not resolved at the meeting. The commissioner promised to draft a set of general directives "to help the editors in knowing what sort of thing that can be printed [sic]," and some wardens subsequently took it upon themselves to tighten censorship controls at their institutions.[74]

Two months later, Commissioner Gibson forwarded the new guidelines for the penal press to Warden Douglass at BC Penitentiary. Reaffirming his awareness of audience, in explaining his purpose, he wrote,

> I am under the impression that public interest in correctional affairs in Canada is increasing ... I believe, also, that the courts, the legal profession,

legislatures and parliament, police, government departments and institutional administrators are all sincerely seeking to improve the treatment of the offender ... I fail to see how an inmate publication can generate greater interest on the part of these authorities by slapping their faces through the medium of its columns.[75]

A set of six regulations followed. The commissioner approved of material describing prison activities; articles discussing subjects of general interest, provided that they displayed literary merit; and reprints from other penal publications, although he cautioned that these would be subject to local censorship. He warned that penal magazines were not to be used to pass messages to prisoners housed elsewhere or to advance individual "beefs." Most pointedly, he assured the prisoners that they would be permitted to publish "articles which discuss matters of current interest in penal administration, provided that criticism contained therein is constructive, and not merely destructive and sarcastic."[76] Note that these rules were only sent to the *Transition* editorial staff. They were not circulated to the other institutions.[77]

Later in 1955, a new *Transition* editorial board was appointed. Publication resumed in July, with Warden Douglass assuring the commissioner that he would maintain strict censorship of the publication.[78] The *New Westminster British Columbian* and *Vancouver Herald* both carried pieces on the resumption of publication, the latter reporting that the revived magazine was "gay and well-edited in content."[79] Gibson wrote to the warden to express his approval.[80]

Yet if the outcome of the *Transition* controversy suggested that the penal press was easily muzzled, events over the next two years proved the contrary. Editors chafed at the censorship of their publications, which they argued was designed to conceal penal realities from the public, who might have advocated for change.[81] Conflicts were commonplace and were particularly acute at Kingston Penitentiary. On several occasions, entire print runs of *Tele-Scope* were destroyed.[82] In an effort to resolve the ongoing disputes, *Tele-Scope*'s editorial board and the warden agreed to have local John Howard Society (JHS) members act as a "neutral" third-party censorship board. But in December 1956, the warden objected to several articles that had been approved by the JHS and ordered yet another print run destroyed. The offending articles were removed and the issue reprinted.[83] Soon afterwards, another controversy emerged over office space, editorial board membership, and meeting attendance. The warden, facing a space crunch because of overcrowding (see chapter 4), refused to provide *Tele-Scope*'s editors with enough space to hold meetings of all fifteen associate editors. As the conflict heated up, the warden may also have taken away the editorial staff's office space and other privileges. The accounts vary. What is clear is that the heart of the matter was who controlled *Tele-Scope*. The editors resigned. Publication of *Tele-Scope* ceased.[84]

Several months later, a recently released prisoner told the story to a *Globe* columnist, J.V. McAree, who concluded his account of the conflict as follows:

> We are sorry indeed to get this news. In the past, we have praised the Kingston Warden, and the Prison Headquarters in Ottawa for the enlightened policy in letting prisoners, within decent limits, criticize prison affairs. In fact the chief value of the Telescope lay in this freedom. The attack on the magazine will destroy any value it has for us, so we ask whoever is now in charge of the remains to cease sending it to us. ..... [ellipsis in original][85]

That summer at a warden's conference in Ottawa, the commissioner discussed the penal press with his senior staff and the assembled wardens. Looming in the background of this conversation was a suggestion that the press be shut down entirely. According to Kingston Warden Johnstone, articles in *Tele-Scope* frequently incited trouble between prisoners and the administration, and between groups of prisoners, "creat[ing] friction within the institution."[86] He contended that few prisoners would be upset if the magazine was permanently discontinued.[87] Other wardens, the commissioner, and Deputy Commissioner March contested that claim. Wardens described the penal press as important to prisoners. They depicted the editors as wily "politicians,"[88] with prisoners jockeying for control of the magazines, and "good" editors – or rather, those the wardens favoured – often being forced out of their positions owing to disagreements over the direction of editorial policy.[89] They also lamented their experiences with prisoners who refused to follow orders, ignored "good council [sic]," and wanted to appeal local rulings to the commissioner.[90] They spoke of constant battles over censorship, with prisoners often inserting articles or items they had been expressly forbidden to print. As Warden Cummins (BC Penitentiary) lamented, "you try to tell them this will not appear in the magazine and it appears in the magazine."[91] Several wardens also expressed concern that prisoners were using the penal press to pass information from institution to institution. Sometimes, they explained, this occurred overtly, through exchange columns and reprinted articles, and sometimes covertly, through hidden messages in gossip columns or lines slipped stealthily into the proofs.[92] Many administrators also complained that the prisoners were using the information from exchange columns and other penal press magazines to lobby for local improvements – a process one warden referred to as "thresh-rising."[93]

In most cases, however, it appears to have been impossible for the prisoners to sneak forbidden content into columns, features, and articles. They protested censorship so vigorously because it was so frustratingly effective in shutting down criticism and debate. They did, however, want their readers to be aware that they were being censored. In addition to writing editorials that claimed that the next editor needed "either a lighter pen or a more subtle one,"[94] they drew attention to the degree of censorship by typing over pages of text and inserting a header above stating, "Sorry folks, you won't be able to read these two pages. We got ahead of ourselves and ran off a story that shouldn't have gone."[95] More dramatically, they published pages that looked like the ones in Images 6.2 and 6.3.[96]

Overall, the picture that emerges from the 1957 warden's conference is one of prisoners using the penal press as a means to organize and to communicate their interests – in short, it was a mechanism of resistance. In some ways, the press, and the inmate committees that emerged during the 1950s, were functioning as quasi-unions and facilitating collective action among the prison population. Wardens did not appreciate this. As Warden Hall (Saskatchewan Penitentiary) told the 1957 warden's conference: "I find the Penal Press one of the biggest headaches we have to deal with."[97] Those present at the meeting suggested several options to regain control: cutting off prisoners' access to other penal press magazines; cancelling all outside subscriptions; drafting a single, uniform policy for all institutions; hiring a central censor to vet all magazines from Ottawa; and discontinuing the penal press entirely.[98] Both Deputy Commissioner March and Commissioner Gibson spoke against this final option. As Gibson put it, the magazines had "received a lot of publicity from outside and if we accepted to discontinue them, I think we would be subjected to a good deal of ----------."[99] In the end, the commissioner cut off the discussion, and the wardens received no instructions on how to proceed.[100]

It is not clear how strictly the penal press was censored at each institution in the years that followed, but it is clear that censorship took a toll on the press. In the aftermath of the *Transition* controversy, Warden Douglass pledged that a "rigid censorship [would] be maintained" at BC Penitentiary.[101] Writers at his institution wrote that "tight censorship breeds cynicism and insincerity, emotions antithetic to good writing."[102] By the later part of the decade, prisoners were beginning to despair over the deteriorating quality of the press. In the February 1958 edition of *Tele-scope*, the editors wrote:

Once Over Lightly

By John Bruce Haddon

There's a nasty rumour making the rounds. I don't know who started it; but, a little birdie, (a jailbirdie that is), told me that one day last month a dutiful guard opened the front gate in response to a loud, persistant rapping to be greeted by a man who demanded immediate admittance to this crazy refuge of ours.

Now, wasn't that nice of this gentleman. And I suppose he was a gentleman, or at least a respectable citizen because no self-respecting crook would venture an action so foolish.

The guard was nearly nonplussed by this gentleman's request, but retained sufficient presence of mind to realize that in order to gain admittance to our cozy, little nest, one must first have committed a crime. It appeared that the only crime committed by this fellow was to have survived his birth, which did not qualify him. Conse-

| CENSORED |

This incurred that wrath of the

gentleman who, flinging his arms about like wobbly helicopter blades, berated our officer with a heated argument about citizenship, his civil rights, being a taxpayer and so on. And he was only partly convinced when the guard explained that there were ways to obtain admittance here legally, (or illegally if you prefer), but to rap on the front door and request it was not one of them. Such a request would get one into an insane asylum in a hurry, he was told, but not here.

| CENSORED |

But there's no doubt this citizen was driven by compulsion matured by the same misconception that is harboured by many people who have drawn impulsive conclusions about our well being from the pages of Transition. We may intimate that the walls and iron bars which surround us were purposely designed to keep people out. On reflection, though, we find there are 700 scallawags in here willing to testify that the opposite is true.

Image 6.2. Example of censored page from *Transition*. December 1953. Gaucher/Munn penal press collection.

Image 6.3. Example of completely censored page from *Transition*. February 1957. Gaucher/Munn penal press collection.

The Canadian Penal Press is seven years old. During that time it attained a technique and polish which was almost professional, but what has happened to it? Three of Canada's six penitentiary magazines have deteriorated into bi-monthlys and one into quarterly. The contents of the December issues were conspicuously skimpy, obviously padded, and bread-and-milkish in tone. Why?

Is it censorship?.... Is it *indifference* and indolence born of restrictions, frustrations, criticisms and prison politics? Is that the reason?

Can it be inability? Canadian prison writers have sometimes been panned for their efforts but they have also been praised for their growing interest in penological and sociological problems. And much of their work has been reprinted by the free world newspapers beyond the wall.

It would be interesting to know what the reason is. It is true that the quality of a prison magazine usually reflects the stature of the writers in that prison at that time, and individual writers come and go, but, in a population as large as Canada's penitentiaries, they should remain consistent as a group. Canadian prison magazines should never sacrifice quality to convenience ... Will the Canadian Penal Press regain the virility it achieved a few years ago? Where is the meat of yesterday?[103]

According to criminologist Bob Gaucher, the answer to those questions was no. In the coming years, prisoners lost faith in penal reform programs, and penal publications were hamstrung by prisoners' "demand that their magazines more stridently air prisoners' grievances ... in a period when censorship was heavy."[104] These conflicting pressures led to a constant turnover of editorial staff and irregular publication. By the mid-1960s, the majority of the original magazines had ceased operation.[105] The most obvious marker of the New Deal was becoming invisible.

Conclusion

This year has seen a record number of prisoners escape custody from Federal Penal Institutions, it has also seen a number of uprisings in various Penitentiaries across Canada, [*sic*] these are times when some people hold the old cry: "Lock them all up and throw away the key," "Give them better treatment," "Punish them," all this at the same time yet!

Dorchester Beacon, November–December 1961

This was a difficult and exhilarating book to research and write because it disturbed many of our received traditions. What began as a simple task – to document the emergence and life of the penal press in Canada – quickly became a more complicated one about mid-century prison reform. During the research, the tropes that Melissa had absorbed about penal reform in her years in criminology classrooms began falling apart. Chris kept looking at histories of penal reform in Canada to corroborate what we were seeing in the archival documents and found the literature on the subject quite thin. Our disciplinary training made us want to make sense of the stacks of documents in our possession, but the existing analyses were only partly satisfying or, worse, were being disrupted at the most fundamental level. The strongest of these disruptions related to the existing work about the Archambault Commission, and as a result, much of this book has been about making better sense of the commission's report and the New Deal that followed. The new administrative and prisoner-generated primary sources we had found shook up the long-embedded narrative of reform-as-progress, placed the subjects of reform at the centre, and made them active participants in Canada's penal history. This recast the entire reform project as more tentative and uncertain, and ultimately (perhaps expectedly) as unfulfilled. For Melissa, who during the writing of this text was working with federally sentenced prisoners as a rights activist, it seemed that in the eighty years since the Archambault Commission Report became the blueprint for changing a brutal, oppressive, and dehumanizing carceral regime, little of substance has changed. So we end this book by considering the merit of the position that reform is "all a con."

Talk of Violence, Mismanagement, and Progressive Reform

Reform is a tough thing to be negative about. Stanley Cohen has written that reform is "a word with no negative connotations." In conventional narratives, "all reform is motivated by benevolence, altruism, philanthropy and humanitarianism, and the eventual record of success of reforms must be read as an incremental story of progress."[1] Indeed, in Canadian criminological texts, the Archambault Report has become synonymous with progressive reform. It has been characterized as a unique moment in the Canadian penal system,[2] but this representation is in some ways ahistorical and in other ways inaccurate. As Ted McCoy and others have shown, inquiries into the prison system began barely a decade after Kingston Penitentiary opened.[3] They have continued ever since.

Each of these reports can be cynically summarized as follows: prisons are violent and fail to reform prisoners; poor organization and mismanagement are to blame (and a prominent scapegoat is often identified by name); humanitarian reform is needed.[4] The Brown Commission Report of 1849 was a scathing indictment of the conditions of confinement: prisoners were being "tortured"; they were subjected to "absolute starvation" and other forms of brutality; and Warden Henry Smith should be dismissed, guilty as he was of "neglect of his duties – incapacity – mismanagement – cruelty – falsehood – peculation." The same report recommended a new emphasis on "moral, religious, and secular instruction" to secure the reformation of prisoners.[5] This would be a recurring theme. In 1913, the Macdonnell Commission was appointed to investigate Kingston Penitentiary and found conditions to be humiliating, "cruel and inhuman."[6] The commissioners condemned the penitentiary's administration[7] and suggested reforms that might "conduce to the permanent reformation of the convicts" and reduce the suffering of prisoners.[8] Among other recommendations, it called for the creation of a three-member penitentiary commission and the implementation of both a prisoner classification system and state-supervised parole.[9] A mere seven years later, the Biggar, Nickle, and Draper Committee was appointed to advise the minister of justice on revisions to the penitentiary regulations and the Penitentiaries Act. The committee members described the penitentiary system as "needlessly cruel," adding that "beyond food and clothing the convict is without rights and the conduct prescribed for him is that of an automaton; he is prohibited from feeling, or at least from exhibiting, any human emotion."[10] They contended that overseeing the prison system was too much responsibility for one person and recommended that a Penitentiary Board be created to permit the involvement of various medical and psychiatric experts.[11] In addition to echoing many of Macdonnell's recommendations, they called for more permissive visitation and correspondence rules, access to "ordinary newspapers" for prisoners, and a graduated pay-scale for convict labour.[12] In the light of these precursors, the Archambault Commission appears less unique and in many aspects less progressive. In fact, the earlier investigations often recommended more radical reforms. For example, the Biggar, Nickle, and Draper Committee called for an end to the silent system, whereas the Archambault commissioners objected to the tone of prisoner conversations and recommended permitting conversation among prisoners outdoors only.[13] So the Archambault Commission was not unique in terms of its mandate, findings, or recommendations.

A Story of Uneven Progress

Setting aside the repetitive nature of these investigations and reports, the administrative record shows that Archambault was in fact an impetus for reform. The historical analyses derived from these documents tell a story that Stanley Cohen has categorized as one of "Uneven Progress."[14] In such accounts, "the system is capable of being humanized by good intentions and made more efficient by the application of scientific principles."[15] Before Archambault, prisoners entered a penal system imperfectly organized around silence and hard labour (see chapter 2). After Archambault, a convict's daily life was changed in meaningful, appreciable ways. Wardens and prisoners viewed the Archambault Report with optimism. So did politicians, the press, and the public, all of whom urged immediate action. And, as the records show, they got it. A prisoner in the 1950s could converse openly without fear of punishment, and *some* might qualify for educational or vocational training. A new system of payment for convict labour was implemented, and prisoners could purchase previously unobtainable items at the prison canteen or save for their eventual release. By the end of the decade, a new system of parole had been instituted, intended to inspire reformation and shorten prisoners' time behind bars (see chapter 5). In addition, administrators introduced initiatives to break the well-documented monotony of prison life. Prisoners could play baseball, hockey, and table games in the hallways; they could engage in hobbycraft in their cells; and they enjoyed increased access to musical instruments, concerts, and movies (see chapter 4). Also, communication between prisoners and the outside world increased. The penal press offered prisoners a new mechanism to discuss reforms in a constructive manner and to make the public aware of daily life in prison. Likewise, radio shows, "inside" entertainment by "outside" performers, and sporting competitions involving local and professional athletes collectively acted to bridge the divide between prison and community. Moreover, these activities served as a kind of relief mechanism to prevent future riots.

In the story as told from this perspective, the reformative ideals will, given time, be achieved, and the limits of the transformation and the unexpected disturbances of the 1950s are rather meaningless – mere bumps in the road of progress. Yet this accounting requires *only* bureaucratic narratives as source material. These are documents in which the authors are compelled to show that they are taking action, that progress is being made, and that they are responsible for continuous improvements. Moreover, to focus on these records alone is to encourage "an implicit identification between the analyst and the historical reformers being analysed."[16] In the absence of contradictory accounts, when we read the documents produced by Commissioner Gibson, Joseph McCulley, or R.E. March, we begin, unselfconsciously, to adopt their point of view. But this is dangerous. The administrative record is a filtered and audience-aware auto-history[17] of the planners' objectives, complete with their account of the outcomes. Without a doubt, the exclusive use of these documents has produced a shallow, biased, and incomplete history. And this history has been reproduced to the point of becoming reified as Truth. When we add documents generated from different perspectives, the administrative trope is disrupted, which points to the importance of methodology.

Disrupting Methodology: On the Importance of Mutivocality/History from Below

The penal press offers a crucial source of evidence: one that includes prisoners' voices and, in doing so, repopulates history and augments and complicates the administrative and public accounts of prisons. In the introduction, we quoted Appleby, Hunt, and Jacob's dictum that "telling the truth takes a collective effort."[18] From the outset of this project, we have committed ourselves to writing an inclusionary social history, one that incorporates "history from below." Why did we choose this approach? To ignore the history of subaltern and regulated groups is to argue that only the history and actions of the ruling elite matter and hold meaning and that subordinated groups are merely the recipients of action. Social history has taught us that we cannot understand societies, communities, and institutions simply by studying elites: the actions of entire populations matter. Ordinary people – including prisoners – have agency and exert a collective influence. They drive change, and they understand and experience life differently. Yet in the histories of institutions of confinement, the voices of the captive inmates are barely audible.[19] In most cases, their silence reflects the record, in that they have left no significant documentary trace. Historians have nothing to work with.[20] However, the observations of subordinated groups are also often discounted. As Michel Foucault has argued, subaltern knowledges are often "disqualified as inadequate to their task or insufficiently elaborated: naïve knowledges, located low down on the hierarchy, beneath the required level of cognition or scientificity."[21] In this book, we have used the penal press as a major source, thus allowing the subjects of regulation to offer their own accounts, which we have made central rather than peripheral to the analysis.

In the penal press, prisoners reveal the presence or absence of reform and its importance as well. They provide nuance. As we saw in previous chapters, because they were writing to please different audiences than the administrators (both the "inside" prisoner population and "outside" subscribers), prisoners painted a different picture. Even while constrained by penal policies regarding what was suitable for publication, prison editors strove to avoid producing "house organs" and to write more critically about administrative goals and actions. Freed from the demands faced by their keepers and politicians, but not from censorship, they could both celebrate achievements in penal reform and offer constructive (or sarcastic and scurrilous!) criticisms of its implementation. In short, prisoners could document the limits of reform as well as the continuities in the conditions of their confinement. In so doing, they showed how they were attempting to accommodate, influence, and resist the reforms. This project does not simply write a *more comprehensive* history of Canada's prisons; using the penal press, it tells a fundamentally *different* story of the prison system.

Disrupting the Idea That Change Comes from the Top

Our research indicates that prisoners were more than passive recipients of change. The Biggar, Nickle, and Draper Commission had been established in the wake of disturbances staged by prisoners.

Likewise, as we saw in chapter 2, the 1932 riot at Kingston Penitentiary, and the resulting public outcry, led the newly elected Liberal
government to appoint the Archambault Commission in 1936. In
both cases, prisoners had drawn the attention of elected officials.
Prisoners initiated change. They also sustained it. The penal press
has allowed us to write a history that demonstrates that prisoners
acted in constitutive ways, influencing the shape and outcome of the
policies imposed upon them.

A cogent example of prisoners' influence is the creation of the penal
press. An administrative history of the penal press might emphasize
the role of Joseph McCulley, but a social-historical approach would
draw attention to the suggestions of prisoner-editor Gord Marr,
whose input informed the direction and character of the penal press.
His early memo on the purpose of the press was co-opted almost
verbatim by the commissioner in his statement of the aims of that
press.[22] Indeed, prisoner participation was crucial. The administration might have set the parameters (regarding finances and content,
for example), but the penal press was largely organized, operated,
and expanded by prisoners. Similarly, many other reform-era activities, including sports, entertainment, and hobbycraft, were organized and financed by elected inmate committees. It seems fair to
say that the New Deal reforms could only succeed to the extent that
the prisoners supported them.

Prisoners also resisted, and this was instructive in two ways.
On the one hand, as we saw in previous chapters, their resistance
reveals their impact on conditions; on the other, prisoners' resistance made relations of power more visible. It is easy to see the exercise of sovereign and disciplinary power, but the prisoner narrative
shows that they are not fully disempowered within the penal apparatus. Convicts forced administrators to respond, and in so doing,
to reveal their values, ideals, and objectives. Again, the penal press
provides salient examples. Prisoners forced administrators to censor
their magazines, and this revealed cracks in the underpinnings of
the New Deal. On some occasions, entire editorial boards resigned,
refusing to compromise or be co-opted. At other times, prisoners
circumvented the Penitentiary Service hierarchy to appeal directly
to the commissioner. In their resistance, they triggered conversations among administrators, which led to new policies. By defy-
ing the authorities and pushing up against often invisible bound-
aries, convicts revealed to both the incarcerated and their keepers
the parameters of free speech and the limits of the "prisoners are
people" mantra.

Disrupting the Idea That "We Blew It"

Furthermore, the prisoners' voices demonstrate that the New Deal was as much a tale of stagnation as of progress. Their accounts produce a story similar to the "Good (but Complicated) intentions – Disastrous Consequences" narrative described by Cohen.[23] According to that story, the consequences of prison reform were other than intended: these "closed institutions hardly changed and were certainly not humanized; the programmes became supplements, not alternatives, thus expanding the scope and reach of the system; discretion actually became more arbitrary; individual treatment was barely attempted, let alone successful."[24] Outside criticism of the system had no effect. As Cohen explains, "the institutions were kept going because of their functionalism and the enduring power of the rhetoric of benevolence."[25] Cohen dubs this the "*we* blew it" narrative.[26] In this interpretation, bureaucratic and administrative interests complicated the reform process and made a simple progressive narrative problematic. As Stanley Cohen explains, "when reforms reach the existing system, they confront a series of powerful managerial, administrative and organizational imperatives. The reform impulse is resisted and blocked or (more frequently) it is welcomed, only to be absorbed and co-opted (for the wrong reasons) and in the process completely transformed, even in directions diametrically opposed to the original vision."[27]

Another – and perhaps more instructive – variant of the "*we* blew it" interpretation was advanced by Thomas Mathiesen in 1987. This model might be termed "we'll always blow it." Mathiesen emphasized the inherent contradictions between the rehabilitative impulse and the carceral apparatus. He pointed out that for more than four hundred years, the four "core components" of rehabilitation programs – work, schooling, moral treatment, and discipline – had remained remarkably consistent. Throughout the modern history of prisons, convicts have been subjected to a "duty to work" ethos, indoctrination through education, religious and secular remoralization programs and treatments, and the application of prison regimens that include punishments for infractions. Reformers periodically devise new mechanisms to better achieve these objectives but inevitably encounter the same two obstacles – the fiscal and security requirements of the prison system. Mathiesen argued that administrators and workers within the system counter reforms by "defining ideas as irrelevant, defining them as impossible to implement, postponing ideas, puncturing ideas (feigning interest while the practical significance of the new idea is diminished), and absorbing ideas (accepting them nominally, while altering the principle to fit the existing system)."[28] Whenever rehabilitation programs and the operational requirements of prisons come into conflict, the latter are prioritized. As a consequence, reforms always fail.[29] In reflecting on his time inside, Frank Anderson concluded: "Penitentiaries do not change, they adjust to absorb, neutralize and sanitize the interference of the ego-mad prison reformers who periodically surface in both society and parliament."[30]

In examining the history of the New Deal, we could use these variants of the "*we* blew it" model. The Archambault commissioners proposed their reforms as a comprehensive package (reorganization of the penal administration; classification and segregation; reformative and treatment services; specific recommendations for improvements within individual penitentiaries; the centralization of prisons under a single administration; special institutions for young offenders; juvenile court reform; and ticket-of-leave/parole), the parts of which were interdependent. But complications emerged as a result of jurisdictional issues. Commissioner Gibson could not unilaterally act on all of Archambault's eight major groups of recommendations because four fell under the purview of other levels of government or under shared authority.[31] Also, there is considerable evidence that administrators prioritized particular reforms, neglected others, and added their own initiatives. We know, for example, that the policy changes related to correspondence and visitation regulations were largely ignored by the Penitentiary Service. Two core elements of the rehabilitation program – education and vocational training – were available to only a limited number of prisoners (and as previously noted, prison trade credentials were often not recognized in the field, which further stigmatized the holder). It may be that the neglect of these priorities was a result of overcrowding, but that aside, in the absence of a comprehensive slate of initiatives, Canada's prisons remained, for the most part, "mere custodial institutions."[32]

Other elements of the New Deal were, as the "*we* blew it/we'll always blow it" models suggest, discarded or completely transformed.[33] For example, the classification system envisioned by Archambault was intended to provide individualized treatment programs tailored to prisoners' characteristics and rehabilitative needs. However, the classification system as implemented in the 1950s focused more on creating groups that could be managed in ways that would serve the control and financial interests of the institution. Classification procedures were often used to group prisoners into aggregates ineligible for training opportunities, educational programs, and parole. Rather than being about serving the needs of the individual, classification was about slotting them into statistical groups. In effect, the rehabilitative ideals behind classification had been absorbed into the system to enhance control and security.[34] As we saw in chapter 4, the classification system contributed to an expansionist dynamic: new professionals were hired to serve as classification officers, and new institutions were built and designated to house specific prisoner groups. The penal press suffered a similar fate. The press was originally devised to boost morale among prisoners, improve communication between convicts and the administration, and serve as a vehicle for constructive criticism – and therein, continual improvement of the penitentiaries. Within a decade of its inception, however, control of the press, in terms of tone, content, and influence over public opinion, became the principal concern of wardens and the Commissioner's Office.

The sentiment that "we'll always blow it" is confirmed by our research. Additionally, we add new contours to Mathiesen's ideas around the reform project. First, in the particular historical context of mid-twentieth-century Canada, moral re-education took on new dimensions not envisioned by Mathiesen. Administrators focused on the formation of democratic personalities and the creation of good citizens. There is no more poignant example of this aim than the introduction of both the free and penal press to the prisons. As Benedict Anderson has noted, newspapers are crucial to creating a sense of attachment between individuals and nations.[35] Second, we emphasize the particular importance of public relations. While Mathiesen did not incorporate public relations as a system requirement, he did emphasize that "the system interests ... are defined, formulated and communicated to the prison *from the outside*," and that it is necessary to legitimize the prison in the public political sphere by demonstrating its rehabilitative efficacy.[36] The public and governmental demand for prison reform after the riots of the 1930s left administrators with a heightened awareness of the importance of public support to both their own tenure and the continuation of their reform program. They carefully crafted a public image and took actions to maintain that image, actions that sometimes increased and sometimes limited the impact of reform.

Disrupting the "Con"

Mathiesen's model predicted the ongoing failure of penal reform, and that is exactly where we found ourselves five years after we stood in the college corridor talking about the penal press. Our manuscript was almost complete. We had written about the New Deal, the advent of the parole system, the frustrations that led prisoners to revolt, and the studies of the carceral conducted by government. We had looked at penal reforms between 1935 and 1960 and made arguments about continuity and change. But now we stood in another corridor – actually at the confluence of several corridors and cell blocks – and wondered what it all meant. Melissa had just finished delivering a workshop to prisoners at Millhaven Institution – a maximum security penitentiary opened in 1971 with the stated purpose of replacing Kingston Penitentiary, although the latter did not actually close until 2013. Chris looked down a cell block range and could envision a convict pacing back and forth in his cell as Al Parsons had described in 1954. Guards, now called correctional officers, focused on security, never inquiring as to our purpose in the "joint" that day but ensuring we had no contraband on our persons. At times they were visible; at times they remained behind smoke-tinted glass reminiscent of Bentham's panopticon. Prisoners were expressing their frustration over the pay system. Their wages had recently been reduced, which meant they were labouring in the prison for less than they had the year before. Convict after convict detailed the arbitrary nature of who got parole and struggled to figure out if he would have better success in another province. All of them lamented the lack of trades training, and the librarian confirmed that only a few could take correspondence courses at the same time; any more, and her job would be unmanageable. So, how far had we come since the New Deal was introduced?

The Office of the Correctional Investigator (OCI) tells us that overcrowding still plagues Canada's prisons despite there now being fifty-eight federal prisons across the country. In his eleven years as Correctional Investigator, Howard Sapers witnessed exponential growth in the prison population, and in his final report he noted that "prison crowding hit all-time highs" as a result of legislative and policy changes. He expected that prisoner resistance would increase: "I have every expectation that the number of legal challenges will grow as offenders seek judicial relief from conditions of detention and policy reforms that are felt to be unlawful or unjust."[37]

Visitation remains a central concern. Ivan Zinger, the newly appointed Correctional Investigator, has indicated that "visitors are not always treated with courtesy and respect by staff. Family members and friends often experience long delays in entering CSC facilities. It can take weeks or months to be approved for prison visits. Visitors often report feeling highly anxious, stressed and even stigmatized by invasive security checks and measures conducted at the front entrance."[38] Just as the Archambault commissioners had eighty years earlier, he considers the implications of this and notes that "a missed or cancelled visit can have a significant impact on the emotional and psychological well-being [of] incarcerated individuals."[39]

The penal press in Canada is almost non-existent today. *Out of Bounds Magazine* is the only regular publication in the federal prison system, though prisoners periodically introduce new publications, which receive little to no support from the administration or from other prisoners. Thus, one of the main direct (even if censored) avenues for constructive criticism by prisoners has all but disappeared. Even the academically oriented *Journal of Prisoners on Prisons* is periodically banned by prison administrators based on allegations that it jeopardizes the security of their prisons.

Prisoners still look for ways to resist. Zinger's 2017 report on conditions of confinement described the riot that occurred that year in Saskatchewan Penitentiary and concluded: "Prison riots are not random or inevitable events; they are most likely to occur when a certain threshold of defiance and desperation is reached among a group of prisoners who take matters into their own hands to violently force change or express a long-standing grievance."[40] Shortly afterwards, in 2018, the incoming commissioner of Correctional Service Canada was given a mandate letter from the government requiring her to adopt a reform agenda. This chain of events is reminiscent of the era studied in this book. Remember that Oswald Withrow also drew a direct link between prison riots and dehumanizing conditions of confinement and used his articles in the *Globe* (and in his subsequent book) to press the government to reform the prison system. As in the 1930s, the recent riot at Saskatchewan Penitentiary appears to have motivated the Liberal government to give the public a sense that actions are being taken. Minister of Public Safety and Emergency Preparedness Ralph Goodale, in appointing the incoming commissioner of Correctional Service Canada, Anne Kelly, urged her to "regularly [review] policies and operations to identify what works and change what does not ... seeking out innovative ideas and approaches, informed by CSC's own experiences and those of other jurisdictions in Canada and around the world." This approach reminds us of the one employed by the Archambault commissioners, who "investigate[d] the operations of Canadian penitentiaries ... [and made] a thorough study of the problems ... To carry out this latter task it was necessary for the Commission to visit all the Canadian provinces, and other countries, in order to study their penal systems and discuss various problems with their prison officials and penologists."[41] Almost twenty years later, Commissioner Ralph Gibson called on corrections officials from around the world "to scrutinize our own procedures, and to give such assistance and advice as may be helpful in combatting these unfortunate outbreaks [in other countries] which can do much harm to the cause of penal progress."[42] In implementing the Archambault recommendations,

Gibson was committing himself to the ideal of modern penology and to using evidence-based initiatives, progressive educational methods, and the new developments in the psychiatric field to drive his reforms. Similarly, Goodale has directed Kelly to "facilitat[e] the work of independent researchers within CSC; and welcom[e] constructive, good-faith critiques as indispensable drivers of progress." It appears that the ideology of improvement has remained constant. Moreover, the practical points of intervention mirror those of the New Deal era. Goodale's instructions call on Kelly to "fully and transparently" investigate "use-of-force incidents"; address prisoners' "issues related to physical health, mental health and addiction"; improve nutrition; "continue to reduce the use of segregation [solitary confinement] generally"; expand educational and employment opportunities; and "leverage community partnerships to connect people preparing for release."[43] In this letter, we hear echoes of the Macdonnell, Biggar, Nickle, and Draper, Archambault, and Fauteux reports.

Why are we here again? One explanation, captured beautifully in Stanley Cohen's vernacular, is that "it's all a con": the real intentions of the penal system are being masked. To the proponents of this view – including Michel Foucault, Nils Christie, J. Thorsten Sellin, George Rushche, and Otto Kirchheimer[44] – the purpose of penal reform is not to create a kinder, gentler prison. The prison exists to serve "the requirements of the emerging capitalist order."[45] It reproduces the hierarchy of capitalism: it "renders docile the recalcitrant members of the working class, it deters others, it teaches habits of discipline and order."[46] The point is remoralization: "to create a socially safe proletarian ... who has learnt to accept being propertyless."[47] It also succeeds, as Jeffery Reiman and Paul Leighton suggest, in "creat[ing] the image that crime is almost exclusively the work of the poor, an image that serves the interests of the powerful."[48] As such, to focus on whether reforms have succeeded or failed is misguided.[49] The real objective is rooted in the political economy and is often invisible to the reformers themselves. Reformation cannot fail, for it is merely an ideological justification that "conceal[s] the real interests and motives behind the system." The reform "ideology is important then, only insofar as it succeeds at passing off as fair, natural, acceptable or even just and humane, a system which is basically coercive."[50]

How would we emplot our evidence into this narrative, according to which the prison system is designed to reproduce the disciplinary relations of factories and create docile workers? First, despite the reforms of the New Deal, prisoners made it clear in their writing that discipline, regimentation, and confinement continued – sovereign power, as conceptualized by Michel Foucault, remained. The prisons exercised control over convicts' bodies. Convicts spent long hours caged in their cells. As prisoner John Muise made clear, his movements – to and from the kitchen with his tray, to work, and to organized events – were carefully controlled and regimented. Muise's life unfolded according to the dictates of clock time; the prison replicated factory discipline and conditioned its inmates to obedience. Seen this way, we also understand the sports program differently; clearly, it imposed self-discipline and self-regulation.[51] In organized sports, an attempt was made to force prisoners to follow rules, perform roles as members of teams, and participate in organizing activities in cooperation with administrators.[52] As we saw in chapter 4, Commissioner Gibson viewed this development positively,[53] arguing that through their work on inmate committees, prisoners were being responsibilized for their own discipline and made sympathetic to those in power. The prisons during the New Deal also exercised control over prisoners' minds: their correspondence was surveilled and censored, and their writing in the penal press faced similar scrutiny. Indeed, the crucial point for Deputy Commissioner Ralph March during the *Transition* controversy was that prisoners must not criticize law enforcement and penal authorities. They must accept the hierarchy.

Finally, many elements of the New Deal were focused on training prisoners to be competent and, as importantly, willing workers. At one level, prison labour, vocational training, and hobbycraft were meant to promote skills acquisition. At another, these activities were meant to impart a particular work ethos. The Archambault Commission quoted the late chairman of the British Prison Commission, Mr A. Maxwell, with approval: "The spirit in which work is regarded both by the prison officer and by the prisoner is more important than the nature of the work." Maxwell continued: "However laborious or disagreeable a task may be, if the worker feels that he has been set to do it because its accomplishment serves a useful purpose and performs it in a spirit of stoicism or service, he will profit from the experience."[54] While we have no evidence that this transformation occurred, we do know that the prisons benefited by using prisoner labour for operational purposes and to produce items for state use. Nonetheless, the administration was committed to the presentation of work as a moral imperative, so much so that by 1948, vocational instructors had begun to keep records not only of prisoners' performance at their trades but also of their "conduct and ... employment attitude."[55] Soon afterwards, a graduated pay scale was introduced that replicated the pay structure (though certainly not the paycheques) of the wage labour economy, thus incentivizing compliance with prison industrial programs.

Since the official emphasis was on docility, political resistance by prisoners was met with harsh punishment. For their part in the 1932 riot at Kingston Penitentiary, prisoners paid a heavy price. Sam Behan died in a punishment cell, and Tim Buck had nine months added to his sentence.[56] Twenty-two others were flogged. Following the 1954 riot at Kingston Penitentiary, one prisoner spent at least seven months in solitary confinement. His peers were not flogged, but as Chad Marr has noted, the incidence of electroshock treatment increased dramatically in the months that followed. During the New Deal era, solitary confinement and corporal punishment did not disappear. Rather, their form was changed, and both were recast in medicalized terms as a form of "treatment."

Seen this way, the system is actually doing what it is intended to do. Liberal-capitalist states build prisons to uphold a particular and unequal legal order, based on the protection of life, individual liberty, and property. Prisons are created to discipline and punish those who offend against this legal regime. As our evidence shows, reform is a prisoners' demand, shared by humanitarians but not essential to the system. When John Howard demanded that the prisons of England be reformed, England was already imprisoning people. The rationale always comes later. In Amsterdam, as Mathiesen explained, beggars and vagrants were first rounded up because they posed a threat to the emerging mercantilist order. It was only afterwards that the decision was made that they ought to be put to work, educated, and morally resocialized.[57] Reform is the veneer applied to mask the real intentions of the penal system. The acts of studying the problems and attempting to implement change are perceived as evidence of good intentions, though they merely serve to legitimate the extant system. As long as reformative efforts are being made, the exploitative underpinnings of the prison-industrial complex need not be changed, because the humanitarian impulse is satisfied.

This is not to say that reforms have no impact. The New Deal ultimately came to an end, but it left behind residual social deposits and deposits of power – ways of understanding and modes of governance – in a prison system that was different than it had been before.[58] Through their words, we see that prisoners did benefit from the reforms in meaningful and sustained ways. More than sixty years after his release from prison, André Dion recalled the importance of the gains made during the early 1950s. He remembered the visceral impact of the prison and the moments when he felt treated like a person instead of a number. He, like other prison writers, also elaborated on his frustration over the unexpected implications of the changes and the slow pace of reform.

Dion's carceral experience had an enduring impact; as Bob Gaucher points out, "despite his post-imprisonment accomplishments and public celebration of those accomplishments, his focus at the end of his life was to understand and deal with what had happened to him as a young man [in prison]."[59] In the same vein, in his last years, noted historian Peter Brock compiled an anthology of writing by imprisoned conscientious objectors in an effort to understand his own experience of imprisonment during the Second World War.[60]

Disrupting Singular Narratives

Ultimately, the story of penal reform between 1935 and 1960 cannot be written in the singular. As the quotation that opened this chapter demonstrates, there are multiple stories. The narratives of "uneven progress," "*we* blew it/we'll always blow it," and "it's all a con" should not be understood as mutually exclusive. Again we turn to Cohen, who argued that they should not be seen as

> competing abstract explanations, nor as different schools of thought to be contemplated and then purchased in the academic supermarket. Each of these systems of thought is connected with a corresponding system of power. That is to say, the stuff of which the theory speaks, represents certain real social "deposits." The metaphor of a deposit ... conveys a dual meaning: it is something which is *left behind* and something which is *drawn upon*. At each level – ideas, organizations, professionals and political economy – these deposits take the form of descriptions (stories) and causal theories, which are drawn upon and leave behind real forms of power. While the deposits appear to be contradictory, they, in fact, rely on each other ... Each can be emphasized for different purposes, and all might be needed for something like a complete explanation.[61]

These stories, told together and through a multiplicity of voices, offer a stronger analytic of the textures and folds of these historical events. It is important to hear those voices in terms of both the evidence and the analyses they offer. The story would be incomplete without each set of sources. The narrative would also be incomplete without each level of analysis.

This project started as an investigation of the penal press, but it evolved into an effort to challenge the dominant discourse on the Archambault Report and early- to mid-twentieth-century prison reform in general. As we read the prisoners' narratives, the established criminological tropes about that report and the subsequent penal reforms began to seem inadequate and misleading. We know that historical representations are "essentially provisional and contingent [in] nature" and are susceptible "to infinite revision in light of new evidence or more sophisticated conceptualization of problems."[62] We know too that we are guilty of merely following established tropes – of organizing the data along the lines of established story arcs. We told a story of progress. We told a story of unachieved ambition. We told a story of the nefarious imposition of power. These are stories we knew and liked and into which it was easy to inject the evidence. The stories were easily populated by the data at hand.

But the goal of this book had never been to tell *the* definitive story. The aim has always been to render visible subjugated knowledges, to emancipate voices from their historical silence, to listen differently to the extant stories, and to include both the powerholders and the oppressed in an analysis that changes our understanding of prison reform. This book has brought together disparate voices, including those of prisoners (e.g., Andre Dion, Sam Behan, Oswald Withrow, Gord Marr, James P. Carleton, Frank Anderson, and Vic Ashton), of mainstream media figures (Harry Anderson, Sidney Katz, and Andy O'Brien), of politicians (Agnes Macphail and Stuart Garson), of government-appointed investigators (Joseph Archambault and Gerald Fauteux), of administrators (Joseph McCulley and Ralph Gibson), and of those who blurred the lines separating prisoner from politician, including Frank Howard, Tim Buck, and Sam Carr.

Because of *all* of their stories, we now see this history differently.

Appendix A

Excerpts from Commissioner's Annual Reports Detailing Psychiatric Services, 1947–1957

Table 4.1. Excerpts on psychiatric services from the commissioner's annual reports, 1947–57 (emphasis added)

1947–48

132. While consideration has already been given to the development of psychological and psychiatric services, it is planned to **develop such services still further** for it is recognized that **successful reformation and rehabilitation depend upon a thorough study of the causative factors in personality maladjustment** followed by an attempt at re-education of the person and elimination of the still existing causative factors. A limitation in the development of this programme is the scarcity of experienced and competent personnel. Many interviews with convicts considered in need of psychiatric advice and treatment have been carried out by the Deputy Commissioner in the course of his -visits to the penitentiaries. The services of outside psychiatrists are also utilized in some cases where examination and diagnosis appear necessary. In the Officers' Training Courses series of thirty lectures is given by Deputy Commisioner Gendreau on the development of **Normal Human Behaviour, Causative Factors in Aberrant Human Behaviour, Maladjustment leading to Crime, Methods of Re-educating and process of Rehabilitation**. These lectures are considered as basic and fundamental to the process of orientation and education of the Penitentiary Officers towards the goal of reform and rehabilitation for the prisoner. During the period in question visits were made to-the Medical Center for Federal Prisoners at Springfield, Mo., and the Drug Addiction Treatment Centre at Lexington, Ky., operated by the United States Bureau of Prisons and much valuable information obtained as to the methods of treatment employed at these institutions.

1948–49

183. At Kingston Penitentiary the opening of a small Psychiatric Hospital with facilities **for electric shock treatment and occupational therapy** has provided facilities for treatment of pre-psychotic cases and has resulted in the correction of a number of cases of maladjustment which might otherwise have developed into more serious mental illness.

184. The arrangements with the various Provincial authorities for the admission of mentally ill convicts to Provincial Mental Institutions have continued on a satisfactory basis, a total of 46 cases having been transferred during the year. Sixteen cases of pulmonary tuberculosis were transferred to Provincial Sanitoria for care and treatment under temporary Ticket of Leave.

(Continued)

(Continued)

---

185. In addition to the psychiatric examinations carried out by Deputy Commissioner Gendreau during his visits to the penitentiary, examinations by outside psychiatrists were authorized upon request of the Penitentiary Physicians whenever symptoms indicative of mental illness became evident. The counselling carried on by the Classification Officers in cases of maladjustment has had a **beneficial effect** in many cases where psychotherapeutic treatment was indicated.

1949–50

187. The psychiatric ward at Kingston Penitentiary has provided facilities for the treatment of the psychoneurotic and the pre-psychotic. **Electroshock treatment and psychotherapy have shown themselves to be of definite value in the treatment of such convicts**. Further mental deterioration has been prevented and conflictual situations have been resolved without further difficulties. During the year there were 30 admissions to the psychiatric ward for the purpose of observation and required treatment. Seventy-five shock treatments were administered under the direction of the part-time psychiatrist who also had 239 interviews with convicts who were in need of psychiatric help and advice. The **occupational therapy** department of the psychiatric ward began its operation in July, 1949. Its chief purpose is to do away with enforced idleness and also to provide some orientation towards constructive work habits which help towards eventual rehabilitation. Various patients are engaged in shellcraft, leathercraft and the making up of rugs, mats and baskets. The provincial authorities have accepted for treatment those who develop more serious forms of mental illness and require intensive treatment. Thirty-five convicts were transferred during the year to their respective provincial mental institutions to receive the required care and treatment. Two convicts suffering from pulmonary tuberculosis were transferred to provincial sanatoria for care and treatment under temporary ticket-of-leave.

1950–51

205. The psychiatric ward at Kingston Penitentiary continues to provide facilities for the care and treatment of the psychoneurotic and the pre-psychotic. The psychiatric hospital has, during the year, been kept very busy. Three hundred and forty-two consultations were held, 24.4 per cent of the population making use of the facilities for remedial treatment. **General therapy, psychotherapy, electro-convulsive therapy, recreational and occupational therapy** are made use of according to indications. **Psychiatric services will be extended to other penitentiaries**. Thirty-three inmates suffering from mental symptoms who were examined by the psychiatrists were certified as insane and subsequently transferred to their respective provincial institutions for treatment.

1951–52

217. These medical activities are planned not merely to deal with illness or injuries as they occur but in the belief that **good mental and physical health are essential to the rehabilitation of the offender**. It is an important part of the rehabilitation process that the individual who is suffering from physical, nervous or mental conditions should receive treatment that will assist him in overcoming physical handicaps and in developing a better insight into his own personality problems.

218. In addition to the established psychiatric ward at Kingston Penitentiary salaried psychiatrists have been employed during the year at British Columbia and Manitoba penitentiaries. **An increasing number of the inmate population take advantage of the opportunities offered by such services; many return for further interviews**.

219. As an innovation in some of the penitentiaries, **group therapy** under the supervision of the Psychiatrist has been started. Its chief purpose is to help inmate's arrive at a clearer understanding of some of their troubles, resolve some of their conflicts and enable them to use personal resources in developing methods of behaviour acceptable to society. A Narcotics Anonymous group has been initiated in one penitentiary under the supervision of the Penitentiary Psychiatrist.
220. The medical and psychiatric services provided by penitentiary staffs are supplemented where necessary by consultative services from the outside including hospital and surgical treatment when such is required. The cost of such services amounted to $26,481.91 for the year, as compared to $28,804.03 for the previous year. The per capita cost was $5.61.

1952–53

228. **The psychiatric services are being developed more and more to meet the needs.** During the year a psychiatrist was added to the staff of Saskatchewan Penitentiary. **Many inmates suffer from emotional disturbances which often have played a major part in their anti-social behaviour**, and it is felt that unless these emotional disturbances can be alleviated through psychiatric or other means, normal functioning in society cannot be fully re-established. **Psychiatric interviews are available for inmates who ask for them and many problem cases are referred to the psychiatrist for advice and counselling.** Penitentiary psychiatrists are making use of psychotherapy through individual interviews, **occupational therapy, group therapy and, where indicated, electronarcosis is being used. A great deal of benefit** has accrued to the inmate in many instances and very real and acute administrative problems have diminished as the result of adoption of such procedures. **The further development of this trend will require an increase in psychiatric service and facilities.**

1953–54

204. **Increasing demands are being made on the available psychiatric services**, both on the part of the inmates and administration, for the purpose of dealing more wisely with what are commonly referred to as problem cases. **Further development of this trend will necessitate the extension of psychiatric services.**
205. The **various therapies** administered have been on the basis of the individual's indicated needs and use is made of the following forms of therapy: **psychotherapeutic interviews, electronarcosis, electroconvulsive, occupational and group, all of which have resulted in considerable benefit.**

1954–55

200. **The psychiatric services have been extending in scope and activity.** One thousand seven hundred and seventy-five interviews were held by the Psychiatrists in the penitentiaries where it has been possible so far to establish such services. The number of interviews indicates that many **inmates are of their own accord seeking a solution to their own conflicts and deviated behaviour. The indications are that more trained personnel and more space will be required to meet this developing trend** which, in the present state of knowledge, offers the greatest hope for the ultimate reformation of the offender. Various forms of therapy are used depending on the individual's specific needs. **General therapy, psychotherapy, electrostimulative, electroconvulsive, monopolar therapies, group therapy, occupational therapy**, all form part of the general treatment programme. Group therapy has been developed more and more. It has shown itself to be of **considerable benefit** to those who attend the sessions and it has resulted in the development of an increasing **degree of insight into the inmate's own condition, has helped to reduce tension, anxiety, and has brought about a re-direction of the inmate's impulses and drives.**

(Continued)

This is one phase of activity which should be explored and developed more as it seems to afford the greatest possibility for mass treatment in the penitentiary. The penitentiary hospitals have also to look after a number of mentally ill inmates awaiting transfer to provincial mental hospitals. There were seventeen such cases as at March 31, 1955.

1955–56

152. The demand for ever increasing services from the Psychiatric Departments has made it imperative that consideration be given to **enlarging the facilities and increasing the personnel presently employed**. Institutional Psychiatrists held 2,316 interviews with inmates. **Group therapy** sessions were held. The number of inmates who participate varies in each penitentiary from 40 to 80. To make the work easier, such large groups must be divided into smaller groups. This has the disadvantage that more personnel is required, as well as space. Urgent requests have been made by all psychiatric departments for more space and because of the beneficial results obtained it is felt that serious consideration must be given to this very important section of the service which **holds a great deal of promise** both from the standpoint of rehabilitation and also to provide the necessary care and treatment to individuals who show symptoms of mental illness. The compilation of statistics in the course of the past few years has shown that the problem created by those with symptoms of mental illness is of greater magnitude than was ordinarily thought to be. From the time of inception of the psychiatric services, accurate and dependable information has been obtained which makes it possible to conclude that the number of inmates who become psychotic to the extent that they are certified as such is in the ratio of 1:50 to 1:60. It has also been evident that those who seek, the advice of the psychiatrist on the subject of their mental condition, their behaviour and their problems occur in the proportion of 1:3 or 1:4. Improvement is possible for many through various forms of therapy. **Individual psychotherapy is too time-consuming. Group therapy must be resorted to**.

153. The above lends further strong support to the idea expressed some twenty years ago by a foremost student of criminal behaviour that **"criminality is without exception symptomatic of abnormal mental states and is an expression of them."** It would also tend to indicate that a certain proportion of penitentiary inmates' criminal behaviour is a by-product of and is concommitant [sic] with the development of mental abnormality, which abnormality in its not too advanced state is often not recognized as such by the victim but only by trained personnel.

154. The psychotic and pre-psychotic obviously require care. **The treatment seeking inmates** must be provided with the assistance they ask for. **Individual psychotherapy, because of the time requirement, cannot meet the situation because there are not enough available trained personnel. Group therapy must be resorted to** and should be supplemented by careful supervision and observation carried on by personnel who have received special training in rehabilitation procedures: **this will require more facilities both as to buildings and personnel**. The need exists in all the penitentiaries and is felt more acutely at the present time in the institutions having the larger populations.

1956–57

185. In order to provide a more thorough understanding of the penitentiary medical services it can be stated that health is broadly conceived and recognized as having physical and mental components to which consideration must be given. Such a concept forms the basis for constructive ideas directed at eventual reformation. Many physical symptoms are the repercussions of mental stress, tension and anxiety. Man's ability to live as a social being within the type of society he has built for himself depends not only upon a relative degree of attainable physical health but on the extent to which he has or not developed healthy mental attitudes and reactions. **The asocial and antisocial type of individuals who are sentenced by the courts to the penal system have failed through unfortunate circumstances and the vicissitudes of their past life to develop mentally as the average person does.** Proper corrective measures can be applied provided sufficiently qualified and trained personnel be obtained for the purpose of examining, assessing and reporting on the findings. **Reformation, which is the ultimate aim of incarceration, stands to succeed best when the deficiencies and needs of the inmate are known.** These may be many in number. The attempt made to fill these needs constitutes treatment and one in particular stands out, and that is mental therapy. **This situation has been met by the employment of more psychologists** who will have as their chief function the further development of **Group Therapy**. Group therapy makes possible the extension of therapeutic skills to many more persons than would otherwise be the case. It deals chiefly with problems of maladjustment and through sustained discussion provides an opportunity for emotional release. The disappearance of neurotic anxieties brings about a growth in self-acceptance and increases personal effectiveness in society. Group therapy has been conducted in penitentiaries where space and qualified personnel became available. **Additional facilities** are being provided at three institutions through the development of Psychiatric Wards.

186. Past experience has shown that **an increasing number of inmates are, of their own free will, availing themselves of the opportunities afforded for psychiatric help and assistance** in an attempt to find a solution to their mental conflicts and often seeking to find some explanation for their deviant behavior. **This trend which is likely to continue will require more space and accommodation than have been provided for now.** In some areas, those suffering from chronic mental illness continue to overcrowd the existing facilities. The chronicity of their illness makes them fit subjects for admission to provincial mental institutions and we are dependent upon the provincial authorities for their acceptance into provincial mental hospitals for treatment.

Sources: Commissioner's Reports: 1947–48, 33; 1948–49, 43; 1949–50, 36; 1950–51, 43; 1951–52, 47; 1952–53, 50; 1953–54, 50; 1954–55, 43; 1955–56, 40; 1952–53, 47–8.

Appendix B

Article Refused for Publication
in *Pathfinder*, 1953

PICTURE

I am a penitentiary cell. Above (or opp.page) is a picture
of me taken recently in Canada. I have several thousand twin-
brothers in this country and a great multitude of cousins all
over thw world. We are, all of us, engaged in the business of
housing and "Treating" the human species. Times are good and our
business is at an all-time high.

Looking at my picture you may think I haven't much to offer,
but, as my customers can testify, there is more to me than meets
the eye; it's the intangibles that count in this business. My personal popularity is indicated by the statistics. Customers never
spend less than 16 hours out of each 24 in my embrace.

I am not cold, or impersonal either, as alleged by some
humans. I generally come to know my customers much more intim-
ately than their fellow-humans ever do. Yes, I am privileged to
see them with their masks off; all pose, all pretense is abandoned
when they come to me at the close of each trying day. Shortly
after each evening meal I start my "treatments." Oh, you should
see the convincing portrayals of yearning, sorrow, bitterness,
regret and black despair I am able to elicit! Most of my customers would make a Hollywood actor turn green with envy.

With all its changes, the new penal prpgram in my country
hasn't effected me too greatly. Confidentially though, I don't
care for it. There is always the danger those darned humanitarians
may start hollering for changes to be made in me one of these days,
too. What a dreadful prospect! I have changed but little over
the centuries, and my effectiveness never suffered as a result.

But be of good cheer! I too, have powerful defenders. If
you should lose your liberty, it's a safe bet I'll be here to give
you the full 'treatment'. Should your stay be long or short, you
will carry memories of me to your grave.

My family have housed many famous personages and never
failed to affect them all deeply. Consider this fine testimonial
verse composed on our honor by Oscar Wilde:

            "This too I know--and wise it were

            If each could know the same--
            That every prison that men build
            Is built with bricks of Shame,
            And bound with bars lest Christ should see
            How men their brothers maim "

Notes

Foreword

1 Ian Roger Taylor was a co-author of *The New Criminology* (1973), which provided a comprehensive, groundbreaking critique of institutional-based criminology and moved the discipline of criminology into the realm of academic analysis of social control in Western democratic societies.

2 See Goffman's *Asylums* (1961) and *Stigma: Notes on the Management of Spoiled Identity* (1968). His work on the social relations in "total institutions" is essential to this research and informs it.

3 Matza's analysis was instrumental in the development of critical criminology in this era.

4 What was then known as "Scandinavian Criminology" was the most developed and critical school of thought in this emerging academic discipline. Especially see the work of Nils Christie and Thomas Mathiesen, whose influence continues to this day. Because of their influence on state policy at that time, their respective jurisdictions were deemed the most advanced carceral systems in the world.

5 Claire was celebrated by many prisoners for her saintly actions on their behalf. In my lifetime I have encountered no one whose level of commitment and energetic engagement with issues of social justice and prisoners' rights matched that of Claire Culhane. Her involvement with Canadian prisoners and her harassment of penal authorities was legendary. Through her "talks" and writing she encouraged resistance and opposition to state repression across Canadian society. Claire was instrumental in the establishment of "Prison Justice Day, August 10th" as a national day of observance both inside and outside prison walls. She had an important impact on me and my students, including one of the authors of this book. See Culhane: *Barred From Prison;* and *Still Barred from Prison;* and Lowe, *One Women Army.*

6 Notwithstanding our grumbling, this conference had a lasting impact on abolitionist thought. For example, it did much to widen the scope of consideration to include criminal justice as social control, and it led to the relabelling of the conference as "Penal" Abolition to reflect this understanding.

7 We accomplished this by inviting Indigenous rights' and prisoner rights' groups, including the Leonard Peltier Defense Committee and the Native Women's Association of Canada.

8 See Gaucher, "The Canadian Penal Press."

Introduction

1 Appleby, Hunt, and Jacob, 309.

2 Gaucher, "The Canadian Penal Press," 6–7.

3 Over the years, a few students and scholars utilized this collection in their work. Bob also made copies of the materials for the library of the Department of the Solicitor General in Ottawa. However, a search of the present-day Public Safety Canada Library catalogue reveals no record of these publications.

4 The website www.penalpress.com was created by Melissa Munn to allow greater access to these important materials.

5 Richards et al., 16.

6 Tilly, 320.

7 Ibid., 320.

8 Ibid., 321.

9 For an overview of contending analyses, see Cohen, *Visions of Social Control*. See also Mathiesen, *Prison on Trial*; Foucault, *Discipline and Punish*; Ignatieff, *A Just Measure of Pain*; Rothman, *The Discovery of the Asylum*.

10 Bob Gaucher, personal communication with the authors, July 2018.

11 The reader is cautioned that the term segregation is used in two distinct ways in government documents. Most often, segregation is used to describe the process of classifying the prisoner population into categories of prisoners; occasionally, it denotes a punishment practice wherein the individual is subjected to solitary confinement. In this book, we indicate when the latter occurs.

12 *C.B. Diamond*, July 1953, 2.

13 Gosselin, 75.

14 The subsequent appointment of report authors to positions of oversight is a recurring pattern. R.B. Gibson was appointed to implement his own recommendations, and Edmison was appointed to the Parole Board he suggested.

15 Canada, Parliament, Standing Committee, *Report*, 14 (hereafter MacGuigan Report).

16 Between 1934 and 1962, Canada's federal women's prison was administered by the warden of Kingston Penitentiary. See "The Closing of the Prison for Women."

17 See chapter 4. In 1973, prisoners at Kingston Penitentiary for Women would establish *Tightwire* magazine, to give voice to their own uniquely gendered experiences and contribute a feminist perspective to the penal press in Canada. For examples, visit www.penalpress.com.

18 Winterdyk and Wood, 47.

19 Ibid., 47.

20 Canada, Parliament, House of Commons, *Debates*, (hereafter HCD), 18th Parl., 1st sess., vol. 1, 737.

1. Riots and Reform

1 Withrow, 30.

2 Ibid., 10.

3 Ibid., 2.

4 See Judge Deroche's comments at Tim Buck's trial, qtd in the Archambault Report, 82.

5 Marr, 38. Similarly, John Kidman states that the riot at Saint-Vincent-de-Paul in 1932 was triggered by the *cancellation* of cigarette rolling papers, although this too was likely the spark that ignited an already volatile situation. See Kidman, 42.

6 Mathiesen, 134.

7 Two prisoners' "mutinies" took place at Kingston Penitentiary in 1920. Another riot took place in 1927. Canada, Sessional Papers (1922), 9; Withrow, 1.

8 Canada, Department of Justice (hereafter CDOJ), "Extracts from Penitentiary Regulations, 6 (rule 169).

9 Ibid. (rules 170–1).

10 Canada, Committee Appointed by the Rt Hon. C.J. Doherty, 9–10 (hereafter Biggar, Nickle, and Draper Report).

11 Biggar, Nickle, and Draper Report, 9–10.

12 Withrow, 44.

13 Ibid., 44, 55–6.

14 Ibid., 104–10.

15 Ibid., 106. See also Archambault Report, 61–5.

16 *Tele-Scope*, May 1954, 22.

17 Canada, Superintendent of Penitentiaries, *Report … Re: Kingston Penitentiary Disturbances*, 9.

18 Ibid., 4. See also Brock: "Prison Samizdat" and *These Strange Criminals*, 160, 166, 202–3.

19 Withrow, 1–2, 124.
20 Ibid., 2; Canada, Superintendent of Penitentiaries, *Report … Re: Kingston Penitentiary Disturbances*, 4.
21 Ibid., 8.
22 Thompson with Seager, 227.
23 Avakumovic, 87.
24 Buck, 200.
25 Ibid., 208–9; Marr, 37.
26 Buck, 209.
27 Ibid., 206.
28 Ibid., 206–7.
29 *Tele-Scope*, May 1954, 22.
30 Buck, 209–10.
31 Ibid., 212.
32 Canada, Superintendent of Penitentiaries, *Report … Re: Kingston Penitentiary Disturbances*, 4–5.
33 Ibid.,12–13.
34 Ibid., 13.
35 Buck, 214–15.
36 Ibid., 215.
37 Ibid., 215.
38 Marr; Canada, Superintendent of Penitentiaries, *Report … Re: Kingston Penitentiary Disturbances*, 14.
39 Marr, 38; Canada, Superintendent of Penitentiaries, *Report … Re: Kingston Penitentiary Disturbances*, 14–15.
40 Ormond estimated that 300 to 400 prisoners gathered in the shop dome. Tim Buck put the number at 500 to 600. Canada, Superintendent of Penitentiaries, *Report … Re: Kingston Penitentiary Disturbances*, 16; Buck, 215.
41 Canada, Superintendent of Penitentiaries, *Report … Re: Kingston Penitentiary Disturbances*, 15.
42 Marr, 38.
43 Canada, Superintendent of Penitentiaries, *Report … Re: Kingston Penitentiary Disturbances*, 16–17.
44 Ibid., 17.
45 Ibid., 17. For a description of the events, see Marr, 38–9; Canada, Superintendent of Penitentiaries, *Report … Re: Kingston Penitentiary Disturbances*, 16–18.
46 Ibid., 17–18. Ormond's report of the events pinned the blame for the riot squarely on his subordinates; therefore, his account should be read with a certain degree of scepticism. See, for example, ibid., 13, 16, 18, 23, 27. The Archambault Commission's account held Superintendent Ormond responsible for event at Kingston Penitentiary following his arrival. See Archambault Report, 79, 81.

47 Ibid., 18; Marr, 40.
48 When enumerating the causes of the riot, Superintendent Ormond referred
to the "admission in the Kingston Penitentiary during the month of
February, 1932, of certain convicts who were especially adept in organizing
and inciting disturbances against constituted authority." Archambault
Report, 29.
49 Canada, Superintendent of Penitentiaries, *Report ... Re: Kingston Penitentiary
Disturbances*, 20.
50 Ibid., 24.
51 Ibid., 24.
52 Ibid., 20–3.
53 Ibid., 21–2.
54 Ibid., 19–24; cf. Marr, 40, which appears to be in error. Ormond reports
that some prisoners were permitted to circulate through corridors, making
speeches and agitating.
55 Canada, Superintendent of Penitentiaries, *Report ... Re: Kingston Penitentiary
Disturbances*, 21.
56 Buck, 219.
57 Marr, 40.
58 Canada, Superintendent of Penitentiaries, *Report ... Re: Kingston Penitentiary
Disturbances*, 23–24.
59 Ibid., 25.
60 The lack of clarity around these circumstances is typical of the report.
Ormond contended that the prisoners "found or had hidden" the planks,
but explains no further. Ibid., 25.
61 Ibid., 25–6; Marr, 40–1, 44.
62 Archambault Report, 90–1.
63 Ibid., 79–80.
64 Ibid., 85.
65 Avakumovic, 90. Letters calling for an investigation may be found in
Archambault Report, 87–9.
66 Canada, Superintendent of Penitentiaries, *Report ... Re: Kingston
Penitentiary Disturbances*, 26–8.
67 Buck, 222–3; Canada, Superintendent of Penitentiaries, *Report ... Re:
Kingston Penitentiary Disturbances*, 29; Jackson, 39.
68 Marr, 6–15.
69 Ibid., 16–19.
70 Thompson with Seager, 222–44, 267–71.
71 Marr, 17–18.
72 Withrow. Another former prisoner contributed articles to *Maclean's*
magazine. Kidman, 43. For additional information on the contours of this
phase of "deviancy control," see Cohen, *Visions of Social Control*, 16–17.

73 See Strange, 113–15; *Brooks v. the King*, [1927] S.C.R. 633.
74 McSherry, 164–5.
75 Canada, Royal Commission on Penitentiaries, *Report*, 5 (hereafter Macdonnell Report).
76 Canada, Parliament, Sessional Papers (hereafter SP), 1922, 9; Biggar, Nickle, and Draper Report, 7.
77 Macdonnell Report, 5–6; Biggar, Nickle, and Draper Report, 5–6.
78 On the American reforms, see Rotman, 154–60; for American-inspired reform recommendations, see Macdonnell Report, 33–4, 38; Biggar, Nickle, and Draper Report, 62, 67–8.
79 Macdonnell Report, 26.
80 Biggar, Nickle, and Draper Report, 11. See also Macdonnell Report, 26.
81 Macdonnell Report, 26.
82 Ibid., 15–16.
83 Biggar, Nickle, and Draper Report, 42–43.
84 Ibid., 42–4, 47, 54–46, 61. The Macdonnell Report also recommended the introduction of newspapers. Macdonnell Report, 16.
85 Withrow, 30.
86 Crowley, 133.
87 Withrow, 36.
88 Lavell, 70–1; Withrow, 30, 35–6.
89 Ibid., 36.
90 Ibid., 30; Macdonnell Report, 8; Biggar, Nickle, and Draper Report, 9–10.
91 Withrow, 31.
92 According to Withrow, three concerts were held over the thirty months of his imprisonment at Kingston. Ibid., 47.
93 Typically, prisoners spent sixteen of every twenty-four hours during the week (and longer on weekends and holidays) in their cells. Macdonnell Report, 8.
94 Withrow, 30.
95 Ibid., 39.
96 Ibid., 37, 159.
97 Ibid., 37.
98 Macdonnell Report, 8.
99 Withrow, 56.
100 Biggar, Nickle, and Draper Report, 9–10.
101 Withrow, 44.
102 Ibid., 56.
103 Ibid., 8–9, 68, 82.
104 Goffman, in his study of total institutions, argued that the periodic nature of these ceremonies was designed "to give rise to some social excitement. All the groupings in the establishment join in, regardless of rank or

position – but are given a place that expresses their position ... a society dangerously split into inmates and staff can through these ceremonies hold itself together." Goffman, *Asylums*, 109.

105 Withrow, 50.
106 Ibid., 163.
107 Ibid., 8, 138–9.
108 Withrow, 42, 176–8.
109 Ibid., 97–8, 154. Georg Rusche and Otto Kirchheimer assert that the decisions on medical care were based on more than the patient's needs; "the doctor must consider ... the effect of his treatment on the other inmates and on institutional discipline." Rusche and Kirchheimer, 154.
110 Withrow, 74, 75, 99–102, 192.
111 Ibid., 102–3.
112 Ibid., 164–6.
113 Biggar, Nickle, and Draper Report, 20, 41.
114 Ibid., 49.
115 Ibid., 50.
116 Macdonnell Report, 43.
117 Ibid., 17.
118 Withrow, 106.
119 Ibid., 15.
120 Ibid., 108.
121 Topping, 37.
122 Withrow, 107, 109. The range of punishments is confirmed by Topping. However, Topping implied that the use of the strap was rare, since that particular punishment could only be inflicted with the consent of the minister of justice. Topping, 37.
123 Macdonnell Report, 9, 44.
124 Biggar, Nickle, and Draper Report, 38–9.
125 Ibid., 31, 33–34; Macdonnell Report, 32.
126 Biggar, Nickle, and Draper Report, 33–4; Macdonnell Report, 31–2.
127 Regarding wages, see Macdonnell Report, 32; and Biggar, Nickle, and Draper Report, 36. Regarding early release, the Macdonnell Report recommended a form of indeterminate sentencing with minimum and maximum sentence lengths, and with the actual time served to be based on prisoners' conduct. Biggar, Nickle, and Draper suggested that remission of sentences for good conduct be increased. They further recommended that prisoners be automatically considered for parole rather than having to make application. See Macdonnell Report, 44; Biggar, Nickle, and Draper Report, 16, 20, 45–6, 62–4.
128 Rusche and Kirchheimer, 156.
129 Withrow, 64.

130 Biggar, Nickle, and Draper Report, 20.
131 Ibid., 20.
132 Withrow, 65.
133 Ibid., 26, 59, 63, 71, 84. On trades instruction, see also Marr, 33.
134 Withrow, 71.
135 Ibid., 63, italics in original.
136 Ibid., 81–3.
137 Ibid., 59, 61.
138 Ibid., 163–4.
139 Biggar, Nickle, and Draper Report, 57; Topping, 24.
140 Macdonnell Report, 43–4.
141 The government did not create multi-member panels to oversee the
     penitentiaries. Instead, it created the new position of Superintendent of
     Penitentiaries in 1918. See HCD, 13th Parl., 1st sess., vol. 1 (1918), 1176–7;
     An Act to Amend the Penitentiary Act, S.C. 1918, c. 36.
142 Macdonnell Report, 42.
143 Biggar, Nickle, and Draper Report, 13, 26.
144 *Penitentiary Act*, R.S. Canada 1906, c. 147, s. 41; *Penitentiary Act*, R.S.
     Canada 1927, c. 154, s. 40; Withrow, 70–1.
145 Ibid., 71.
146 Crowley, 138–40.
147 SP, 1920, "Report," 8–12; see also Topping, 25–6.
148 On development of the physical plant, see SP, 1926, Paper no. 20, "Report …
     1924–25," 10–11. For a discussion of improvements to the standards of
     prisoner care, see SP, 1923, Paper no. 20, "Report … 1922," 10–13. For
     typical vignettes describing reformed prisoners, see SP, 1922, Paper no. 35,
     "Report … 1921," 15.
149 Ibid., 12–13; SP, "Report … 1923," 11; "Report … 1924," 12–14; "Report …
     1925," 13–16; "Report … 1926," 13.
150 See for example, SP, "Report … 1923," 10; "Report … 1924," 13–14.
151 Kidman, 52–3; Topping, ix, x. Kidman identified C.W. Topping and Alfred
     Lavell as leading Canadian penologists and key figures in the prison
     reform movement. See ibid., 90, 92–4.
152 Topping, a sociology professor at the University of Puget Sound, and
     subsequently at the University of British Columbia, had life experience
     similar to that of many members of the Penitentiary Service administration.
     He had previously served in the Canadian military and had been
     employed as Keeper of the provincial jail in Kingston. That experience and
     his academic credentials may explain why the superintendent trusted him
     and granted him access to the penitentiaries. Topping, ix; Kidman, 53, 93.
153 For Topping's role in the John Howard Society and the prison welfare
     movement, see ibid., 38, 90.

154 Topping, 83–4.
155 Ibid., 26, 33, 84–5.
156 Ibid., 94.
157 Ibid., 94.
158 Ibid., 25–7.
159 Ibid., 7, 87.
160 Ibid., 86.
161 Ibid., 87; Kidman, 11, 90, 94.
162 Lavell, 23–8.
163 Ibid., 70–1.
164 Lavell qtd in Topping, 87.
165 Lavell, 78–93.
166 Ibid., 76.
167 Ibid., vii.
168 Lavell qtd in Topping, 87. This is an interesting assertion, given that many Canadian penal practices were based on American models.
169 Topping, 87.
170 According to Edgardo Rotman, while many prison reforms were championed in Progressive Era American prisons, they remained, for the most part, relatively unchanged: "Shabby facilities, lack of space, inadequate opportunities for work, and more profoundly still, an institutional routine lived under the eyes of guards in which security was the single most important consideration." Nevertheless, as will become evident, it is doubtful that Canadian prisons were much superior to their American counterparts. See Rotman, 163–4.
171 See, for example, *Ottawa Citizen*, 21 October 1932.
172 CDOJ, *Annual Report ... 1933 and General Report to December 1, 1933*, 21–6, 29–31.
173 The superintendent attributed the uprising to four factors: poor prison management, including poorly trained officers, and inadequate inspection; the activities of agitators, among them communist leaders, young and irresponsible prisoners, and a group plotting an escape attempt; a generalized desire to ameliorate prison rules and regulations; and the monotony of prison confinement. Canada, Superintendent of Penitentiaries, *Report ... Re: Kingston Penitentiary Disturbances*, 29.
174 Marr, 25; HCD, 18th Parl., 3rd sess., vol. 4 (1938), 4352. Among the changes introduced in 1933 were the provision of cigarette papers, greater writing and visitation privileges, longer exercise periods, radios, approved conversation periods, compulsory education for "teachable" illiterates, and the moderation of corporal punishment. By 1934, experiments with competitive athletics had begun. In 1935, prisoners began to receive five cents per day in payment for their labour. See Marr,

46; Kidman, 44, 67–8; Crowley, 138–9; HCD, 17th Parl., 5th sess., vol. 4 (1934), 4292.

175 Harry Anderson, cited in Withrow, ix.

176 Crowley, 125; *Ottawa Citizen*, 25 June 1934.

177 Ottawa *Citizen*, 27 June 1934.

178 The campaign was successful. The communist prisoners were released in 1934, and Section 98 was repealed in 1936. Avakumovic, 89–90.

179 Among the team of lawyers who volunteered to represent the prisoners was W.F. Nickle, who had participated in a government inquiry into prison conditions over a decade earlier and who had conducted an investigation of two riots at Kingston in 1921. See Topping, 30; Marr, 25, 45; Harry Anderson, Introduction to Withrow, ix; Crowley, 134; Kidman, 43–4.

180 Marr, 45.

181 HCD, 18th Parl., 3rd sess., vol. 4 (1938), 4378–9.

182 *Gazette* (Montreal), 3 July 1933.

183 Ibid. On tickets of leave, see chapter 5.

184 HCD, 17th Parl., 5th sess., vol. 4 (1934), 4285, 4.

185 *Gazette* (Montreal), 3 July 1933.

186 *Gazette* (Montreal), 28 May 1933.

187 HCD, 17th Parl., 5th sess., vol. 4 (1934), 4285.

188 Kidman, 49.

189 HCD, 17th Parl., 5th sess., vol. 4 (1934), 4289.

190 Crowley, 140.

191 Ibid., 139–40.

192 CDOJ, *Annual Report … 1934*, 24.

193 HCD, 17th Parl., 5th sess., vol. 4 (1934), 4293.

194 HCD, 17th Parl., 5th sess., vol. 4 (1934), 4291; Ottawa *Citizen*, 25 June 1934.

195 HCD, 17th Parl., 5th sess., vol. 4 (1934), 4289.

196 CDOJ, *Annual Report … 1935*, 11.

197 HCD, 17th Parl., 5th sess., vol. 4 (1934), 4289.

198 CDOJ, *Annual Report … 1935*, 12.

199 HCD, 17th Parl., 5th sess., vol. 4 (1934), 4290.

200 HCD, 17th Parl., 5th sess., vol. 4 (1934), 4289.

201 HCD, 17th Parl., 5th sess., vol. 4 (1934), 4285–92; Ottawa *Citizen*, 25 June 1934.

202 Kidman, 54–5, 97.

203 HCD: 18th Parl., 1st sess., vol. 1 (1936), 613; 18th Parl., 3rd sess., vol. 4 (1938), 4360. See also Kidman, 49; Crowley, 144.

2. The Blueprint for the New Deal

1 *The Globe*, 7 November 1932, 4.

2 Archambault Report, 1.

3 Crowley, 138–40, 142, 145.
4 Archambault Report, v.
5 Ibid., 2–5.
6 Kidman, 51, 59; Marr, 48; Crowley, 145.
7 Archambault Report, 162.
8 Quoted from the proposal made by Mr Waller to the International Penal and Penitentiary Commission, in Paul Cornill, *Preparatory Report on the Possible Modifications of the Standard Minimum Rules for the Treatment of Prisoners*, UN paper ESA/SD/AC. 1/1, 2, cited in Kraiem, 1.
9 League of Nations, "Penal and Penitentiary Questions Report … Fifth Committee," United Nations Archives [hereafter UNA].
10 League of Nations, "Penal and Penitentiary Questions Report of the Secretary-General to the Assembly," UNA.
11 Archambault Report, 22–3.
12 Ibid., 23.
13 Ibid., 66.
14 Ibid., 295.
15 Ibid., 24.
16 Ibid., 109, 120.
17 Ibid., 23–4, 109–14.
18 Ibid., 163.
19 Ibid., 23, 114–15.
20 Ibid., 23–4.
21 Ibid., 109. The term rehabilitation has subsequently taken on different connotations. In the early twentieth century, it was used to denote the effort to "readjust … the [convict] to his former status," whereas in the latter part of the century, it came to refer to psychiatric and psychological interventions to change an individual's behaviour. For the older understanding, see Kidman, 87.
22 Archambault Report, 23.
23 Ibid., 100.
24 Ibid., 100–2.
25 Ibid., 23, 116, 126–7.
26 Ibid., 49.
27 Ibid., 26.
28 Ibid., 26–7, 32–3, 44.
29 Ibid., 26, 29–30, 44.
30 Ibid., 51.
31 The superintendent envisioned that "eventually all young convicts for the Province of Ontario may be confined in Collin's Bay Penitentiary," which had been under construction since 1930. D.M. Ormond, "Report of the Superintendent of Penitentiaries on the Study of the Borstal System of England," in CDOJ, *Annual Report … 1935*, 31–42 at 40.

32 Archambault Report, 28, 54.
33 Ibid., 62–3.
34 Withrow, 105–6.
35 Archambault Report, 64.
36 Ibid., 63.
37 Ibid., 47.
38 Ibid., 61.
39 Ibid., 62.
40 Ibid., 44–6, 60, 61.
41 United Province of Canada, Reports of the Commissioners Appointed
    to Inquire into the Conduct, Discipline, & Management of the Provincial
    Penitentiary, With Documents transmitted by the Commissioners
    (Montreal: Rollo Campbell, 1849), 258.
42 Archambault Report, 9.
43 Ibid., 8.
44 Ibid., 9
45 Ibid., 217, 249. For documentation of rising recidivism rates, see 213–14.
    For costs, see 215–17.
46 Ibid., 9–10.
47 Ibid., 100.
48 Ibid., 220.
49 The contemporary language used to address the same issue and the same
    group of convicts is "Dangerous Offender." Canada, *Criminal Code*, R.S.C.
    1985, c. C-46, s. 753.
50 Archambault Report, 222–3. The commission viewed chronic minor offenders
    differently. They recommended that "beggars, vagrants, and drunkards,"
    typically subject to short sentences and routine re-arrest, be sentenced instead
    to lengthier incarceration on special prison farms, so they might "acquire
    industrial habits and gain regular employment after release." Ibid., 211–12.
51 Ibid., 159.
52 Ibid., 161.
53 Ibid., 156–7.
54 Ibid., 210. The commission heard arguments that the *Juvenile Delinquents
    Act* should be amended to increase the age limit from sixteen to eighteen
    years. However, they recommended that the judiciary be granted
    discretion to determine whether cases involving seventeen- and eighteen-
    year-olds should be brought under the act. Ibid., 183, 188–9, 201.
55 Ibid., 201.
56 Ibid., 203.
57 Ibid., 202–3.
58 Ibid., 195–6.
59 Ibid., 176.

60 Ibid., 176–7. The commission expanded on each topic, producing a litany of environmental causes for criminality among the young, including but not limited to parental laxity, parental alcoholism, "irregular" (i.e., common law) unions, the presence of foster parents, various types of domestic abuse, bad neighbourhoods, mass culture, and unsupervised activities. Ibid., 177–9.
61 Ibid., 178–9.
62 Ibid., 176.
63 Ibid., 180.
64 Ibid., 196.
65 Ibid., 196.
66 Ibid., 204.
67 Ibid., 204.
68 Ibid., 203–4.
69 Ibid., 203–4.
70 Ibid., 197.
71 Ibid., 208.
72 Ibid., 209–10.
73 Ibid., 201.
74 Despite the enthusiastic endorsement of the Borstal model by Canadian authorities, it was not a long-lived experiment. For example, Thomas Mathiesen notes that the Borstal system in Norway was abolished during the 1970s. Mathiesen, 41.
75 For eighteenth- and early nineteenth-century examples of similar progressive stage systems, see McConville, "The Victorian Prison," 121–3; for mid-nineteenth-century variants developed by Alexander Maconochie and Sir Walter Crofton, see McCoy, 75–8.
76 Archambault Report, 107.
77 Ibid., 233–5.
78 Ibid., 108, 233.
79 Ibid., 344, 353.
80 Ibid., 345.
81 Ibid., 350, 353.
82 Ibid., 362.
83 Ibid., 234.
84 Weber, 7.
85 Archambault Report, 129, italics in original.
86 Mathiesen, 33.
87 This suggestion had the added benefit of avoiding conflict with unionized labour and the business community. In Upper Canada, workingmen's movements opposed convict labour as unfair competition and "as an affront to their dignity and respectability." McCoy, 36. For more on this potential conflict see Rusche and Kirchheimer.

88 League of Nations, "Penal and Penitentiary Questions Report of the Secretary-General to the Assembly."

89 Archambault Report, 130, 133–5. In 1914, the Macdonnell Commission interviewed two Canadian labour leaders on the subject of prison labour. According to the commission report, James Watt, president of the Toronto Trades and Labour Council, supported the principle of production for state use but urged that prisoners be paid wages. J.C. Watters, president of the Dominion Trades and Labour Congress, stated that all prison labour was in competition with free labour but that production for state use involved the least competition, and he supported it on that basis. Macdonnell Report, 35.

90 Archambault Report, 137–9.

91 Ibid., 129.

92 Ibid., 126, 129.

93 Ibid., 139.

94 Ibid., 139. On pay for prison labour, see 140–1.

95 Ibid., 144.

96 Foucault, *Madness and Civilization*, 59–60.

97 Mathiesen, 34, 41–2.

98 Archambault Report, 115, 117.

99 Ibid., 115.

100 Ibid., 117.

101 Ibid., 115.

102 Ibid., 119.

103 Ibid., 120.

104 On residential schooling in Canada, see Miller; Milloy; and Haig-Brown.

105 Archambault Report, 109–11, 113–14.

106 Ibid., 112–13.

107 Ibid., 265, 278, 357. The commissioners also noted that some prisoners found the conversation periods disruptive. Elsewhere in the report, the commissioners recommended that restrictions on conversations between guards and prisoners be eased slightly. While they disapproved of "any kind of familiarity" between prisoners and guards, they contended that "sometimes a word or two passed by an officer to an inmate may prove to have a very favourable influence in the latter's reformation." Ibid., 66.

108 Ibid., 24, 255–7.

109 Ibid., 113, 250.

110 Ibid., 111, 113, 250.

111 Ibid., 109. Foucault, *Discipline and Punish*, 135; Weber, 181.

112 Archambault Report, 104–6. The commission recommended the adoption of the English model and outlined the English system of classification on 105–6.

113 Ibid., 342.
114 Ibid., 344.
115 Ibid., 344.
116 Ibid., 249. Agnes Macphail, like many prison reformers and administrators of the era, identified recidivism as her chief concern. Crowley, 136.
117 Archambault Report, 251–2.
118 Ibid., 257–8.
119 Ibid., 257–9.
120 Ibid., 263. Prisoners' aid organizations appearing before the commission included "The Prisoners' Welfare Association, Halifax; The Prisoners' Aid and Welfare Association of Montreal; La Jeunesse Ouvriére Catholique, Montreal, Inc.; the Prisoners' Rehabilitation Society of Toronto; The John Howard Society of British Columbia, Vancouver; The Prisoners' Welfare Committee of the Regina Welfare Bureau, Regina; The Manitoba Prisoners' Aid Association, Winnipeg; and the Salvation Army." The commission reported that "it is apparent that the associations are accomplishing very little at any of the Canadian penitentiaries." Ibid., 251–2.
121 Mathiesen, 28.
122 Archambault Report, 263.
123 Ibid., 264.
124 "General Ormond Will Be Retired – Many More to Go," *Globe and Mail*, 15 June 1938.
125 J.S. Woodsworth claimed that he had read favourable editorials from newspapers across the country. HCD, 18th Parl., 3rd sess., vol. 4 (1938), 4358.
126 "Miss Macphail Is Pleased with Report on Prisons," *Ottawa Citizen*, 15 June 1938. See also "Royal Commission Report Strongly Indicts Canada's Prison System," *Ottawa Citizen*, 15 June 1938.
127 "Miss Macphail Is Pleased with Report on Prisons," Ottawa *Citizen*, 15 June 1938.
128 Ibid.
129 "General Ormond Will Be Retired."
130 HCD, 18th Parl., 3rd sess., vol. 4 (1938), 4342.
131 HCD, 18th Parl., 3rd sess., vol. 4 (1938), 4345.
132 Archambault Report, 44.
133 HCD, 18th Parl., 3rd sess., vol. 4 (1938), 4342–3, 4363.
134 HCD, 18th Parl., 3rd sess., vol. 4 (1938), 4344.
135 HCD, 18th Parl., 3rd sess., vol. 4 (1938), 4343, 4374–5.
136 HCD, 18th Parl., 3rd sess., vol. 4 (1938), 4352.
137 HCD, 18th Parl., 3rd sess., vol. 4 (1938), 4358.
138 HCD, 18th Parl., 3rd sess., vol. 4 (1938), 4282–3.
139 HCD, 18th Parl., 3rd sess., vol. 4 (1938), 4360–1.
140 HCD, 18th Parl., 3rd sess., vol. 4 (1938), 4360.

141 Kidman, 60.

142 Ibid., 60.

143 Prisoners used the phrase "New Deal" to describe the reforms implemented in Canadian prisons as early as 1951, and it had become commonplace by 1954. See *Tele-Scope*: June 1951, 18; April 1952, 24; April 1953, 14, 36; May 1953, 9; June 1953, 6, 32; May 1954, 21; June 1954, 2; *Mountain Echoes*, September 1951, 4; *Pen-O-Rama*: January 1953, 6; February 1953, 8; August–September 1953, 2; October 1954, 23–4; December 1954, 53; *C.B. Diamond*: December 1953, 9; April 1954, 7, 48; May 1954, 2; *Transition*, October 1956, 25.

144 Mathiesen, 21.

145 See LAC, RG 73, vol. 42, file 1-20-11, pts 6–8.

146 Keshen, 241.

147 Ibid., 249. Notably, while the arrest rates began to fall in 1943, and continued to decline thereafter, the level of concern remained high. For the statistical data, see ibid., 251.

148 In his analysis of the rising juvenile arrest rate, Keshen refers to a large cohort of teenagers in the early 1940s. He also notes that with many males in the 18–30 age range – the most crime-prone demographic group – serving overseas, the police shifted their focus to less serious issues, which resulted in more children being charged with minor offences, a pattern that is supported by statistical data. See ibid., 251–2.

149 Ibid., 250.

150 Ibid, 250.

151 Ibid, 252.

152 LAC, RG 73, vol. 42, file 1-20-11, pts 6–8.

153 Helen Lewis, on behalf of the League for Women's Rights, to the Honourable Louis St Laurent, K.C., Minister of Justice and Attorney General for Canada, 10 April 1944, LAC, RG 73, vol. 42, 1-20-11, pt 6. Lewis's attempt to create a moral panic is a typical social reform strategy. For more on moral panics, see Cohen, *Folk Devils and Moral Panics*.

154 Ibid.; Constance P. Garneau, President, Ligue pour les Droits de la Femme, Montreal, to the Honourable Louis St Laurent, Minister of Justice, 23 May 1944, LAC, RG 73, vol. 42, 1-20-11, pt 6; League for Women's Rights, Montreal, to the Hon. Louis St Laurent, Minister of Justice, 11 May 1944, LAC, RG 73, vol. 42, 1-20-11, pt 6.

155 R.C.C. Henson, Chairman, Board of Directors, United Welfare Chest, The Federation of Greater Toronto's Social Services, to the Honourable Louis S. St Laurent, K.C., Minister of Justice, 9 November 1945, LAC, RG 73, vol. 42, file 1-20-11, pt 7.

156 Henry B. Peters, President, K.W. Larter, Secretary, Community Welfare Council of Regina, to Hon. Louis St Laurent, Minister of Justice, 30 January 1945, LAC, RG 73, vol. 42, file 1-20-11, pt 7.

157 See, for example, Constance P. Garneau, League for Women's Rights, Montreal, to the Honourable Louis St Laurent, 10 April 1944, LAC, RG 73, vol. 42, file 1-20-11, pt 6; Katherine H. Gallery, Chairman, Delinquency Prevention Committee, Montreal, to Hon. Louis St Laurent, Minister of Justice, 11 May 1944, LAC, RG 73, vol. 42, file 1-20-11, pt 6; Bertha E. Beveridge, Montreal Women's Club, to Hon. Louis St Laurent, Minister of Justice, 15 June 1944, LAC, RG 73, vol. 42, file 1-20-11, pt 7.

158 F.R. Scott, R. Gordon Burgoyne, and John Kidman, Canadian Penal Association, to Hon. Louis St Laurent, M.P., Minister of Justice, 20 November 1945, LAC, RG 73, vol. 42, file 1-20-11, pt 7.

159 LAC, RG 73, v. 42, file 1-20-11, pts 6–8, *passim*.

160 *Ottawa Journal*, 12 December 1945, newspaper clipping, LAC, RG 73, vol. 42, file 1-20-11, pt 7.

161 Clarkson, 124–9.

162 Francis, Jones, and Smith, 295–6, 337.

163 Kidman, 103.

164 Rev. Canon W.W. Judd, The Church of England in Canada, Department of Christian Social Service, to the Rt Honourable W.L. Mackenzie King, C.M.G., Prime Minister, and the Premiers of the Nine Provinces, 3 October 1946, LAC, RG 73, vol. 42, file 1-20-11, pt 8.

165 Kidman, 60; *An Act to amend The Penitentiary Act, 1939*, S.C. 1945, c. 28. There was an immediate public response. Petitions and resolutions began to arrive at the Ministry of Justice and Prime Minister's Office. Many of the petitioners worried that a single commissioner would lack the range of competencies of the three-member commission envisioned by Archambault. See F.R. Scott, R. Gordon Burgoyne, and John Kidman, Canadian Penal Association, to Hon. Louis St Laurent, M.P., Minister of Justice, 20 November 1945, LAC, RG 73, vol. 42, file 1-20-11, pt 7; J. Dinnage Hobden, Executive Secretary, the John Howard Society of British Columbia, to Major General Ralph B. Gibson, H.M. Canadian Prison Commission, 9 May 1946, LAC, RG 73, vol. 42, file 1-20-11, pt 7; G.J. Matte, Private Secretary, Prime Minister's Office, to Reverend R.W. Hardy, United Church of Canada [including an enclosed copy of several resolutions], 5 June 1946, LAC, RG 73, vol. 42, file 1-20-11, pt 7; LAC RG 73, vol. 42, file 1-20-11, pt 8, *passim*.

166 *The Canadian Who's Who*, vol. 8 (1958–60), s.v. "Gibson, Maj.-Gen. Ralph Burgess"; Law Society of Upper Canada, Ontario Weekly Notes, 1917–1921, Meeting of Convocation, Thursday, 21st October, 1920, 268, 270, https://archive.org/details/meetingconvocation1721.

167 Memorandum to the Right Honourable The Minister of Justice, Re: Answers to questions 1 to 8 of Mr T.L. Church, M.P., 20 May 1940, LAC, RG 73, vol. 42, file 1-20-11, pt 5.

168 CDOJ, *Report of General R.B. Gibson*, 4–5.There is also a typewritten (and differently paginated) original manuscript of the report at LAC, RG 73, vol. 16, file 1-12-76.

169 CDOJ, *Report of General R.B. Gibson*, 7–8, 13.

170 Frank Anderson, who was incarcerated at Prince Albert, noted that in 1939 the "radio was set up in the Roll Call room and two loud speakers were installed in each cell block. The only station it could pick up was CKBI in Prince Albert and in the beginning only news broadcasts were permitted, each carefully monitored to censor any reference to the taboo subjects. A guard actually sat beside the radio so that he could instantly shut it off at the mere hint that a verboten topic was about to be broadcast." He goes on to note that "even this minimal contact with the outside world had a dramatic impact on the inmates, making some withdraw further into themselves while encouraging others to blossom under the spray of sound." Anderson, *Up The Ladder*, 117.

171 CDOJ, *Report of General R.B. Gibson*, 5.

172 Ibid., 5.

173 Ibid., 6.

174 Ibid., 5–6.

175 Ibid., 6.

176 W.S. Lawson, Memorandum to the Deputy Minister of Justice, 18 December 1943, LAC, RG 73, vol. 42, file 1-20-11, pt 5.

177 Memorandum for the Deputy Minister of Justice, 18 May 1943, LAC, RG 73, vol. 42, file 1-20-11, pt 5; Memorandum to the Right Honourable the Minister of Justice. Re: Answers to questions 1 to 8 of Mr T.L. Church, M.P., 20 May 1940, LAC, RG 73, vol. 42, file 1-20-11, pt 5; Memorandum Re: Recommendations of the Royal Commission, 1938. Re: Action already taken or about to be taken thereon, 20 December 1943, LAC, RG 73, vol. 42, file 1-20-11, pt 5; Memorandum to the Deputy Minister of Justice: Re: Parliamentary Inquiries – Re: Questions of Mr Church, M.P. March 1944, 31 March 1944, LAC, RG 73, vol. 42, file 1-20-11, pt 6; W.S. Lawson, Memorandum to the Deputy Minister of Justice, 14 June 1944, 2, LAC, RG 73, vol. 42, file 1-20-11, pt 6.

178 CDOJ, *Report of General R.B. Gibson*, 8.

179 Ibid., 13.

180 Ibid., 13. Gibson recommended that private prisoners' aid societies continue to provide post-carceral support. He wrote that "the activities of these Societies should be encouraged and recognized" and recommended that the penitentiary service cooperate with their representatives and provide financial aid to organizations that had demonstrated their efficiency. CDOJ, *Report of General R. B. Gibson*, 16–17.

181 Ibid., 13–14.

182 Ibid., 13.

183 Ibid., 13.
184 Ibid., 13.
185 Ibid., 13.
186 Ibid., 10.
187 Ibid., 10.
188 Manuscript copy of ibid., LAC, RG 73, vol. 16, file 1-12-76, 16–17. This material is missing from the copy available online, in which page 11 is in French and is differently paginated. The commissioner also recommended that existing arrangements for housing insane prisoners in provincial mental hospitals be continued and suggested that the operation of habitual offender legislation in the United States and England be studied before any arrangements were made for the construction of special facilities for their separate incarceration. Manuscript copy of ibid., 18–19.
189 CDOJ, *Report of General R. B. Gibson*, 12.
190 Ibid., 14.
191 Ibid., 17.
192 Bob Gaucher, personal communication with the authors, July 2018.
193 CDOJ, *Report of General R.B. Gibson*, 8–9.
194 CDOJ, *Annual Report … 1946*, 37.
195 CDOJ, *Annual Report … 1948*, 7–8.
196 The Commissioner's annual reports contain only a brief accounting of Gendreau's annual activities, generally under a page in length. See Appendix A.
197 See, for example, the *C.B. Diamond*, July 1952, 2.
198 Kropf, 300.
199 Ibid., 306.
200 Niergarth, 173, 190.
201 Ibid., 182, 189.
202 Ibid.
203 Kropf, 350. Italics original.
204 Ibid., 346.
205 Ibid., 311–12; Niergarth, 172, 175–6, 182, 195.
206 Ibid., 177.
207 Ibid., 176–7.
208 Kropf, 314.
209 Ibid., 326–7.
210 Ibid., 314–16.
211 Ibid., 315.
212 Ibid., 303.
213 Ibid., 302, 341–2.
214 Ibid., 345.
215 Ibid., 340.

3. "Men Who Beefed"

1 Joseph McCulley, Memorandum to the Commissioner, "Re: Prison Newspaper," 19 May 1948, LAC, RG 73, vol. 65, file 1-11-26. A Canadian prison, Burwash Industrial Farm, which ran under provincial jurisdiction, already had a publication, but this was not to be the model that McCulley advanced – likely because it was not enjoying much success. McCulley, Memorandum to the Commissioner, December 7, 1948, LAC, RG 73, vol. 65, file 1-11-26.
2 McCulley, Memorandum, "Re: Prison Newspaper."
3 On the American penal press, see Baird, *The Penal Press*.
4 McCulley, Memorandum, "Re: Prison Newspaper."
5 J. McCulley, Deputy Commissioner to The Warden, The Penitentiary, Collins Bay, Ontario, "Re: Prison Newspaper," 16 June 1949, LAC, RG 73, vol. 65, file 1-11-26.
6 R.M. Allan, Warden, Kingston Penitentiary to Commissioner of Penitentiaries, 14 July 1950, LAC, RG 73, vol. 65, file 1-11-26.
7 R.M. Allan, Warden, Kingston Penitentiary to Commissioner of Penitentiaries, 14 July 1950, LAC RG 73, vol. 65, file 1-11-26. His support is not surprising. In his 1949–50 Commissioner's Report, Gibson noted: "At two institutions a bulletin was prepared, edited and' illustrated by inmates – the bulletin either being circulated to inmates or posted for their perusal. It is hoped that the publication of such a bulletin will become a regular feature in all the institutions and that it may perhaps develop into an inmate newspaper or magazine which will serve as an opportunity for expression for convicts with literary ability and also as a medium of contact between the inmates and the authorities." CDOJ, *Annual Report ... 1950*, 18.
8 Baird, 170.
9 Commissioner Gibson to Warden Allan, "Re: Softball Bulletin, Re: Prison Newspaper," 21 July 1950, LAC, RG 73, vol. 65, file 1-11-26.
10 R.M. Allan, Warden, Kingston Penitentiary to Commissioner of Penitentiaries, "Re: Penitentiary Newspaper," 11 August 1950, LAC, RG 73, vol. 65, file 1-11-26.
11 Author unknown, Handwritten notation on R.M. Allan, Warden, Kingston Penitentiary, to Commissioner of Penitentiaries, "Re: Penitentiary Newspaper," 11 August 1950, LAC, RG 73, vol. 65, file 1-11-26.
12 Gordon Marr, #598, Editor, The K.P. Tele-scope to letter to Warden R.M. Allan, 8 August 1950, LAC, RG 73, vol. 65, file 1-11-26.
13 J. McCulley, Deputy Commissioner, Memorandum to the Commissioner, "Re: Penitentiary Newspaper – Kingston," 15 August 1950, LAC, RG 73, vol. 65, file 1-11-26.

14 R.M. Allan, Warden, Kingston Penitentiary to Commissioner of Penitentiaries, "Re: Penitentiary Newspaper," 11 August 1950, LAC, RG 73, vol. 65, file 1-11-26.
15 *Tele-Scope*, 1 September 1950.
16 Gordon Marr, #598, Editor, The K.P. Tele-scope to Warden R.M. Allan, 8 August 1950, LAC, RG 73, vol. 65, file 1-11-26.
17 Ibid.
18 Ibid.
19 *Tele-Scope*, 1 September 1950, 1.
20 In fact, in December 1958, *Mountain Echo*es indicated that the warden planned to contribute to their magazine on a regular basis, and they noted: "Should this take fruit, it will be the first among the Canadian Penal Publications." *Mountain Echoes*, December 1958, 8.
21 Minutes of the 1957 Wardens Conference, 4 June 1957, 3:30 to 5:00 p.m., LAC, RG 73, vol. 33, file 1-18-17, pt 2.
22 R.B. Gibson, Commissioner to The Warden, The Penitentiary, Prince Albert, Sask., 9 November 1953, LAC, RG 73, vol. 121, file 7-11-26, pt 1.
23 G.T. Crofton, A/Warden to Commissioner of Penitentiaries, "Re: Recreational Activities – Inmates," 12 November 1953, LAC, RG 73, vol. 121, file 7-11-26, pt 1.
24 R.E. March, Deputy Commissioner, Memorandum to the Commissioner, "Re: 'Pathfinder' Magazine," 3 December 1953, LAC, RG 73, vol. 121, file 7-11-26, pt 1.
25 *Tele-Scope*, April 1951, 15.
26 Letter to the editor from Bill W., *Beacon*, 19 October 1951, 2.
27 *Beacon*, 12 October 1951, 7.
28 Gaucher, "The Canadian Penal Press," 4.
29 Marks, 89.
30 *Tele-Scope*, March 1951, 18.
31 The JHS donated a typewriter to *C.B. Diamond. C.B. Diamond*, September 1952, 9.
32 CDOJ, *Annual Report ... 1951*, 17.
33 *Pen-O-Rama*, November 1952, 2.
34 J. McCulley, Deputy Commissioner to The Warden, The Penitentiary, Stony Mountain, Manitoba, "Re: *Prison Newspaper*," 12 October 1951, LAC, RG 73, vol. 117, file 6-11-26.
35 *Pen-O-Rama*, November 1952, 2.
36 R.B. Gibson, Commissioner to The Warden, The Penitentiary, Prince Albert, Sask., "RE: 'Pathfinder' Magazine," 2 December 1953, LAC, RG 73, vol. 121, file 7-11-26, pt 1; R.E. March, Deputy Commissioner, Memorandum to the Commissioner, "Re: 'Pathfinder' Magazine," 3 December 1953, LAC, RG 73, vol. 121, file 7-11-26, pt 1.

37 *Pen-O-Rama*, October 1952, back cover.

38 *Pen-O-Rama*, December 1952, back cover.

39 J.A.M. Grignon, Liaison Officer to Warden LeBel, "Re:- Penorama; Subscriptions and Financing," 29 August 1952, LAC, RG 73, vol. 96, file 3-11-26, pt 1.

40 "Policy for financing Inmate Prison Newspapers," LAC, RG 73, vol. 65, file 1-11-26.

41 Ibid.

42 Advertising sales was a point of contention with the commissioner, who, as early as 1952, wondered about the ethics of prisoners soliciting companies for advertisement sales. R.B. Gibson, Commissioner to the Warden, St. Vincent de Paul Penitentiary, "Re: Anniversary Bulletin," 16 July 1952, LAC, RG 73, vol. 96, file 3-11-26, pt 1. However, he ultimately relented when they were framed as "good will" acts by the businesses. G. LeBel, Warden to Commissioner of Penitentiaries, "Re:- Anniversary Bulletin, Re:- Financing by Advertisements, 31 July 1952 LAC, RG 73, vol. 96, file 3-11-26, pt 1. The presence and volume of advertising in *Pen-O-Rama* also caused some jealousy in the penal press circuit, with one publication writing, "sometimes we wonder if you come under the same Department of Justice we do." *Transition*, October 1955, 25.

43 Memorandum to the Commissioner, "Re: Prison Newspapers, Re: Policy re Financing," 8 July 1953, 2, LAC, RG 73, vol. 117, file 6-11-26.

44 Memorandum to the Commissioner, "Re: Prison Newspapers, Re: Policy re Financing," 8 July 1953, 2, LAC, RG 73, vol. 117, file 6-11-26; *Transition*, August 1955, 4.

45 *Sports Bulletin* 1, no. 10 (1950), 3.

46 Andre Dion (former prisoner at St. Vincent de Paul Penitentiary), in discussion with Melissa Munn and Robert Gaucher, 20 January 2016, Magog Quebec.

47 *C.B. Diamond*, February 1958, 2.

48 Access to equipment was understandably a source of tension in the penal press. *Pen-O-Rama* writers called out *Tele-Scope* staff for being smug, noting: "Yes, it is a good magazine, working under a minimum of handicaps. It has more facilities at its disposal than all other Canadian institutions combined, including good writers." *Pen-O-Rama*, April 1953, 10. CDOJ, *Annual Report ... 1951*, 33.

49 *Pathfinder*, March 1955, 21.

50 CDOJ, *Annual Report ... 1951*, 17.

51 *Mountain Echoes*, November 1951, 6.

52 Some magazines thought it important to have a slogan to guide their publication. *Tele-Scope* borrowed from Shakespeare when they popularized the idea of making time serve them rather than serving time. *Transition*

said that their aim was to "be an able servant to all who serve the tyrant, time." *Transition*, March 1953, 2. *Beacon* lamented the absence of a slogan, while *Pen-O-Rama* staff wrote that their work was designed to "promote goodwill and understanding between the inside and outside." *Pen-O-Rama*, February 1955, back cover.

53 *Tele-Scope*, September 1954, back cover.
54 *Tele-Scope*, November 1952, 8–9.
55 The reprinted image can be found in *Transition*, September–October 1957, 29.
56 Sykes and Messinger, 18.
57 Goffman, "The Underlife of a Public Institution," in *Asylums*, 319.
58 *Mountain Echoes*, November 1951, 1.
59 *Tele-Scope*, September 1951, 23. There is evidence that the penal press did create dialogue about the daily lives of the prisoners. For example, in September 1954 an article was published in *Mountain Echoes* that questioned the way that tobacco was being dispersed to prisoners who were to be released imminently; the commissioner wrote to the warden after reading the article, and this created a flurry of correspondence between administrators and staff about procedures. *Mountain Echoes*, September 1954, 12; Commissioner of Penitentiaries to the Warden, Stony Mountain [Manitoba] Penitentiary, "RE: Tobacco Issues," 17 September 1954, LAC, RG 73, vol. 117, file 6-11-26; E. McKeown, Clerk Personnel to the Warden, Manitoba Penitentiary, "Re: Tobacco Issues," 22 September 1954, 1954, LAC, RG 73, vol. 117, file 6-11-26; Warden Campbell, Manitoba Penitentiary to Commissioner of Penitentiaries, "Re: Tobacco Issues," 25 September 1954, LAC, RG 73, vol. 117, file 6-11-26; R.B. Gibson, Commissioner of Penitentiaries to the Warden, Stony Mountain [Manitoba] Penitentiary, "Re: Tobacco Issues," 5 October 1954, LAC, RG 73, vol. 117, file 6-11-26; Warden Campbell, Manitoba Penitentiary to Commissioner of Penitentiaries, "Re: Tobacco Issues," 9 October 1954, LAC, RG 73, vol. 117, file 6-11-26.
60 *C.B. Diamond*, March 1952, 1. Interestingly, by June 1954, their platform had changed to one that was much more moralistic in tone. For example, they wrote the following platform, which seemed to run counter to the new penal reforms: "To inspire and cultivate moral and intellectual improvement amongst the men of Collin's Bay. To aid in overcoming the arbitrary bias which is one of the numerous 'bars sinister' to a wayward man's redemption. To discuss progressive and revolutionary penological data, with a report to particularity, favor or affection. To evince Stoicism and humour, to the end that lights shall obtain even in darkness. To elicit the support of Society in welcoming the return of a man from prison who needs help and who is genuinely desirous of seeking his reformation in the highly competitive life of the free world." *C.B. Diamond*, June 1954, 1.

61 *Tele-Scope*, September 1951, 11.

62 *Transition*, January 1953, 12.

63 *Tele-Scope*, September 1951, 8.

64 *Tele-Scope*, December 1951, 22.

65 *Tele-Scope*, April 1958, 32.

66 "From Behind the Wall," *Edmonton Journal*, 13 October 1953, newspaper clipping, LAC, RG 73, vol. 121, file 7-11-26, pt 1.

67 *Pen-O-Rama*, December 1952, 61. This idea appeared repeatedly in various sources. Harold Weir, in a piece titled "Wisdom from the cells," in the *Vancouver Sun*, noted that "if I had a son and wanted to keep him out of jail, which would be likely, I'd like him to read these magazines for the level-headed aspects from which they view crime." Reprinted in *Pathfinder*, March 1955, 3–4.

68 Albert N. Forcier in *Pathfinder*, October 1958, 27.

69 While most were optimistic about the penal press and the New Deal, others recognized that conditions were, at their root, the same. For example, an editorial in the *Winnipeg Free Press* commented on the high calibre of writing in *Mountain Echoes* but noted that its contents were written from "a dungeon, no matter however modern, efficient and humane it may be." "Mountain Echoes," *Winnipeg Free Press*, 1 December 1953, newspaper clipping, LAC, RG 73, vol. 117, file 6-11-26.

70 HCD, 22nd Parl., 1st sess., vol. 6 (1954), 6573.

71 Sidney Katz, Assistant Editor, Maclean's Magazine to General Ralph Gibson, Commissioner of Penitentiaries, 6 February 1955, LAC, RG 73, vol. 65, file 1-11-26. By 1957, prisoners at SVP are able to apprentice under another prisoner who had been a journeyman typesetter prior to his incarceration. Ben Jauvin and Leo Leblanc, *Pen-O-Rama* to the Commissioner, 25 March 1957, LAC, RG 73, vol. 96, file 3-11-26, pt 2.

72 Don Lobb, Editor, *Mountain Echoes* to R.B. Gibson, Commissioner of Penitentiaries, 14 November 1957, LAC, RG 73, vol. 117, file 6-11-26.

73 Reprinted in *Tele-Scope*, June 1953, 6–7.

74 Gaucher, "The Canadian Penal Press," 2–4.

75 Prior to their launch, McCulley noted that he had no real objection to outside subscriptions, which he thought "could serve nothing other than a good purpose that immediate families should be aware that inmates do have opportunity for some constructive activities as will be recorded in the pages of the magazine and it is possible for them to laugh at prison jokes." J. McCulley, Deputy Commissioner, Memorandum to the Commissioner, "Re: Penitentiary Newspaper – Kingston," 15 August 1950, LAC, RG 73, vol. 65, file 1-11-26.

76 *Tele-Scope*, September 1951, 13. A notable exception to this is *Pathfinder*. Up to March 1952, *Pathfinder* did not receive other penal press publications from Canada or the United States. J.W. Everatt, Warden, Saskatchewan

Penitentiary to the Commissioner of Penitentiaries, "Re: Prison Publications," 26 March 1952, LAC, RG 73, vol. 121, file 7-11-26, pt 1. The warden planned to relax this ban but delayed doing so because his staff did not want other publications "tipping off" the *Pathfinder* staff that mail was being intercepted from the International Prisoners Association. J.W. Everatt, Warden, Saskatchewan Penitentiary to the Commissioner of Penitentiaries, "Re: Penal Press, Re: Magazine 'The Alabama Pen Point,'" 31 March 1952, LAC, RG 73, vol. 121, file 7-11-26, pt 1.

77 *Tele-Scope*, September 1951, 13.
78 *Tele-Scope*, September 1951, 13.
79 James F. Clark, Assistant Editor, on behalf of the Editorial Staff of *Pathfinder* Magazine to Warden Everatt, Saskatchewan Penitentiary, 14 October 1952, LAC, RG 73, vol. 121, file 7-11-26, pt 1.
80 R.B. Gibson, Commissioner of Penitentiaries to Warden, Saskatchewan Penitentiary, "Re: Editorial Policy, 'Pathfinder' Magazine," 21 October 1952, LAC, RG 73, vol. 121, file 7-11-26, pt 1; J.W. Everatt, Warden, Saskatchewan Penitentiary to the Commissioner of Penitentiaries, "Re: Pathfinder Magazine, Re: Editorial Policy," 14 October 1952, LAC, RG 73, vol. 121, file 7-11-26, pt 1.
81 *Tele-Scope*, March 1953, 32.
82 *C.B. Diamond*, December 1957, inside front cover.
83 *Tele-Scope*, January 1958, 7.
84 *Pen-O-Rama*, February 1954, 6.
85 Clint Sanders, Alabama Pen Point to the C.B. Diamond, 30 January 1952, RG 73, vol. 114, file 5-11-26, pt 1; Clint Sanders, Alabama Pen Point to the editor, C.B. Diamond, 20 April 1952, RG 73, vol. 114, file 5-11-26, pt 1; G. L. Sauvant, Senior Assistant Commissioner to the Warden, New Westminster, B.C., "Re: Penal Press, Re: Magazine 'The Alabama Pen Point,'" 27 March 1952, RG 73, vol. 114, file 5-11-26, pt 1; H. Cleeton, Warden, Collin's Bay Penitentiary to the Commissioner of Penitentiaries, "Re: Penal Press, Re: Alabama Pen Point," 22 March 1952, LAC, RG 73, vol. 114, file 5-11-26, pt 1.
86 G. Lebel, Warden, St. Vincent de Paul Penitentiary to the Commissioner of Penitentiaries, "Re:- Penal Press, Re:- 2598 Zarbatany, Emile," 12 April 1952, LAC, RG 73, vol. 114, file 5-11-26, pt 1.
87 H. Cleeton, Warden, Collin's Bay Penitentiary to the Commissioner of Penitentiaries, "Re: Penal Press, Re: Alabama Pen Point," 22 March 1952, LAC, RG 73, vol. 114, file 5-11-26, pt 1.
88 G.L. Sauvant, Senior Assistant Commissioner to the Warden, New Westminster, B.C., "Re: Penal Press, Re: Magazine "The Alabama Pen Point," 27 March 1952, RG 73, vol. 65, file 1-11-26; Commissioner R.B. Gibson to the Warden, Prince Albert, Saskatchewan, "Re: Prison Magazines," 8 April 1952, RG 73, vol. 65, file 1-11-26.

89 Baird, 10.
90 Ibid., 71–2.
91 *Sports Bulletin* 1, no. 24 (1950), 2.
92 *C.B. Diamond*, June 1957, 8–9.
93 *Transition*, April 1956, 6.
94 *Pen-O-Rama*, June 1953, 2.
95 *Tele-Scope*, January 1957, 43.
96 A prisoner at Kingston Penitentiary provided an apt description of the magnitude of diversity when he implored the editors of *Tele-Scope* to write "articles about us and our problems. Articles of interest to us and our friends. Articles that speak for us – all of us: the first offender and the 10th offender, the short timer and the long-timer, the booster and the heistman, the junkie and the junk-dealers, the paper-hanger and the prowler, the Peterman and all of us. It doesn't make any difference what we've done or what we are. We're all alike in our hopes and fears. We're all in the same boat and we sink or float together. So let your magazine speak for us all." *Tele-Scope*, January 1953, 11.
97 In 1950, the editor of *Sports Bulletin* pointed out that even a second person would be helpful: "Having had the real pleasure of reading two recent issues of the Kingston penitentiary paper, with its four *able* associate editors and many inmates contributing clever articles, and its smart format, one cannot but deplore that our Sports Bulletin is confined almost exclusively to the continually overstressed an egotistical viewpoint, vacuous outpourings, and biased opinions of one man only." *Sports Bulletin* 1, no. 21 (1950), 7.
98 The staff at the prisoner-written magazines often did this work in their spare time as they often had other full-time work in the institution. *C.B. Diamond*: January 1957, 2; April 1958, 24.
99 *Beacon*, 2 November 1951, 1.
100 *Beacon*, 30 November 1951, 4.
101 *Tele-Scope*, November 1954, 2.
102 *Tele-Scope*, December 1952, 9.
103 *Transition*, January 1953, 18.
104 *Transition*, January 1953, 18.
105 *Tele-Scope*, March 1954, 39.
106 *Tele-Scope*, May 1954, 23.
107 Goffman, "On the Characteristics of Total Institutions," in *Asylums*, 97.
108 *C.B. Diamond*, June 1954, 34.
109 *Transition*, March 1953, 3–4.
110 *Transition*, December 1955, 29. *C.B. Diamond* reprinted this criticism in their February 1956 edition but attempted to deflect the criticism by blaming a former editor. They concluded their piece by stating: "In closing, we know

we are the junior member of the Canadian Penal Press, further we know we are rank amateurs; but at least we do not engage in rebounding brickbats from one magazine to another. *C.B. Diamond*, February 1956, 39.

111 Bill Blair, "On First Impression," *Transition*, August 1958, 6.

112 R.B. Gibson, Commissioner of Penitentiaries to the Warden, Saskatchewan Penitentiary, "Re:'Pathfinder' Magazine," 25 August 1955, 3, LAC, RG 73, vol. 121, file 7-11-26, pt 1; Gibson's use of the term "tolerance" seems to be a direct response to the editors of *Pathfinder* who wrote to him on 20 July 1953 with their concerns over censorship. In their letter, the prisoners suggest that "perhaps the best that any honest and sincerely written inmate publication can hope to win from Administration is *tolerance*" (emphasis in original). James F. Clark, Editor, *Pathfinder* to Commissioner of Penitentiaries, 20 July 1953, 2, LAC, RG 73, vol. 121, file 7-11-26, pt 1.

113 Gaucher, "The Canadian Penal Press," 1.

114 Ibid., 4–5.

115 Al Parsons, *Pen-O-Rama*, June 1955, 20.

116 Gaucher, "The Canadian Penal Press," 1.

117 "The Sharp and Bright Sword," C.B. Diamond, July 1955, 4.

118 Gaucher, "The Canadian Penal Press," 3.

119 "The Sharp and Bright Sword," C.B. Diamond, July 1955, 4.

4. The New Deal – Same as the Old Deal?

1 CDOJ, *Annual Report ... 1949*, 7.

2 Joseph McCulley, Deputy Commissioner of Penitentiaries to the Editor, *C.B. Diamond*, 5 August 1952, LAC, RG 73, vol. 65, file 1-11-26; Joseph McCulley, Deputy Commissioner of Penitentiaries to the Editor, *Tele-Scope*, 6 August 1952, LAC, RG 73, vol. 65, file 1-11-26; *Tele-Scope*, April 1953, 36; *Pen-O-Rama*, August–September 1953, 29; *Pen-O-Rama*, October 1954, 23; *C.B. Diamond*, May 1956, 27; *Tele-Scope*, January 1957, 25; HCD, 24th Parl., 1st sess., vol. 1 (1958), 624; CDOJ, Committee Appointed to Inquire into the Principles and Procedures Followed in the Remission Service of the Department of Justice of Canada, *Report*, 79 (hereafter Fauteux Report).

3 CDOJ, *Annual Report ... 1951*, 8.

4 Taylor and Baskerville, 402; Canada, Parliament, House of Commons, *Budget Speech ... 1953*, 18.

5 See Mathiesen, 29–31, in which the author discusses the consistent rehabilitative emphases of prison programs and the repeated failure of those efforts over a four-hundred=year period.

6 HCD, 21st Parl., 6th sess., vol. 3 (May 29, 1952), 2716.

7 *Tele-Scope*, November 1952, 8–9.

8 Gibson, Presidential Address, 5.
9 Gibson, *"The Penitentiaries Move Forward,"* 4.
10 Cohen, *Visions of Social Control*, 225–6.
11 Foucault, *Discipline and Punish*, 268.
12 Ibid., 269.
13 Cohen, *Visions of Social Control*, 194.
14 Gibson, *"The Penitentiaries Move Forward,"* 4.
15 Frank Anderson contends that the silent system broke down before it was officially abolished. He argues that the war depleted the number of officers in the prisons so that by 1939, the new officers were "untrained" and not only tolerated dialogue between convicts but "guards and convicts conversed freely about every topic under the sun." See *Up the Ladder*, 125. Anderson's account, like Withrow's before him, demonstrates that change (or stagnation) does not always originate from the top, as the administrative record would suggest.
16 Foucault, *Discipline and Punish*, 101, 167, 203.
17 Gamberg and Thomson, 53.
18 "Staff Selection and Training in the Canadian (Federal) Penitentiary Service," 2, LAC, RG 73, vol. 32, file 1-18-15, pt 1.
19 Cohen, *Visions of Social Control*, 161–5.
20 Anderson, *Up the Ladder*, 124.
21 Archambault Report, 202.
22 CDOJ, *Annual Report ... 1948*, 10.
23 Gibson, *"The Penitentiaries Move Forward,"* 4.
24 CDOJ, *Annual Report ... 1950*, 21.
25 HCD, 21st Parl., 6th sess., vol. 3 (1952), 2721.
26 HCD, 21st Parl., 6th sess., vol. 3, 2721–2.
27 CDOJ, *Annual Report ... 1955*, 8–9.
28 *Tele-Scope*, January 1953, 5. Mainstream publications also advocated for diversion of youth from prison. See for example, Sidney Katz, "It's a Tough Time to Be a Kid," *Maclean's*, 15 January 1951, 14–15, 44–5.
29 *C.B. Diamond*, May 1955, 2.
30 John Fortano in Gamberg and Thomson, 53.
31 Gamberg and Thomson, 53.
32 Despite the platitudes, and the commissioner's clear recognition of the importance of psychiatric interventions, medical and psychiatric services received less than two pages of coverage in the commissioner's annual reports during the 1950s, and most of that space was devoted to medical services. While Gibson's reports are meticulous in their detail on other matters – for example, his tables, descriptions, and pontifications on prison industries and prisoner labour emphasize progress in painstaking detail – his coverage of psychological services is cursory, vague, repetitive,

and non-instructive. Appendix A provides the complete reports on psychological services between 1947 and 1957. In these reports, five major tropes developed and were repeated *ad nauseam*: the link between psychiatric disorders and crime; autonomous prisoner demand for psychiatric services; the types of therapies available; the benefits attained; and the need to hire more personnel and expand facilities.

33 For information on staffing, see Canada, Department of Justice: *Annual Report … 1951*, 43; *Annual Report … 1953*, 50; *Annual Report … 1957*, 18–19, 47.

34 CDOJ, *Annual Report … 1957*, 47.

35 Cohen, *Visions of Social Control*, 25, 166.

36 CDOJ, *Annual Report … 1956*, 40.

37 Gibson, "The Penitentiaries Move Forward," 5; CDOJ, *Annual Report … 1950*, 20. These classification practices continue to the present day.

38 Gibson, "The Penitentiaries Move Forward," 5; Canada, Department of Justice: *Annual Report … 1949*, 20; *Annual Report … 1950*, 20; *Annual Report … 1951*, 23-24; *Annual Report … 1953*, 18–19.

39 For information on group and electroconvulsive therapy, see Canada, Department of Justice: *Annual Report 1949*, 42; *Annual Report … 1950*, 36; *Annual Report … 1952*, 47; *Annual Report … 1957*, 47.

40 For further consideration see Osborne.

41 Reprint of Tyler, "Prisoners Used."

42 Ibid.

43 Between 1947 and 1952, 366 new positions were created in the Penitentiary Service. CDOJ, *Annual Report … 1952*, 14.

44 Canada, Department of Justice: *Annual Report … 1948*, 10; *Annual Report … 1949*, 7–8; Gibson, "The Penitentiaries Move Forward," 4.

45 HCD, 21st Parl., 6th sess., vol. 3, 2717.

46 "Education for Penal Inmates is Broader Says Commissioner," *Victoria Colonist*, 4 October 1950, newspaper clipping, RG 73, vol. 43, file 1-20-36, pt 1. A document titled "Staff Selection and Training in the Canadian (Federal) Penitentiary System" details the ways that selection of staff, and their new training, was conducted. LAC, RG 73, vol. 32, file 1-18-15, pt 1.

47 *Tele-Scope*, August 1952, 2–3.

48 Gibson, "The Penitentiaries Move Forward," 4.

49 HCD, *Debates*, 21st Parl., 6th sess., vol. 3, 2725.

50 *Tele-Scope*, August 1952, 4.

51 *Tele-Scope*, August 1952, 4, 19.

52 Archambault Report, 344–5.

53 Between 1948 and 1951, 469 officers had either attended training courses or participated in conferences; 455 of these individuals remained with the service in June 1951. However, these men were selected by their wardens. Among those who did not attend, staff turnover was significant. Annual rates of

turnover averaged between 10 and 15 per cent in the late 1940s and early 1950s (among a total staff complement that exceeded 1,100 members by 1953), which means that turnover among non-trainees likely exceeded 25 per cent per year at times. Minutes of the 1949 Wardens' Conference, 15 June 1949, morning session, LAC, RG 73, vol. 31, file 1-18-11; Minutes of the 1951 Wardens' Conference, 21 June 1951, 9:30 a.m., LAC, RG 73, vol. 31, file 1-18-1, 11.

54 *Tele-Scope*, May 1954, 5.

55 Frankie Watson, Inmate Committee Chair at Kingston Penitentiary, commented, in regard to Warden Allan's retirement, that despite the speculation and the fear of others, if the new warden "lives up to Little Dick [Allan], in so far as his attitude towards the new deal is concerned, we won't go far wrong." *Tele-Scope*, May 1954, 21.

56 Goffman, "On the Characteristics of Total Institutions," in *Asylums*, 114.

57 "Static minds?," *Transition*, October 1954, 8–9.

58 Archambault Report, 345.

59 According to Rusche and Kirchheimer, staffing penitentiaries with the members of the "military caste" was intentional, because "conformism" was considered "a prime virtue." Rusche and Kirchheimer, 156.

60 Archambault Report, 330.

61 *C.B. Diamond*, February 1958, 7.

62 Mathiesen, 35, 42.

63 See chapter 2 for more discussion on the lack of criteria used to define incorrigibility.

64 Gamberg and Thomson, 54.

65 *Pathfinder*, June 1955, 19.

66 *Tele-Scope*, June 1952, 21.

67 *C.B. Diamond*, December 1952, 39. While this reform did not fully happen in the period under consideration, it bears mention that this is now standard practice in the "cascading" system currently used in federal corrections.

68 Al Parsons, "My Cell," *Pen-O-Rama*, November 1954, 18; Andre Dion, a former prisoner at St. Vincent DePaul, noted that during his incarceration, in-cell toilets were not available; prisoners used a bucket, which they emptied daily. Andre Dion (former prisoner at St. Vincent de Paul Penitentiary), in discussion with Melissa Munn and Robert Gaucher, 20 January 2016, Magog, Quebec.

69 *Tele-Scope*, March 1954, 4.

70 "1940–1959: Times of Change," http://www.csc-scc.gc.ca/about-us/006 -2003-eng.shtml.

71 Goffman, "On the Characteristics of Total Institutions," in *Asylums*, 6.

72 HCD, 22nd Parl., 2nd sess., vol. 6, 5909.

73 Mathiesen, 45.

74 Ibid., 44.

75 Gamberg and Thomson, 54.

76 Gibson, *"The Penitentiaries Move Forward,"* 2–3.

77 McCulley, *Rehabilitation*, 4.

78 Ibid., 4.

79 R.B. Gibson to Joseph McCulley, 20 November 1948, LAC, RG 73, vol. 43, file 1-20-31.

80 Some prisons permitted prisoners to participate in organized sports in the 1930s, although the practice was discontinued. See Archambault Report, 289.

81 Canada, Department of Justice: *Annual Report … 1950*, 17; *Annual Report … 1952*, 26.

82 Vic Ashton, "Prison Utopia," *Transition*, April 1953, 18.

83 *Pen-O-Rama*, December 1954, 53.

84 *Pen-O-Rama*, December 1954, 53–4.

85 Goffman, "On the Characteristics of Total Institutions," in *Asylums*, 107.

86 In May 1952 the Minister of Justice indicated to the House of Commons that "considerable use already is being made of inmate committees in order to develop a sense of community responsibility." HCD, 21st Parl., 6th sess., vol. 3, 2718. While these committees undoubtedly gave the prisoners a sense of control over their daily lives inside, counter-arguments can be made. For example, there is some indication that these committees offered the "necessary illusion" that they had say and some power when their participation was just a means of ensuring self-regulation and acceptance of the regulation inside a total institution. See Herman and Chomsky; and Chomsky. See also Goffman's contention that many institutional practices and ceremonies are designed to bring "staff and inmates … close enough together to get a somewhat favourable image of the other and to identify sympathetically with the other's situation," an analysis echoed by Commissioner Gibson (below, main text). Goffman, "On the Characteristics of Total Institutions," in *Asylums*, 94. Some prisoners were aware of this dichotomy (power vs powerlessness), and it was discussed repeatedly in the penal press, with several commenting on the futility of these committees: "[Committee] acts and policies are subject to the approval of the prison administration … Custody and discipline, the responsibility of the administration, have not been lessened." *Tele-Scope*, May 1953, 6. Another prisoner, Keith Munro, wrote in the *C.B. Diamond* of the irony that prisoners were "encouraged to think freely but must obey orders without question" (August 1956, 29).

87 CDOJ, *Annual Report … 1951*, 19. Over the course of the 1950s, inmate committees would take on an expanded role, administering various inmate funds and organizing new activities. At the same time, their relationship with administrators grew more confrontational and at times openly hostile. Minutes of the 1957 Wardens' Conference, 4 June 1957, 3:30 to 5:00 p.m., LAC, RG 73, vol. 33, file 1-18-17, pt 2.

88 CDOJ, *Annual Report … 1950*, 17.

89 Foucault, "Governmentality," 87–104. The Chief Keeper at Kingston Penitentiary noted that "it has been proved beyond a shadow of a doubt that the playing of softball within the institution has improved the morale of everybody. Not only has it been an emotional outlet, it has also been the means of teaching self-discipline and control." J.E. Atkins in *Tele-Scope*, September 1950, 5.

90 *Sports Bulletin* 1, no. 9 (1950), 11, emphasis in original.

91 *Sports Bulletin* 1, no. 19 (1950), 6. This kind of reward system reinforced the prisoners' notion that they were being treated like people. For example, Joe Bennett wrote in *Tele-Scope* that participation in sports "has enabled personalities overburdened by the deteriorating anonymity of regimented numbers, to become in a small way individualized, by the opening of opportunities, small as they are, for exerting relatively unchaperoned individual efforts." *Tele-Scope*, September 1951, 21.

92 *Softball Bulletin* 1, no. 10 (August 1950), 2.

93 *C.B. Diamond*, August 1956, 30.

94 Goffman, "On the Characteristics of Total Institutions," in *Asylums*, 108.

95 *Tele-Scope*, June 1951, 12.

96 *Tele-Scope*, September 1, 1950, 9. In May 1952, the minister of justice, Stuart Garson, took time in Parliament to praise the sports program: "It is interesting to note that in at least two areas penitentiary teams have been included in local city softball leagues and the standard of sportsmanship displayed in these contests has been a credit to the men in our institutions. Furthermore, such visits to the institutions have provided opportunities for certain members of the outside public to [see] something of the inside of prisons and to become familiar with a policy of administration which is humane and dedicated to the idea of rehabilitation." HCD, 21st Parl., 6th sess., vol. 3, 2718.

97 *Tele-Scope*, August 1951, 11.

98 *Pen-O-Rama*, April 1953, 37.

99 Given his positive coverage of the sports program at Kingston Penitentiary, the prisoners were shocked when Andy O'Brien authored a piece in the *Weekend Picture Magazine* (15 July 1951) that, they felt, minimized the severity and austerity of the prison conditions. *Tele-Scope*, October 1951, 18.

100 *Toronto Daily Star*, qtd in *Tele-Scope*, June 1951, 18.

101 CDOJ, *Annual Report … 1950*, 16.

102 *Pen-O-Rama*, December 1952, 21.

103 On the radio upgrade, see CDOJ, *Annual Report of the Commissioner of Penitentiaries for the Fiscal Year ended March 31, 1954* (Ottawa: Queen's Printer, 1955), 23.

104 CDOJ, *Annual Report … 1955*, 72; *Tele-Scope*, March 1954, 4.

105 These orchestras were dependent on donations of instruments. *Transition*, February 1953, 13.

106 The calibre of the prisoners' artistry was even noted in the House of Commons: "A final item which I would like to mention was the participation by a male chorus consisting of member[s] of the Catholic and Protestant choirs of Dorchester penitentiary in the maritime music festival. The choir had been trained by the penitentiary organist, and their selections were transmitted by telephone line from the prison to the hall in Moncton where the contest was being held. The adjudicator awarded to the penitentiary choir the highest marks given to competitors in all classes. The program and the remarks of the adjudicator were relayed back to the prison and heard by all inmates over the prison public address system." HCD, 21st Parl., 6th sess., vol. 3, 2719.

107 Minutes of the 1957 Wardens Conference, 4 June 1957, 3:30 to 5:00 p.m., LAC, RG 73, vol. 33, file 1-18-17, pt 2. For evidence of entertainers donating their time, see *Pen-O-Rama*, December 1952, 21; *Tele-Scope*, July 1952, 23.

108 The other opportunity that the men had to see women was during Red Cross Blood Donation clinics. Prisoners were exceptionally generous in their participation and took the opportunity to congratulate themselves, and encourage future donations, by running photos of the nurses drawing blood. *Pen-O-Rama*, September 1953, front cover, 20, 21, 27, 28; *C.B. Diamond*, July 1953, 20, 21; *Transition*, February 1956, 11.

109 HCD, 21st Parl., 6th sess., vol. 3, 2719.

110 Canada, Department of Justice: *Annual Report … 1952*, 26; *Annual Report … 1954*, 22.

111 Canada, Department of Justice: *Annual Report … 1952*, 26; *Annual Report … 1953*, 24.

112 CDOJ, *Annual Report … 1950*, 19.

113 CDOJ, *Annual Report … 1950*, 19.

114 Minutes of the 1955 Wardens' Conference, 29 January 1955, a.m. 2nd session, 11–12:30, LAC, RG 73, vol. 32, file 1-18-15, pt 1; CDOJ, *Annual Report … 1957*, 22.

115 These acts of generosity were known by the prisoners but also by government officials at the highest levels. For example, the following speech was given by the minister of justice in 1952: "At Christmas of last year inmates for the first time were permitted to receive Christmas parcels from the outside. These were standard parcels of a value from $1 to $5, and arrangements were made by the individual wardens to have such parcels prepared by outside commercial suppliers provided the inmates themselves or their relatives made necessary funds available. The Christmas season in the institutions has in times past been a period of

considerable emotional tension. The granting of this privilege in keeping with the sentiments of the season seemed to be a reasonable and humane act, and it was also much appreciated by the inmates. There were of course some inmates who did not have funds available, but various arrangements were made that assured that no inmate would suffer because of lack of personal funds. It is only fair to the inmates to state that in many cases more fortunately placed inmates generously shared the contents of their parcels with their less fortunate fellows." HCD, 21st Parl., 6th sess., vol. 3, 2717.

116 There is evidence that some of the products could easily have been sold had there been a way to market them to potential purchasers. For example, hobbycraft from BC Penitentiary won first place at the Pacific National Exhibition in 1953. *Transition*, October 1953, 9.

117 Minutes of the 1951 Wardens' Conference, 14 June 1951, 2:30 p.m., LAC, RG 73, vol. 31, file 1-18-13, pt 1.

118 HCD, 22nd Parl., 1st sess., vol. 6, 6572.

119 Assistant Editor, *Pathfinder* to Commissioner of Penitentiaries, 31 August 1954, LAC, RG 73, vol. 121, file 7-11-26, pt 1.

120 R.B. Gibson, Commissioner of Penitentiaries to the Warden, Saskatchewan Penitentiary, 18 October 1954, LAC, RG 73, vol. 121, file 7-11-26, pt 1.

121 Minutes of the 1951 Wardens' Conference, 22 June 1951, 3:45–5:00 p.m., 1–3, LAC, RG 73, vol. 31, file 1-18-13, pt 1.

122 Anderson, *Up the Ladder*, 117.

123 *Toronto Daily Star*, qtd in *Tele-Scope*, October 1951, 22.

124 W.F. Johnstone, Supervisor of Training, Memorandum to Deputy Commissioner McCulley, "RE: Censorship in Penitentiaries, RE: Reader's Digest for March, 1951," 24 February 1951, LAC, RG 73, vol. 48, file 1-1-54; J. McCulley, Memorandum for File, "Re: Censorship Generally," 26 February 1951, LAC, RG 73, vol. 48, file 1-1-54.

125 By the end of the 1950s, many prisoners had access to some television. *Tele-Scope* noted that by July 1958 there were nine televisions at Kingston Penitentiary, and around 24 per cent of the inmate population had access to it. *Tele-Scope*, July 1958, 18. A TV was donated to the pre-release block at Dorchester in August 1958, and this expanded their prisoner's access to news. *Beacon*, August 1958, 16.

126 HCD, 21st Parl., 6th sess., vol. 3, 2717.

127 David Croll, qtd in *CB Diamond*, May 1957, 21.

128 *Transition*, May 1952, 9.

129 Archambault Report, 255.

130 *Transition*, November 1953, 3.

131 *Transition*, November 1953, 3.

132 Unknown Author, Handwritten Note to Commissioner, 25 November 1953, written in margin of G.T. Crofton, Acting Warden, Saskatchewan Penitentiary to Commissioner of Penitentiaries, "Re: Pathfinder Magazine," 20 November 1953, LAC, RG 73, vol. 121, file 7-11-26, pt 1.

133 *C.B. Diamond*, July 1956, 11.

134 *Tele-Scope*, March 1952, 7.

135 G.T. Crofton, Acting Warden, Saskatchewan Penitentiary to Commissioner of Penitentiaries, "Re: Pathfinder Magazine," 20 November 1953, LAC, RG 73, vol. 121, file 7-11-26, pt 1.

136 *Transition*, November 1952, 6–7.

137 Jack Grady, *Tele-Scope*, February 1953, 20.

138 CDOJ, *Penitentiary Regulations, 1933*, Regulation 101. Oswald Withrow noted that friends were permitted to visit but that such visits were discouraged and infrequent. Withrow, 37–8, 162.

139 *Transition*, June 1954, 4.

140 League of Nations, "Penal and Penitentiary Questions … the Fifth Committee," 24 September 1934.

141 *Transition*, April 1953, 21.

142 For example, on 23 June 1954, the following exchange occurred in the House of Commons: Mr. Winch: "The time has come for the revision of some of these regulations. I think they are a little bit too onerous. For example, I think an inmate of the penitentiary is allowed two letters per month. If a man is in a penitentiary for a considerable number of years it seems to me a little bit tough that he should be tied down to two letters a month, or three if he does not have any visitors for a period of four weeks. I have spoken to men in the penitentiary and they tell me they can send a letter to their wives, one to their mothers, and that is all. They cannot write their brothers, sisters, or others. I am wondering if there is any possibility of reconsidering regulations such as that and introducing some slight change for the better." Mr. Garson: "The hon. member must be clairvoyant because it so happens that that particular matter is under consideration at the present time." HCD, 22nd Parl., 1st sess., vol. 6, 6569.

143 J.A. McLaughlin, Assistant Commissioner of Penitentiaries, "MEMORANDUM FOR FILE," 13 April 1949, LAC, RG 73, vol. 48, file 1-1-54.

144 Interestingly, there is some early evidence of the emergence of the prison-industrial complex in the file. The warden of Kingston Penitentiary sent Commissioner Gibson an article that verged on being promotional material from an electrical journal. The article contended that "the ingenuity of prisoners in using a wide variety of liquids as sympathetic or 'invisible' inks is well known to crime detection agencies," and held out the promise that the use of ultraviolet lamps would make

such messages "instantly readable." "Filtered Ultraviolent Light Aids Crime Detection and Identification," *Electrical Digest*, undated clipping, LAC, RG 73, vol. 48, file 1-1-54. See also R.B. Gibson, Commissioner of Penitentiaries to the Commissioner, Royal Canadian Mounted Police, "RE: Training of Penitentiary Officers," 16 October 1952, LAC, RG 73, vol. 48, file 1-1-54; R.M. Allan, Warden, Kingston Penitentiary to Commissioner of Penitentiaries, "Re: detection of invisible writing, Re: Black Light," 29 December 1950, LAC, RG 73, vol. 48, file 1-1-54; S.C. Davidson, Deputy Warden, Kingston Penitentiary to the Warden, "Re: Detection of Invisible Writing, Re: Black Light," 23 December 1950, LAC, RG 73, vol. 48, file 1-1-54; L.P. Gendreau, Deputy Commissioner to Warden, Kingston Penitentiary, "Re: Detection of Invisible Writing, Re: Black Light," 5 January 1951, LAC, RG 73, vol. 48, file 1-1-54; L.P. Gendreau, Deputy Commissioner to Warden, Kingston Penitentiary, "Re: Detection of Invisible Writing, Re: Black Light," 26 January 1951, LAC, RG 73, vol. 48, file 1-1-54; G.L. Sauvant, Senior Assistant Commissioner to the Warden, Kingston Penitentiary, "Re: Censoring of Mail and Detection of Invisible Ink, Re: Black Light," 23 February 1950, LAC, RG 73, vol. 48, file 1-1-54; R.M. Allan, Warden, Kingston Penitentiary to Commissioner of Penitentiaries, "Re: Censoring of Mail and Detection of Invisible Ink, Re: Black Light," 10 February 1950, LAC, RG 73, vol. 48, file 1-1-54.

145 L.P. Gendreau, Deputy Commissioner to Warden, Kingston Penitentiary, "Re: Detection of Invisible Writing, Re: Black Light," 20 December 1950, LAC, RG 73, vol. 48, file 1-1-54; S.C. Davidson, Deputy Warden, Kingston Penitentiary to the Warden, "Re: Detection of Invisible Writing, Re: Black Light," 23 December 1950, LAC, RG 73, vol. 48, file 1-1-54.

146 *Beacon*, 30 November 1951, 8.

147 *Tele-Scope*, June 1954, 2.

148 *Tele-Scope*, May 1954, 4.

149 HCD, 21st Parl., 6th sess., vol. 3, 2725–6.

150 CDOJ, *Annual Report … 1949*, 16.

151 CDOJ, *Annual Report … 1951*, 15.

152 R.B. Gibson drew attention the DVA's contribution when he wrote in his annual report: "Thanks are, however, extended to the Department of Veterans Affairs for their continued co-operation. During the year a total of 1,680 inmates registered for D.V.A. courses – of these 683 being veterans and 997 non-veterans. Courses were successfully completed by a total of 637 inmates (283 veterans and 354 non-veterans) and certificates of achievement awarded." CDOJ, *Annual Report … 1950*, 15.

153 CDOJ, *Annual Report … 1950*, 15.

154 *Tele-Scope*, September 1951, 32; *C.B. Diamond*, March 1952, 8.

155 *Tele-Scope*, November 1951, 7.

156 See, for example, *Mountain Echoes*: March 1952, 21; August 1958, 21.

157 Smith, 52.

158 Prisoners laboured in various locations – in the kitchen, in the tailor shop, on cleaning crews, and in yard crews. In a somewhat morbid turn, members in the stone shed crew carved the numbered gravestones of those who died in prison but did not have their bodies claimed. *Pen-O-Rama*, August–September 1953, 33.

159 See CDOJ, *Annual Report ... 1948*, 19–20, on the creation of the new program.

160 *Transition*, June 1954, 6.

161 "DATA SHEET, Inmate Work Assignments, Wardens' Conference '55," LAC, RG 73, vol. 32, file 1-18-15, pt 2.

162 Gamberg and Thomson, 52.

163 CDOJ, *Annual Report ... 1951*, 30; *Annual Report ... 1952*, 35.

164 CDOJ, *Annual Report ... 1949*; *Annual Report ... 1957*, 42;, 26; *Annual Report ... 1958*, 39.

165 CDOJ, *Annual ... 1958*, 17–18.

166 CDOJ, *Annual Report ... 1958*, 40–1.

167 See CDOJ, *Annual Report ... 1948*, 94; *Annual Report ... 1949*, 116; *Annual Report ... 1950*, 106; *Annual Report ... 1951*, 122; *Annual Report ... 1952*, 136; *Annual Report ... 1953*, 46; *Annual Report ... 1954*, 146; *Annual Report ... 1955*, 144; *Annual Report ... 1956*, 144; *Annual Report ... 1957*, 158; *Annual Report ... 1958*, 190.

168 CDOJ, *Annual Report ... 1955*, 26.

169 *Tele-Scope*, April 1953, 20.

170 *Beacon*, 30 November 1951, n.p.

171 Gamberg and Thomson noted that only 38 per cent of inmates were employed in penitentiary shops by 1960. Gamberg and Thomson, 52.

172 HCD, 22nd Parl., 1st sess., vol. 6 (23 June 1954), 6574.

173 *Tele-Scope*, November 1951, 24. As criminologist Bob Gaucher has pointed out, in the 1960s, "whatever 'certificates' prisoners obtained were not recognized outside; and therefore, in providing such certificates to prospective employers only succeeded in highlighting that the applicant had been in prison." Bob Gaucher, personal communication with the authors, July 2018.

174 Archambault Report, 129.

175 Archambault Report, 128.

176 CDOJ, *Annual Report ... 1953*, 34.

177 CDOJ, *Annual Report ... 1953*, 34.

178 CDOJ, *Annual Report ... 1953*, 40.

179 This amount was predicated on the prisoner being of good behaviour; if he was not, his pay was docked.

180 HCD, 21st Parl., 6th sess., vol. 3, 2716–17.

181 Andre Dion (former prisoner at St. Vincent de Paul Penitentiary), in discussion with Melissa Munn and Robert Gaucher, 20 January 2016, Magog, Quebec.

182 Minutes of the 1955 Wardens Conference, 28 January 1955, 9:30 to 11:00 a.m., LAC, RG 73, vol. 32, file 1-18-15, pt 1.

183 *Transition*: January 1953, 3; March 1953, 3, 26

184 *Transition*, July 1953, 10.

185 HCD, 21st Parl., 6th sess., vol. 3, 2717.

186 Minutes of the 1955 Wardens Conference, 28 January 1955, 9:30 to 11:00 a.m., LAC, RG 73, vol. 32, file 1-18-15, pt 1.

187 Rusche and Kirchheimer argued that fair wages for prisoners was, given the social structures in place, an impossibility because convicts could not earn the same as free labour or prison would lose its deterrent value. Rusche and Kirchheimer, 153.

188 *Transition*, April 1952, 2.

189 Arnold Abrams noted that there was no mechanism built into the pay scale to adjust for inflation and that this would result in future prisoners being in worse economic shape on release. *Transition*, April 1952, 3.

190 *Transition*, August 1956, 5–6.

191 HCD, 24th Parl., 2nd sess., vol. 1, 1017.

192 Bothwell, Drummond, and English, 15–16, 20–1, 198–9.

193 CDOJ, *Annual Report … 1952*, 33–4.

194 Canada, Department of Justice: *Annual Report … 1948*, 17–18; *Annual Report … 1949*, 21; *Annual Report … 1950*, 25; *Annual Report … 1951*, 29; *Annual Report … 1952*, 33; *Annual Report … 1954*, 26–7; *Annual Report … 1955*, 23–4; *Annual Report … 1956*, 22–3; *Annual Report … 1957*, 24; *Annual Report … 1958*, 20.

195 Garfinkel, 420–4.

196 *Montreal Star*, October 1954, in *Pen-O-Rama*, October 1954, 23.

197 See chapter 4 for further discussion of how the penal press helped propagate an image of prisons as better than they were.

198 HCD, 21st Parl., 6th sess., vol. 3, 2721.

199 Rusche and Kirchheimer, 159.

200 *Tele-Scope*, October 1951, 22.

201 *Transition*, March 1953, 7.

202 *Transition*, June 1957, 11. Canada did not start keeping official crime statistics until 1961, so reliable data before that time are not available.

203 "There is no substitute," *Mountain Echoes*, December 1958, 16.

204 Brownie, "Gentlemen's Club? Well … let's see," *Pen-O-Rama*, October 1954, 23.

205 *C.B. Diamond*, July 1953, 2.

206 *Pathfinder*, February 1955, 4.

207 The reasons for McCulley's resignation do not appear in the official
record. Memorandums and notes in his personal correspondence file at
the University of Toronto archives indicate that individuals within the
corrections fields were "shocked" by his departure and that McCulley
made a great effort to reassure them of the difficulty of his decision and
his continued commitment to work on penal reform in an unofficial
capacity. Indeed, while he left the Penitentiary Service to take a warden's
position at Hart House (a space for "co-curricular activities") at the
University of Toronto, he maintained his involvement in penal reform,
writing to and visiting prisoners, participating actively in penal reform
organizations, and serving on the Fauteaux Committee from 1953 to
1956. It is clear that people involved in education were pleased that he
had accepted the warden position – one he had been considered for in
1943, prior to his appointment as Deputy Commissioner – but some
commented that it appeared to be a demotion of sorts, especially given
that he had been headhunted by organizations like the United Nations.
McCulley's personal correspondence makes it possible to hypothesize
two main reasons for his decision. First, he had experienced periods of
illness, and in 1950 his physician had cautioned him to "avoid prolonged
emotional tensions," opining that "the greatest hazard in this regard
would be in connection with your present position and programme
of penal reform." In his personal correspondence, McCulley validated
the physician's notion that he was working too hard as he repeatedly
discussed the immense workload and challenges of his job. So it may
be that he took the Hart House position to protect his health. There is
also tantalizing but inconclusive evidence that McCulley may have had
difficulty working within the military-style hierarchy of the Penitentiaries
Branch under General R.B. Gibson. It is clear from the Penitentiary
Branch records that there was a definite chain of command and authority
within the branch, and we can speculate that the bureaucratic structure
may have been a sticking point. For twenty years at Pickering, McCulley
had been at the top of the chain of command, though he worked to
minimize hierarchies and to encourage two-way dialogue. A series of
letters from friends and former colleagues following his resignation
from the Deputy Commissioner position adds weight to this theory. For
example, in a letter of congratulations on his new appointment, his friend
Blackie at Pickering College noted that "one or two knowing ones are
glad to see you freer from political influence and pressures," concluding
with a postscript reminding him that "Old Abe sure had his troubles with
generals." A letter from lawyer Charles Krug also lends credibility to this
theory. Krug suggested that McCulley's replacement would need to be
someone "accustomed to General Gibson's methods of operation and the

particular political exigencies of your service ... The Public Service ... has a very slow digestive rate for ideas. From all reports you've given them in five years a good generation of solid chewing." For more information on Hart House, see "History," Hart House, http://harthouse.ca/about-us/history. For his correspondence with prisoners, see *Transition*, February 1953, 12; *C.B. Diamond*, July 1953, 16. There is a photograph of McCulley visiting the Pen-O-Rama "office" in Pen-O-Rama, November 1952, 4. On McCulley's continued involvement with the Canadian Penal Congress, see *Pen-O-Rama*, September 1953, 2. The personal correspondence referred to in this note can be viewed at the Joseph McCulley, Personal Correspondence, Penitentiaries Branch, University of Toronto Archives, Reference Code UTA 1540-B1992-0013/006, in the folders labelled "Personal J. McCulley Re Hart House" and "Re Personal File Generally I."

208 McCulley, qtd in Leo Leblanc, "The Fauteux Report: Second Part," *Pen-O-Rama*, April 1957, 12.

209 This article, which was deemed by administrators as unfit for publication, is included in Appendix B.

210 James F. Clark, Editor, *Pathfinder* to Commissioner of Penitentiaries, 20 July 1953, 2, LAC, RG 73, vol. 121, file 7-11-26, pt 1.

211 Ben Jauvin, Manager, *Pen-O-Rama* and J.A.M. Grignon, Liaison Officer to Col. G. LeBel, Warden, St. Vincent de Paul Penitentiary, 22 January 1957, LAC, RG 73, vol. 96, file 3-11-26, pt 1; G. LeBel, Director, St. Vincent de Paul Penitentiary to Commissioner of Penitentiaries, "Re:- Pen-O-Rama," 25 January 1957, LAC, RG 73, vol. 96, file 3-11-26, pt 1; G.L. Sauvant, Deputy Commissioner to Director, St. Vincent de Paul Penitentiary, "Re: Pen-O-Rama," 29 January 1957, LAC, RG 73, vol. 96, file 3-11-26, pt 1.

212 *Pen-O-Rama*, September 1957, 31.

213 Bill Martin, "What's it like?" *Tele-Scope*, July 1958, 30.

214 *Tele-Scope*, June 1953, 6.

215 *Transition*, January 1954, 12.

216 *Transition*, October 1954, 8.

217 James P. Carleton, "Before and After Durance Vile," *Tele-Scope*, April 1954, 8–11.

5. Time Off: Clemency, Remission, and Parole

1 *Transition*, January 1953, 22.

2 Prisoners referred to time received for good behaviour as "crumb time." Bob Gaucher, personal communication with the authors, July 2018.

3 Archambault Report, 243.

4 CDOJ, *Report of General R.B. Gibson*, 3.

5 Fauteux Report, 1.

6 Ibid., 5.
7 Canada, *Penitentiary Act*, R.S.C. 1906, c. 147, s. 64
8 Fauteux Report, 60.
9 Ibid., 60.
10 CDOJ, *Annual Report ... 1939*, 31; Withrow, 107.
11 Fauteux Report, 60.
12 Ibid., 60.
13 Ibid., 60.
14 Tommy Nickols, "Remission Changes?" *Tele-Scope*, November 1951, 19.
15 *Tele-Scope*, April 1951, 24.
16 Fauteux Report, 60.
17 *Beacon*, October 1958, 3.
18 *Beacon*, October 1958, 4.
19 Virginia A, a prisoner in the Women's Prison, argued in an article titled "Remission Win or Lose" that the ability to earn remission was important and more validating than simply losing it for poor conduct. This seemed to be a minority opinion in the press. *Transition*, September 1951, 9.
20 *Sports Bulletin* 1, no. 23 (1950), 8–10.
21 *Tele-Scope*, 1951, 19.
22 Fauteux Report, 61.
23 *Sports Bulletin* 1, no. 23 (1950), 8.
24 G.T. Crofton, Acting Warden, Saskatchewan Penitentiary to Commissioner of Penitentiaries, "Re: Pathfinder Magazine," 20 February 1956, LAC, RG 73, vol. 121, file 7-11-26, pt 1.
25 When the Penitentiary Act was revised in 1961, the remission system was overhauled. At the time of admission, prisoners were automatically credited with good time equal to 25 per cent of their court-imposed sentence; this credit could be reduced as a form of punishment. They were also allowed to earn an additional three days per month for good conduct in the institution; once earned, this "good time" was not removed from the prisoner. *An Act respecting Penitentiaries*, S.C. 1961, c. 53, ss. 22–24.
26 Fauteux Report, 32.
27 *Pen-O-Rama*, April 1953, 15.
28 *Tele-Scope*, April 1953, 36.
29 HCD, 21st Parl., 7th sess., vol. 5, 4426.
30 "A Coronation precedent to be considered," *Montreal Star*, reprinted in *Tele-Scope*, February 1953, 25.
31 *Tele-Scope*, April 1953, 36.
32 CDOJ, *Annual Report ... 1953*, 12.
33 *Pen-O-Rama*, April 1953, 7.
34 *Tele-Scope*, May 1953, back cover.
35 CDOJ, *Annual Report ... 1953*, 12.

36 Fauteux Report, 8.

37 Ibid., 28.

38 A "free" pardon was a pardon granted by the governor general when the innocence of the accused was established and admitted by the Crown; in effect it was a pardon to which the wrongly accused was morally entitled. An ordinary pardon was seen more as an act of mercy, which was granted "on special considerations of an unusual character." In both instances, the pardon erased the offence completely, as if it never occurred. See Fauteux Report, 32.

39 Ibid., 102.

40 Ibid., 102–3.

41 Ibid., 115.

42 The Fauteux Report recommended that pardons be more liberally granted and that the authority for this should come from the Criminal Code rather than through a RPM. Ibid., 88.

43 Ibid., 55–6.

44 Ibid., 55.

45 Ibid., 91.

46 Anderson, *Up the Ladder*, 148.

47 See chapters 4 and 6 for more details.

48 CDOJ, *Annual Report … 1955*, 8.

49 Indeed, parliamentary debate in 1954 indicated that one of the main reasons the Fauteux Comission was established was "to see if we cannot by some different system of parole, not only remission in the federal field but also parole in the provincial field, have a smaller number of inmates in our provincial prisons or federal prisons to take care of in proportion to the total number of prisoners convicted." HCD, 22nd Parl., 1st sess., vol. 6, 6575.

50 Minutes of the 1955 Wardens Conference, 4 February 4, 1955, 9:30 to 11:00 a.m., LAC, RG 73, vol. 32, file 1-18-15, pt 1.

51 CDOJ, *Annual Report … 1955*, 13.

52 The following exchange took place in Parliament: "Mr. Garson: I wonder whether my hon. friend is aware, for example, that in 1954 – and that is fairly recently – there were 915 tickets of leave, of whom 576 had supervision by trained social workers or representatives of the remission service." HCD, 22 Parl., 2nd sess., vol. 6, 5914.

53 *Tele-Scope*, July 1954, 36.

54 *Tele-Scope*, August 1955, 17.

55 Fauteux Report, 62.

56 Ibid., 63.

57 Ibid., 63. Gibson noted in his 1955–56 report that if a prisoner was sick or lacked outside assistance, the remission service would not grant a ticket-of-leave. CDOJ, *Annual Report … 1956*, 39.

58 For individuals serving a sentence of preventative detention that was indeterminate, Section 666 of the *Criminal Code* required the minister of justice to review all circumstances to see if a person should be granted a parole. Fauteux Report, 65.

59 HCD, 22nd Parl., 3rd sess., vol. 2, 2120. During his interview with us, Andre Dion, former editor of *Pen-O-Rama*, indicated that he was granted a leave in 1951 after serving five of fourteen years. Andre Dion (former prisoner at St. Vincent de Paul Penitentiary), in discussion with Melissa Munn and Robert Gaucher, 20 January 2016, Magog, Quebec.

60 HCD, 22nd Parl., 3rd sess., vol. 2, 2121.

61 Fauteux Report, 65.

62 In 1949, the Remission Branch added an office in Vancouver (one officer) and one in Montreal (one officer) to the already operational one in Ottawa (seven officers). F. Ward Cook operated the Vancouver office with the help of a filing clerk and a secretary while Mr. Tremblay operated the Montreal office with four support staff. Ibid., 8–9.

63 Ibid., 9.

64 Anderson, *Up the Ladder*, 135.

65 *Tele-Scope*, December 1952, 20–21.

66 Dave Nolan, "The Case for Parole: Part II," *Tele-Scope*, February 1951, 17.

67 Ibid., 17.

68 HCD, 24th Parl., 1st sess., vol. 4, 3727.

69 Fauteux Report, 1.

70 HCD, 22nd Parl., 3rd sess., vol. 1, 416.

71 *Pen-O-Rama*, December 1957, 2.

72 The Parole Board of Canada argues, on the basis of information from Frank Miller, Assistant Director with the Remission Service, that "change was already under way when the Fauteux committee started its work, and that the committee simply helped the changes along." In Miller's words, "We didn't sit back and wait for the report." "History of Parole in Canada," Parole Board of Canada.

73 HCD, 24th Parl., 1st sess., vol. 3, 3375.

74 Fauteux Report, 80.

75 *Tele-Scope*, April 1958, 24.

76 Nolan, "The Case for Parole: Part II," *Tele-Scope*, February 1951, 16.

77 Fauteux Report, 81.

78 Appointments were to be for a ten-year period, so initial selection would have long-lasting implications. Ibid., 81.

79 *Tele-Scope*, April 1958, 24.

80 *Tele-Scope*, October 1958, 12. The issue of "carry-over" was perhaps bigger than the prisoners realized. The minister of justice confirmed that "in actual fact, our present plans contemplate the transfer of virtually all of the staff of the remission service to the staff of the new parole board." HCD, 24th Parl., 1st sess., vol. 4, 3732.

81 HCD, 24th Parl., 1st sess., vol. 4, 3729.
82 HCD, 24th Parl., 2nd sess., vol. 4, 4896. The first woman member, Mary Louise Lynch, was appointed to the board in 1960. CDOJ, National Parole Board, *Annual Report ... 1960*, ii.
83 "What about parole!," *Mountain Echoes*, February 1952, 21.
84 HCD, 23rd Parl., 1st sess., vol. 3, 3107.
85 HCD, 23rd Parl., 1st sess., vol. 2, 1388.
86 HCD, 23rd Parl., 2nd sess., vol. 1, 1012.
87 Garfinkel, 420–4.
88 Fauteux Report, 82.
89 Ibid., 82.
90 In addition, these representatives were liaisons between the institutions and the board, arranged for the hearings to take place, made arrangements for the supervision of parolees, and performed other duties of an administrative nature. Ibid., 68.
91 CDOJ, National Parole Board, *First Annual Report ... 1959*; *An Act to provide for the Conditional Liberation of Persons Undergoing Sentences of Imprisonment*, S.C. 1958, c. 38, s. 8.
92 CDOJ, National Parole Board, *Annual Report ... 1960*, 18.
93 "Parole," *C.B. Diamond*, December 1960, 36.
94 Street, 3.
95 Ibid., 3.
96 *Beacon*, November–December 1960, 14.
97 *Beacon*, November–December 1960, 14.
98 "Parole," *C.B. Diamond*, December 1960, 37.
99 *Transition*, August 1956, 14.
100 Fauteux Report, 62.
101 Street, 4.
102 Ibid., 3.
103 See, for example, CDOJ, National Parole Board, *Annual Report ... 1961*, 2.
104 "History of Parole in Canada," Parole Board of Canada.
105 Fauteux Report, 87.
106 See United Nations, Department of Social Affairs, "Justification for Parole" (New York, 1954) in ibid., 126–9, App. L.
107 HCD, 24th Parl., 3rd sess., vol. 5, 5623.
108 See for example, *C.B. Diamond*, May 1960, 23.
109 The minister's statistics do not match those provided by the National Parole Board. In this case, it is possible that the minister simply inverted two numbers by stating 2,830 rather than the 2,038 noted in the board's annual report. CDOJ, National Parole Board, *First Annual Report ... 1959*, 6.
110 HCD, 24th Parl., 3rd sess., vol. 5, 5623.

111 CDOJ, National Parole Board, *First Annual Report ... 1959*, 16.
112 *C.B. Diamond*, December 1960, 37. The 70 per cent figure often appears in the penal press, though no official sources are cited. For another example of this statistic, see *Transition*, January–February 1960, 2.
113 *C.B. Diamond*, May 1960, 27.
114 Mathiesen, 42.
115 See CDOJ, *Annual Report ... 1960*, 13; *Annual Report ... 1961*, 2.
116 *Transition*, May June 1960, 2.
117 Cohen, *Visions of Social Control*, 89.

6. New Deal/Old Deal: Discontent and Censorship

1 The four estates were, from first to fourth, the clergy, the nobility, the commoners, and the press.
2 Gordon Marr to Warden R.M. Allan, 8 August 1950, LAC, RG 73, vol. 65, file 1-11-26.
3 Minutes of the 1957 Wardens' Conference, 30 May 1957, 1st Section, 09:30 a.m. to 11:00 a.m., LAC, RG 73, vol. 33, file 1-18-17, pt 2.
4 CDOJ, *Annual Report ... 1953*, 22.
5 John Muise, "A Day in Prison," *Tele-Scope*, July 1958, 34–5.
6 R.B. Gibson, "Treatment of the Offender in Federal Institutions," *Tele-Scope*, May 1954, 6.
7 Gibson, *"The Penitentiaries Move Forward."*
8 CDOJ, *Annual Report ... 1954*, 8–9.
9 Marr, 64–5.
10 Ibid., 64.
11 Ibid., 65–6.
12 Ibid., 66–7.
13 Ibid., 67.
14 Correctional Service of Canada, "History of the Canadian Correctional System," 3.
15 Marr, 68.
16 Ibid., 68–9.
17 Ibid., 73.
18 Ibid., 71. For some time now, there has been concern over the ethics of electroshock therapy with prisoners. For an interesting examination of how this was used in combination with other experiments on brainwashing, see the transcript of Avril Benoit's interview of Rosie Rowbotham (which also includes transcripts of portions of Rowbotham's interviews of Allen Hornblum, a researcher who investigated medical experiments in American prisons; Dorothy Proctor, who received electroshock and LSD treatment at the federal Prison for Women in Kingston; and Dr George

Scott, the psychologist alleged to have supervised Proctor's treatment) at Canada, Groupe en éthique de la recherché, Le didacticiel EPTC 2 Formation en éthique de la recherche (FER), Module 6, http://eptc2fer.ca/files/module6/Dorothy_Proctor_radio_documentary_transcript_EN.pdf.

19 Tyler, "Prisoners Used."
20 CDOJ, *Annual Report … 1950*, 36. See Appendix A for more detail.
21 Marr, 70. Scholars have advanced several theories of causation for the riot. See ibid., 105–16.
22 CDOJ, *Annual Report … 1955*, 8.
23 Gibson qtd in Marr, 70.
24 Ibid., 70–1.
25 Gibson qtd in ibid., 71.
26 Gamberg and Thomson, 40; cf. Marr 70–1.
27 Ibid., 72.
28 Ibid., 72.
29 Minutes of the 1951 Wardens' Conference, 15 June 1951, 2:30 p.m., LAC, RG 73, vol. 31, file 1-18-13, pt 1.
30 Minutes of the 1951 Wardens' Conference, 21 June 1951, 11:30 a.m.–12:30 p.m., LAC, RG 73, vol. 31, file 1-18-13, pt 1. It was common for prisoners to be held in solitary confinement for extended periods of time. This issue was raised in Parliament by Mr Winch, who had this to say about the practice: "Let me tell you what solitary is, straight from my visit to Kingston penitentiary, where I saw and spoke with the inmates and the warden. There is a small cell about 4 ½ by 10 feet. There is a mattress, a concrete floor, a lavatory, a sink, earphones on the radio and steel bars. Yet this is not like any other cell in the penitentiary, because outside of the barred door there is a solid door with a four-inch peephole. If a man had to stay there for a day – perhaps he should, but you and I would not like it. If we had to stay there for several days it would result in claustrophobia. For a man to be locked in a room without being able to hear or see anybody, and being let out for only half an hour a day, may be all very well for a few days, if a man is bad … Sir, I cannot understand it. I do not believe in coddling or pampering, but I do not believe in a man, irrespective of his guilt, being kept for nine months or a year in solitary confinement. I thank the Hon. Minister for giving me the authority to call two of the men out of solitary and speak to them. It took me ten minutes before I could even speak to them, because they just could not speak; they were shaking. They were on an indeterminate sentence; they did not know whether they would ever get out. I cannot understand why the Minister of Justice, as I know him, will allow even criminals to be kept for nine months or a year in solitary confinement, locked in a cell and allowed out for only half or three-quarters of an hour a day for exercise." HCD, 22nd Parl., 2nd sess., vol. 5, 5281.

31 Minutes of the 1951 Wardens' Conference, 15 June 1951, 2:30 p.m., 6, LAC, RG 73, vol. 31, file 1-18-13, pt 1.
32 HCD, 24th Parl., 2nd sess., vol. 1, 1012.
33 "Standard Minimum Rules."
34 *Beacon*, December 1958, 5.
35 HCD, 24th Parl., 2nd sess., vol. 1, 1016.
36 HCD, 24th Parl., 2nd sess., vol. 6, 6881.
37 HCD, 24th Parl., 6th sess., vol. 3, 2717.
38 CDOJ, *Annual Report ... 1950*, 14. This exemplifies Stanley Cohen's idea of organizational convenience, which he describes as follows: "When reforms reach the existing system, they confront a series of powerful managerial, administrative and organisational imperatives. The reform impulse is resisted and blocked or (more frequently) it is welcomed, only to be absorbed and co-opted (for the wrong reasons) and in the process completely transformed, even in directions diametrically opposed to the original vision." Cohen, *Visions of Social Control*, 92.
39 HCD, 24th Parl., 1st sess., vol. 3, 3195.
40 Many articles in the penal press argued that one of the major judicial issues was the increased use of indeterminate sentences, which, Al Young argued, went "against the 'people are prisoners' mantra because it treats them inhumanely." *Tele-Scope*, January 1957, 25.
41 *Transition*, June 1952, 23.
42 *Pathfinder*, January 1955, 2.
43 Mr. Fulton noted: "We recognize, therefore, that this new building program is designed only to take care of the portion of the penitentiary population for which we are responsible now and even then we know we shall soon have to be starting new buildings in addition to those I have mentioned just to take care of our own responsibilities." HCD, 24th Parl., 1st sess., vol. 3, 3196.
44 McCulley, *Rehabilitation*, 3.
45 Joe McCulley, "Guest Editorial, *Tele-Scope*, June 1952, 3. In *Visions of Social Control*, Stanley Cohen pointed out the importance of the message that McCulley was presenting when he noted: "Ideology is important, then, only insofar as it succeeded passing off as fair, natural, acceptable or even just and humane, a system which is basically coercive." Cohen, *Visions of Social Control*, 22.
46 Marr, 74.
47 Ibid., 74–5.
48 Ibid., 75.
49 Archambault Report, 45.
50 CDOJ, *Annual Report ... 1955*, 8.
51 See "Public Distrust Grows for Peace Guardians," "Young Offenders," and "Across the Editor's Desk," *Transition*, November 1954, 6, 10–11, 18–19;

March discusses each of these articles in his memorandum. R.E. March, Memorandum to the Commissioner, "Re: 'Transition'" (Nov. 1954), LAC, RG 73, vol. 126, file 8-11-26.

52 "Yardbird Echoes," *Transition*, November 1954, 27.

53 R.E. March, Memorandum to the Commissioner, "Re: 'Transition' (Nov. 1954)," LAC, RG 73, vol. 126, file 8-11-26; "Charity or Wages," *Transition*, November 1954, 5.

54 "Across the Editor's Desk," *Transition*, November 1954, 6.

55 Al Sieben, "A Living Monument," *Transition*, November 1954, 12–13, 26.

56 R.E. March, Memorandum to the Commissioner, "Re: 'Transition' (Nov. 1954)," LAC, RG 73, vol. 126, file 8-11-26.

57 Commissioner R.B. Gibson to the Warden, New Westminster, "Re: Prison Magazine 'Transition,'" 15 December 1954, LAC, RG 73, vol. 126, file 8-11-26.

58 W.J. Slack, D.J. Gillies, and M.J. Barry to the Warden, British Columbia Penitentiary, 22 December 1954, "Re: Transition, Re: Censoring, Re: November, 1954, issue," LAC, RG 73, vol. 126, file 8-11-26.

59 Ibid.

60 Warden Douglass, British Columbia Penitentiary, to the Commissioner of Penitentiaries, "Re: Prison Magazine 'Transition,'" 28 December 1954, LAC, RG 73, vol. 126, file 8-11-26.

61 Ibid.

62 Ibid.

63 James F. Clark, Editor, *Pathfinder* to Commissioner of Penitentiaries, 20 July 1953, 2, LAC, RG 73, vol. 121, file 7-11-26, pt 1.

64 *Transition* Staff to Recreation and Welfare Committee, 6 January 1955, LAC, RG 73, vol. 126, file 8-11-26.

65 "Six 'Pen' Editors Resign," *Vancouver Sun*, undated newspaper clipping, LAC, RG 73, vol. 126, file 8-11-26.

66 Harvey Blackstock, "Special Treatment for Drug Addicts," *Tele-Scope*, July 1954, 15.

67 Ibid.

68 Minutes of the 1955 Wardens' Conference, 29 January 1955, A.M., 2nd session (1100–1230), p. 2, LAC, RG 73, vol. 32, file 1-18-15, pt 1.

69 Ibid.

70 Ibid.

71 James F. Clark, Editor, *Pathfinder* to Commissioner of Penitentiaries, 20 July 1953, 2, LAC, RG 73, vol. 121, file 7-11-26, pt 1.

72 R.B. Gibson, Commissioner of Penitentiaries to the Warden, Saskatchewan Penitentiary, "Re:'Pathfinder' Magazine," 25 August 1955, 3, LAC, RG 73, vol. 121, file 7-11-26, pt 1.

73 Minutes of the 1955 Wardens' Conference, 29 January 1955, A.M., 2nd session (1100–1230), p. 2, LAC, RG 73, vol. 32, file 1-18-15, pt 1.

74 Ibid.

75 Commissioner of Penitentiaries to the Warden, New Westminster, British Columbia, "Re: Prison Newspaper," 17 March 1955, LAC, RG 73, vol. 126, file 8-11-26.

76 Ibid.

77 Minutes of the 1957 Wardens' Conference, 4 June 1957, 3.30 to 5 P.M., p. 5, LAC, RG 73, vol. 33, file 1-18-17, pt 2.

78 Warden Douglass, British Columbia Penitentiary to the Commissioner of Penitentiaries, "Re: Inmate Magazine 'Transition,'" 3 May 1955, LAC, RG 73, vol. 126, file 8-11-26.

79 "Real Transition," *New Westminster British Columbian*, 11 August 1955, newspaper clipping, LAC, RG 73, vol. 126, file 8-11-26; "New Penitentiary Journal Gives Life Behind Walls," *Vancouver Herald*, 12 August 1955, newspaper clipping, LAC, RG 73, vol. 126, file 8-11-26.

80 R.B. Gibson, Commissioner to the Warden, New Westminster, British Columbia, "Re: Prison Magazine 'Transition,'" 17 August 1955, LAC, RG 73, vol. 126, file 8-11-26.

81 *Transition*, February 1957, 3.

82 R.B. Gibson, Commissioner to the Warden, Kingston, Ontario, "Re: K.P. Telescope," 28 January 1957, LAC, RG 73, vol. 105, file 4-11-26, pt 3. For evidence surrounding one of the conflicts, see R.B. Gibson, Commissioner to the Warden, Kingston, Ontario, "Re: Inmate Publications, Re: 'Tele-Scope,'" 21 March 1955, LAC, RG 73, vol. 65, file 1-11-26, in which the commissioner advised Warden Johnstone not to publish two articles (one was characterized as "a direct and violent attack on the police," and the other as containing "bitter and sarcastic references to Government officials" and an attack on parliamentary legislation). The commissioner also suggested that the Kingston editorial board consult the "Handbook for Penal Press Editors" as a guide to appropriate submissions.

83 "EXTRACT FROM TORONTO GLOBE & MAIL EDITORIAL PAGE – SAT. 20 Apr 57," LAC, RG 73, vol. 105, file 4-11-26, pt 3.

84 Ibid.; Minutes of the 1957 Wardens' Conference, 4 June 1957, 3.30 to 5 P.M., LAC, RG 73, vol. 33, file 1-18-17, pt 2.

85 "EXTRACT FROM TORONTO GLOBE & MAIL EDITORIAL PAGE – SAT. 20 Apr 57," LAC, RG 73, vol. 105, file 4-11-26, pt 3.

86 Minutes of the 1957 Wardens' Conference, 4 June 1957, 3.30 to 5 P.M., p. 6, LAC, RG 73, vol. 33, file 1-18-17, pt 2.

87 Ibid.

88 Ibid.

89 Ibid.

90 Ibid.

91 Ibid.

92 Warden Hall of Saskatchewan Penitentiary described having to "examine that magazine with a fine tooth comb before you can let it out of the

institution. After telling them not to do something, what do you find; they've slipped it in just in one little line down somewhere else." Ibid.

93 Ibid.
94 *Transition*, October 1955, 12.
95 *Transition*, December 1953, 8–9.
96 *Transition*, February 1957, 6; The wording of this edit reads: "Dear Reader. {illegible} copy scheduled for this page has been rejected by the Administration." *Transition*, September–October 1958.
97 Minutes of the 1957 Wardens' Conference, June 4, 1957, 3.30 to 5 P.M., p. 3, LAC, RG 73, vol. 33, file 1-18-17, part 2.
98 Ibid.
99 Ibid.
100 Ibid.
101 Warden Douglass, British Columbia Penitentiary to the Commissioner of Penitentiaries, "Re: Inmate Magazine 'Transition,'" 3 May 1955, LAC, RG 73, vol. 126, file 8-11-26.
102 *Transition*, December 1956, 4.
103 *Tele-Scope*, February 1958, 3.
104 Gaucher, 5.
105 Gaucher, 5.

Conclusion

1 Cohen, *Visions of Social Control*, 18.
2 Osborne, 296.
3 McCoy, 1–2; United Province of Canada, Reports of the Commissioners Appointed to Inquire into the Conduct, Discipline, & Management of the Provincial Penitentiary, With Documents transmitted by the Commissioners (Montreal: Rollo Campbell, 1849).
4 United Province of Canada, *Reports*; Macdonnell Report; Biggar, Nickle, and Draper Report; Archambault Report; CDOJ, Correctional Planning Committee, *Summary of Recommendations Contained in the Report* (Ottawa, 1960); Canada, Canadian Committee on Corrections, *Report*; MacGuigan Report; Canada, Solicitor General, *Commission of Inquiry*.
5 United Province of Canada, *Reports*, 89, 258, 289–93; see also McCoy, 47–57.
6 Macdonnell Report, 15, 17, 18, 21.
7 Ibid., 41.
8 Ibid., 5.
9 Ibid., 30, 41–2.
10 Biggar, Nickle, and Draper Report, 9, 65.
11 Ibid., 13.
12 Ibid., 9, 38, 44.

13 Ibid., 41; Archambault Report, 278.

14 Cohen, *Visions of Social Control*, 15.

15 Ibid., 18.

16 Ibid., 21.

17 An auto-history is a self-history, written from the viewpoint of the writer and his or her social group. It is akin to autobiography. See Sioui, xxi–xxiii.

18 Appleby, Hunt, and Jacob, 309.

19 This near silence undoubtedly reflects the nature of the available source material and, sometimes, the age and condition of the inmates. While historians have endeavoured to capture the experiences of the inmates of institutions through the lens of official documents and case files, statistical evidence, and family members' correspondence, the voices and perspectives of the inmates themselves appear infrequently. See, for example, Robert Adamoski, "Their Duties towards the Children: Citizenship and the Practice of Child Rescue in Early Twentieth Century British Columbia" (PhD diss., Simon Fraser University, 1995), 316, 324, in which Adamoski, who made significant efforts to produce an outline of children's experiences while in the care of the Vancouver Children's Aid Society, often in the Children's Home, admitted that "historical evidence of life within the Children's Home is limited" and "the case files examined for this dissertation offer little insight into the experiences of wards residing in the Children's Home"; See also Edgar-Andre Montigny, *Foisted upon the Government?: State Responsibilities, Family Obligations, and the Care of the Dependent Aged in Late Nineteenth-Century Ontario* (Montreal and Kingston: McGill-Queen's University Press, 1997), 108–29 passim. Montigny, in his chapter on the experiences of elderly patients in Ontario's Rockwood Asylum, is able to provide little in the way of patients' accounts of their experiences.

20 Since the 1990s, the work of convict criminologists has begun to rectify this lacuna in the record. This "diverse collection of individuals who believe that convict voices have been ignored, minimized, or misinterpreted in scholarly research on jails, prisons, convicts, correctional officers, and associated policies and practices that affect these individuals" have been documenting and analysing the lived experiences of the carceral subject. Ross, Jones, Lenza, and Richards, n.p.

21 Foucault, *Discipline and Punish*, 82.

22 Gordon Marr, #598, Editor, The K.P. Tele-scope to letter to Warden R.M. Allan, 8 August 1950, LAC, RG 73, vol. 65, file 1-11-26; *Tele-Scope*, September 1, 1950, 1.

23 Cohen, *Visions of Social Control*, 19.

24 Ibid., 20.

25 Ibid., 20.

26 Ibid., 21.

27 Ibid., 92.
28 Mathiesen, 44–6.
29 Ibid., 31–2, 40–2.
30 Anderson, *Up the Ladder*, 137.
31 CDOJ, *Report of General R.B. Gibson*, 4.
32 Cohen, *Visions of Social Control*, 20.
33 Ibid., 20–1.
34 For more information on neutralization techniques, see Mathiesen, 44–5.
35 Anderson, *Imagined Communities*, 34–6.
36 Mathiesen, 42–3.
37 Canada, Ministry of Public Safety, *Annual Report of the Correctional Investigator, 2014–2015* (Ottawa: The Correctional Investigator of Canada, 2015), 5, http://www.oci-bec.gc.ca/cnt/rpt/pdf/annrpt/annrpt20142015 -eng.pdf.
38 Canada, Ministry of Public Safety, *Annual Report … 2016–2017*, 44. It is intriguing, to say the least, that Zinger expresses such concern for the temporary mental anxiety experienced by discomfited visitors, but of prisoners subjected to solitary confinement for months, he wrote, "there was no evidence that over a period of 60 days the mental health and psychological functioning of segregated offenders significantly deteriorated." See Zinger, iii.
39 Canada, Ministry of Public Safety, *Annual Report … 2016–2017*, 44.
40 Ibid., 31.
41 Archambault Report, 2.
42 *Pen-O-Rama*, February 1953, 5.
43 Goodale, "Commissioner's mandate letter."
44 Foucault, *Discipline and Punish*; Nils Christie, *Crime Control as Industry*; Sellin, *Slavery and the Penal System*; Rusche and Kirchheimer, *Punishment and Social Structure*.
45 Cohen, *Visions of Social Control*, 22.
46 Ibid., 23.
47 Ibid., 23.
48 Reiman and Leighton, 8.
49 Cohen, *Visions of Social Control*, 27.
50 Ibid., 22.
51 Foucault, "Governmentality," in *The Foucault Effect*, 87–104.
52 Foucault, *Discipline and Punish*, 136.
53 CDOJ, *Annual Report … 1951*, 19; Minutes of the 1957 Wardens' Conference, 4 June 1957, 3:30 to 5:00 p.m., LAC, RG 73, vol. 33, file 1-18-17, pt 2.
54 Maxwell quoted in Archambault Report, 129.
55 CDOJ, *Annual Report … 1948*, 20.
56 Buck, 241.

57 Mathiesen, 19, 32–7.
58 Cohen, *Visions of Social Control*, 89.
59 Bob Gaucher, personal communication with the authors, July 2018.
60 Brock, *These Strange Criminals*.
61 Cohen, *Visions of Social Control*, 89.
62 White, 82.

Bibliography

Primary Sources: Unpublished

Canada. Department of Justice. Penitentiary Branch. Operational Files. LAC. RG 73, vol. 16, file 1-12-76, "Report of Commissioner of Penitentiaries."

Canada. Department of Justice. Penitentiary Branch. Operational Files. LAC. RG 73, vol. 31, file 1-18-11, Wardens' Conference, 1949.

Canada. Department of Justice. Penitentiary Branch. Operational Files. LAC. RG 73, vol. 31, file 1-18-13, pt 1, Wardens' Conference, 1951.

Canada. Department of Justice. Penitentiary Branch. Operational Files. LAC. RG 73, vol. 32, file 1-18-15, pts 1–2, Wardens' Conference, 1955.

Canada. Department of Justice. Penitentiary Branch. Operational Files. LAC. RG 73, vol. 33, file 1-18-17, pt 2, Wardens' Conference, 1957.

Canada. Department of Justice. Penitentiary Branch. Operational Files. LAC. RG 73, vol. 42, file 1-20-11, pts 5–8, "Commission appointed in 1936 to Investigate the Penal System of Canada."

Canada. Department of Justice. Penitentiary Branch. Operational Files. LAC. RG 73, vol. 43, file 1-20-31, "Inspections by Commissioner Gibson, Generally."

Canada. Department of Justice. Penitentiary Branch. Operational Files. LAC, RG 73, vol. 48, file 1-1-54, "Censorship Policy, Re:"

Canada. Department of Justice. Penitentiary Branch. Operational Files. LAC. RG 73, vol. 65, file 1-11-26, "Prison Newspapers – Generally."

Canada. Department of Justice. Penitentiary Branch. Operational Files. LAC. RG 73, vol. 96, file 3-11-26, pts 1–2, "Prison Newspaper, St. Vincent de Paul."

Canada. Department of Justice. Penitentiary Branch. Operational Files. LAC. RG 73, vol. 105, file 4-11-26, pt 3, "Prison Newspaper, Kingston."

Canada. Department of Justice. Penitentiary Branch. Operational Files. LAC. RG 73, vol. 114, file 5-11-26, pt 1, "Prison Newspaper, Collin's Bay."

Canada. Department of Justice. Penitentiary Branch. Operational Files. LAC. RG 73, vol. 117, file 6-11-26, "Prison Newspaper, Manitoba."

Canada. Department of Justice. Penitentiary Branch. Operational Files. LAC. RG 73, vol. 121, file 7-11-26, pt 1, "Prison Newspaper, Saskatchewan."
Canada. Department of Justice. Penitentiary Branch. Operational Files. LAC. RG 73, vol. 126, file 8-11-26, "Prison Newspaper, British Columbia."

Primary Sources: Published

Blackstock, Harvey. *Bitter Humour*. Toronto: Burns and MacEachern, 1967.
Brooks v. the King. [1927] S.C.R. 633. https://scc-csc.lexum.com/scc-csc/scc -csc/en/item/3423/index.do#_ftnref1.
Canada. *An Act to amend the Penitentiary Act*, S.C. 1918, c. 36.
Canada. *An Act to amend the Penitentiary Act, 1939*, S.C. 1945, c. 28.
Canada. *An Act to provide for the Conditional Liberation of Persons Undergoing Sentences of Imprisonment*, S.C. 1958, c. 38, https://archive.org/details /actsofparl1958v01cana.
Canada. Committee Appointed by the Rt. Hon. C.J. Doherty, Minister of Justice, to Advise upon the Revision of the Penitentiary Regulations and the Amendment of the Penitentiary Act. *Report*. Ottawa: King's Printer, 1921.
Canada. *Criminal Code*, R.S.C. 1985, c. C-46, s. 753.
Canada. Department of Justice. *Annual Report of the Commissioner of Penitentiaries for the Fiscal Year ended March 31, 1948*. Ottawa: King's Printer, 1949.
Canada. Department of Justice. *Annual Report of the Commissioner of Penitentiaries for the Fiscal Year ended March 31, 1949*. Ottawa: King's Printer, 1949.
Canada. Department of Justice. *Annual Report of the Commissioner of Penitentiaries for the Fiscal Year ended March 31, 1950*. Ottawa: King's Printer, 1951.
Canada. Department of Justice. *Annual Report of the Commissioner of Penitentiaries for the Fiscal Year ended March 31, 1951*. Ottawa: King's Printer, 1952.
Canada. Department of Justice. *Annual Report of the Commissioner of Penitentiaries for the Fiscal Year ended March 31, 1952*. Ottawa: Queen's Printer, 1953.
Canada. Department of Justice. *Annual Report of the Commissioner of Penitentiaries for the Fiscal Year ended March 31, 1953*. Ottawa: Queen's Printer, 1953.
Canada. Department of Justice. *Annual Report of the Commissioner of Penitentiaries for the Fiscal Year ended March 31, 1954*. Ottawa: Queen's Printer, 1955.
Canada. Department of Justice. *Annual Report of the Commissioner of Penitentiaries for the Fiscal Year ended March 31, 1955*. Ottawa: Queen's Printer, 1956.
Canada. Department of Justice. *Annual Report of the Commissioner of Penitentiaries for the Fiscal Year ended March 31, 1956*. Ottawa: Queen's Printer, 1957.
Canada. Department of Justice. *Annual Report of the Commissioner of Penitentiaries for the Fiscal Year ended March 31, 1957*. Ottawa: Queen's Printer, 1958.
Canada. Department of Justice. *Annual Report of the Commissioner of Penitentiaries for the Fiscal Year ended March 31, 1960*. Ottawa: Queen's Printer, 1961.
Canada. Department of Justice. *Annual Report of the Commissioner of Penitentiaries for the Fiscal Year ended March 31, 1961*. Ottawa: Queen's Printer, 1962.

Canada. Department of Justice. *Annual Report of the Superintendent of Penitentiaries for the Fiscal Year ended March 31, 1935*. Ottawa: King's Printer, 1935.

Canada. Department of Justice. *Annual Report of the Superintendent of Penitentiaries for the Fiscal Year ended March 31, 1939*. Ottawa: King's Printer, 1939.

Canada. Department of Justice. Committee Appointed to Inquire into the Principles and Procedures Followed in the Remission Service of the Department of Justice of Canada. *Report*. Ottawa: Queen's Printer, 1956.

Canada. Department of Justice. Correctional Planning Committee. *Summary of Recommendations Contained in the Report*. Ottawa, 1960.

Canada. Department of Justice. *Penitentiary Regulations, 1933*. Ottawa: King's Printer, 1934.

Canada. Department of Justice. *Penitentiary Regulations, 1938* .

Canada. Department of Justice. "Extracts from Penitentiary Regulations, 123 to 143 inclusive, 158 to 178 inclusive," Ottawa: King's Printer, 1929, 6 (rule 169), Public Safety Canada Library, http://www.publicsafety.gc.ca/lbrr /archives/ke%2097%20p452%201929-eng.pdf.

Canada. Parliament. House of Commons. *Budget Speech delivered by Honourable D.C. Abbott, Minister of Finance, Member for St. Antoine-Westmount, in the House of Commons, February 19, 1953* (Ottawa: Queen's Printer, 1953), 18, http:// publications.gc.ca/collections/collection_2016/fin/F1-23-1-1953-eng.pdf.

Canada. Parliament. House of Commons. *Debates*, 13th Parl., 1st sess., vol. 1 (1918); 17th Parl., 5th sess., vol. 4 (1934); 18th Parl., 1st sess., vol. 1 (1936); 18th Parl., 3rd sess., vol. 4 (1938); 21st Parl., 6th sess., vol. 3 (1952); 21st Parl., 7th sess., vol. 5 (1953); 22nd Parl., 1st sess., vol. 6 (1954); 22nd Parl., 2nd sess., vols. 5–6 (1955); 22nd Parl., 3rd sess., vols. 1–2 (1956); 23rd Parl., 1st sess., vol. 3 (1958); 24th Parl., 1st sess., vols. 1–4 (1958); 24th Parl., 2nd sess., vols. 1, 4 (1959); 24th Parl., 3rd sess., vol. 5 (1960). http://parl .canadiana.ca.

Canada. Parliament. *Sessional Papers*, 1920, Paper no. 35, "Report of the Superintendent of Penitentiaries for the Fiscal Year Ended March 31, 1919."

Canada. Parliament. *Sessional Papers*, 1922, Paper no. 35, "Report of the Superintendent of Penitentiaries for the Fiscal Year Ended March 31, 1921."

Canada. Parliament. *Sessional Papers*, 1923, Paper no. 20, "Report of the Superintendent of Penitentiaries for the Fiscal Year Ended March 31, 1922."

Canada. Parliament. *Sessional Papers*, 1924, Paper no. 20, "Report of the Superintendent of Penitentiaries for the Fiscal Year Ended March 31, 1923."

Canada. Parliament. *Sessional Papers*, 1925, Paper no. 20, "Report of the Superintendent of Penitentiaries for the Year 1923–24."

Canada. Parliament. *Sessional Papers*, 1926, Paper no. 20, "Report of the Superintendent of Penitentiaries for the Year 1924–25."

Canada. Parliament. Standing Committee on Justice and Legal Affairs. Sub-Committee on the Penitentiary System in Canada. *Report*. Ottawa: Minister of Supply and Services Canada, 1977.

Canada. *Penitentiary Act*, R.S.C. 1906, c. 147, s. 41.

Canada. *Penitentiary Act*, R.S.C. 1927, c.154, s. 40.

Canada. *Penitentiary Act*, S.C. 1961, c. 53. https://ia802607.us.archive.org/31
/items/actsofparl196061v01cana/actsofparl196061v01cana.pdf

Canada. Department of Justice. National Parole Board. *Annual Report of the
National Parole Board for the Calendar Year Ended December 31, 1960*. Ottawa:
Queen's Printer, 1961.

Canada. Department of Justice. National Parole Board. *Annual Report of the
National Parole Board for the Calendar Year Ended December 31, 1961*. Ottawa:
Queen's Printer, 1962.

Canada. Department of Justice. National Parole Board. *First Annual Report of
the National Parole Board for the Calendar Year 1959*. Ottawa: National Parole
Board, 1960.

Canada. Department of Justice. *Report of General R. B. Gibson, A Commissioner
appointed under Order in Council P. C. 1313, regarding the Penitentiary System
of Canada*. Ottawa, February 5, 1947. http://www.lareau-legal.ca
/ReportGibson1947E.pdf.

Canada. Ministry of Public Safety. *Annual Report of the Correctional Investigator,
2014–2015*. Ottawa: The Correctional Investigator of Canada, 2015. http://
www.oci-bec.gc.ca/cnt/rpt/pdf/annrpt/annrpt20142015-eng.pdf.

Canada. Ministry of Public Safety. *Annual Report of the Correctional Investigator,
2016–2017*. Ottawa: The Correctional Investigator of Canada, 2017. http://
www.oci-bec.gc.ca/cnt/rpt/pdf/annrpt/annrpt20162017-eng.pdf.

Canada. Royal Commission on Penitentiaries. *Report*. Ottawa: King's Printer, 1914.

Canada. Royal Commission to Investigate the Penal System of Canada. *Report*.
Ottawa: King's Printer, 1938.

Canada. Solicitor General. *Commission of Inquiry into Certain Events and the
Prison for Women in Kingston*. Ottawa: Public Works and Government
Services Canada, 1996.

Canada. Superintendent of Penitentiaries. *Report of the Superintendent of
Penitentiaries Re: Kingston Penitentiary Disturbances*. Ottawa: King's Printer, 1933.

Canadian Committee on Corrections. *Report of the Canadian Committee on Corrections.
Toward Unity: Criminal Justice and Corrections*. Ottawa: Queen's Printer, 1969.

Gibson, R.B. *"The Penitentiaries Move Forward." An address given by Maj.-Gen.
R. B. Gibson, C.B., C.B.E., K.C., Commissioner of Penitentiaries, at the Canadian
Penal Congress, Kingston, Ontario, 1949*. Ottawa: Canadian Penitentiary
Service, 1949. Public Safety Canada Library. http://www.publicsafety
.gc.ca/lbrr/archives/hv%208501%20g53%201949-eng.pdf.

Gibson, Ralph B. Presidential Address, *Proceedings of the Eighty-third Annual
Congress of Correction of the American Prison Association, 1953*. https://
heinonline.org/HOL/Page?collection=journals&handle=hein.journals
/panectiop67&id=23

Goodale, Ralph. "Commissioner's mandate letter." Correctional Service
Canada. Last modified 5 September 2018. Accessed 25 September 2018.
http://www.csc-scc.gc.ca/about-us/006-0006-en.shtml.

League of Nations. "Penal and Penitentiary Questions Report of the Secretary-
General to the Assembly." Communicated to the Assembly, the Council and
the Members of the League, Geneva, September 24, 1934. Official No. A. 14.
1934. IV., 2, United Nations Archive.

League of Nations. "Penal and Penitentiary Questions Report Submitted by
the Fifth Committee to the Assembly." Communicated to the Assembly,
the Council, and the Members of the League, Geneva, September 24, 1934.
Official No. A. 45. 1934. IV., 6, United Nations Archives.

McCulley, Joseph. *Rehabilitation from the Point of View of an Administrator, An
Address by Joseph McCulley, Joseph M.A., Deputy Commissioner of Penitentiaries,
Ottawa, Canada, at the American Prison Association, 1951.* Ottawa: Canadian
Penitentiary Service, 1951.

"Standard Minimum Rules for the Treatment of Prisoners, adopted Aug.
30, 1955 by the First United Nations Congress on the Prevention of Crime
and the Treatment of Offenders," U.N. Doc. A/CONF/611, annex I, E.S.C.
res. 663C, 24 U.N. ESCOR Supp. (No. 1) at 11, U.N. Doc. E/3048 (1957),
amended E.S.C. res. 2076, 62 U.N. ESCOR Supp. (No. 1) at 35, U.N. Doc.
E/5988 (1977)." University of Minnesota Human Rights Library. Accessed
June 26, 2018. http://hrlibrary.umn.edu/instree/g1smr.htm.

United Province of Canada. *Reports of the Commissioners Appointed to Inquire
into the Conduct, Discipline, & Management of the Provincial Penitentiary, With
Documents transmitted by the Commissioners.* Montreal: Rollo Campbell, 1849.

Primary Sources: Penal Press

Beacon (Dorchester Penitentiary). 1951–60.
C.B. Diamond (Collins Bay Penitentiary). 1952–60.
Mountain Echoes (Manitoba Penitentiary). 1951–58.
Pathfinder (Saskatchewan Penitentiary). 1955, 1958.
Pen-O-Rama (St. Vincent de Paul Penitentiary). 1952–57.
Softball Bulletin (Kingston Penitentiary). 1950.
Sports Bulletin (St. Vincent de Paul Penitentiary). 1950.
Tele-Scope (Kingston Penitentiary). 1950–58.
Transition (British Columbia Penitentiary). 1951–60.

Primary Sources: Mainstream Periodicals

Edmonton Journal. 1953.
Gazette (Montreal). 1933.

Globe (Toronto). 1932, 1938, 1957.
Maclean's. 1951.
New Westminster British Columbian. 1955.
Ottawa Citizen. 1932, 1934, 1938.
Ottawa Journal. 1945.
Vancouver Herald. 1955.
Victoria Colonist. 1950.
Winnipeg Free Press. 1953.

Secondary Sources

Adamoski, Robert. "Their Duties towards the Children: Citizenship and the Practice of Child Rescue in Early Twentieth Century British Columbia." PhD diss., Simon Fraser University, 1995.

Anderson, Benedict. *Imagined Communities: Reflections on the Origin and Spread of Nationalism*, rev. ed. London: Verso, 1991.

Anderson, Frank. *Up the Ladder*. Saskatoon: Gopher, 1997.

Appleby, Joyce, Lynn Hunt, and Margaret Jacob. *Telling the Truth about History*. New York: W.W. Norton, 1994.

Avakumovic, Ivan. *The Communist Party in Canada: A History*. Toronto: McClelland and Stewart, 1975.

Baird, Russell N. *The Penal Press*. Evanston: Northwestern University Press, 1967.

Becker, Howard S. "Whose Side Are We On?" *Social Problems* 14, no. 3 (1967): 239–47.

Bothwell, Robert Ian Drummond, and John English. *Canada Since 1945: Power, Politics, and Provincialism*, rev. ed. Toronto: University of Toronto Press, 1989.

Brock, Peter. "Prison Samizdat of British Conscientious Objectors in the First World War." *Journal of Prisoners on Prison* 12 (2003): 8–21.

Brock, Peter. *These Strange Criminals: An Anthology of Prison Memoirs by Conscientious Objectors from the Great War to the Cold War*. Toronto: University of Toronto Press, 2004.

Buck, Tim. *Yours in the Struggle: Reminiscences of Tim Buck*, edited by William Beeching and Phyllis Clarke Toronto: NC Press, 1977.

Canada. Groupe en éthique de la recherché. "Le didacticiel EPTC 2 Formation en éthique de la recherche (FER). Module 6." http://eptc2fer.ca/files /module6/Dorothy_Proctor_radio_documentary_transcript_EN.pdf.

Chomsky, Noam. *Necessary Illusions*. Boston: South End Press, 1989.

Christie, Nils. *Crime Control as Industry: Toward Gulags, Western Style*, 3rd ed. New York: Routledge, 2000.

Clarkson, Chris. *Domestic Reforms: Political Visions and Family Regulation in British Columbia, 1862–1940*. Vancouver: UBC Press, 2007.

Cohen, Stanley. *Folk Devils and Moral Panics: The Creation of the Mods and Rockers*. London: MacGibbon and Kee, 1972.

Cohen, Stanley. *Visions of Social Control: Crime, Punishment, and Classification*. Malden: Polity Press, 1985.

Cohen, Stanley, and Laurie Taylor. *Psychological Survival: The Experience of Long-Term Imprisonment*. Harmondsworth: Penguin, 1972.

Correctional Service Canada. "History of the Canadian Correctional System." n.p., n.d. http://www.csc-scc.gc.ca/educational-resources/092/ha-student -etudiant-eng.pdf.

Correctional Service Canada. "1940–1959: Times of Change." Last modified 20 October 2014. Accessed 1 June 2018. http://www.csc-scc.gc.ca/about -us/006-2003-eng.shtml.

Crowley, Terry. *Agnes Macphail and the Politics of Equality*. Toronto: J. Lorimer, 1990.

Culhane, Claire. *Barred from Prison: A Personal Account*. Vancouver: Pulp Press, 1979.

Culhane, Claire. *Still Barred from Prison: Social Injustice in Canada*. Montreal: Black Rose Books, 1985.

Foucault, Michel. *Discipline and Punish: The Birth of the Prison*, trans. Alan Sheridan, 2nd ed. New York: Vintage Books, 1995.

Foucault, Michel. "Governmentality." In *The Foucault Effect: Studies in Governmentality*, edited by Graham Burchell, Colin Gordon, and Peter Miller. Chicago: University of Chicago Press, 1991.

Foucault, Michel. *Madness and Civilization: A History of Insanity in the Age of Reason*. Translated by Richard Howard. London: Tavistock, 1967.

Francis, R. Douglas, Richard Jones, and Donald B. Smith. *Destinies: Canadian History Since Confederation*, 6th ed. Toronto: Nelson Education, 2008.

Gamberg, Herbert, and Anthony Thomson. *The Illusion of Prison Reform: Corrections in Canada*. New York: Peter Lang, 1984.

Garfinkel, Harold. "Conditions of Successful Degradation Ceremonies." *American Journal of Sociology* 61, no. 5 (March 1956): 420–4.

Gaucher, Robert. "The Canadian Penal Press: A Documentation and Analysis." *Journal of Prisoners on Prison* 2, no. 1 (1989): 1–12.

Gaucher, Robert. "Response: The Prisoner as Ethnographer: The Journal of Prisoners on Prisons." *Journal of Prisoners on Prisons* 1, no. 1, 1988: 49–62.

Goffman, Erving. *Asylums: Essays on the Social Situation of Mental Patients and Other Inmates*. New York: Anchor Books, 1961.

Goffman, Erving. *Stigma: Notes on the Management of Spoiled Identity*. New York: Simon and Schuster, 1963.

Gosselin, Luc. *Prisons in Canada*. Montreal: Black Rose Books, 1982.

Haig-Brown, Celia. *Resistance and Renewal: Surviving the Indian Residential School*. Vancouver: Tillacum Library, 1988.

Herman, Edward S., and Noam Chomsky. *Manufacturing Consent: The Political Economy of the Mass Media*. New York: Pantheon Books, 1988.

"History." Hart House. Accessed 29 August 2018. http://harthouse.ca/about -us/history.

"History of Parole in Canada." Parole Board of Canada. Last modified 10 April 2018. Accessed 1 June 2018. https://www.canada.ca/en/parole -board/corporate/history-of-parole-in-canada.html.

Ignatieff, Michael. *A Just Measure of Pain: The Penitentiary in the Industrial Revolution, 1750–1850*. New York: Pantheon Books, 1978.

Jackson, Michael. *Prisoners of Isolation: Solitary Confinement in Canada*. Toronto: University of Toronto Press, 1983.

Katz, Sidney. "It's a Tough Time to Be a Kid." *Maclean's*. 15 January 1951.

Keshen, Jeff. "Revisiting Canada's Civilian Women during World War II." *Histoire sociale / Social History* 60, no. 30 (November 1997): 239–66.

Kidman, John. *The Canadian Prison: The Story of a Tragedy*. Toronto: Ryerson, 1947.

Kraiem, Rubin. "Prisoners' Rights and the Standard Minimum Rules for the Treatment of Offenders." *International Journal of Offender Therapy and Comparative Criminology* 22, no. 2 (1978): 156–63. https://doi.org/10.1177 /0306624X7802200208.

Kropf, Joel. "Pursuing Human Techniques of Progressive Justice: The Ethical Assumptions of Early-to-Mid-Twentieth-Century English-Canadian Penal Reformers." PhD diss., Carleton University, 2014.

Lavell, Alfred E. *The Convicted Criminal and his Re-establishment as a Citizen: With Special Reference to the Province of Ontario, Canada*. Toronto: The Ryerson Press, 1926.

Lemert, Edwin M. *Human Deviance, Social Problems, and Social Control*. New York: Prentice Hall, 1967.

Lowe, Mick. *One Woman Army: The Life of Claire Culhane*, Toronto: Macmillan of Canada, 1992.

Marks, Michael P. *The Prison as Metaphor: Re-Imagining International Relations*. New York: Peter Lang, 2004.

Marr, Chadwick Alem. "'A Series of Nasty Situations': The Causes and Effects of Riots at Kingston Penitentiary." MA thesis, Queen's University, 1998.

Mathiesen, Thomas. *Prison on Trial*, 3rd English ed., Criminal Policy Series, edited by Andrew Rutherford. Winchester: Waterside Press, 2006.

Matza, David. *Becoming Deviant*. New York: Prentice Hall, 1969.

Matza, David. *Delinquency and Drift*. New York: Wiley, 1964.

McConville, Sean. "The Victorian Prison, 1865–1965." In *The Oxford History of the Prison: The Practice of Punishment in Western Society*, edited by Norval Morris and David J. Rothman. New York: Oxford University Press, 1995, 121–3.

McCoy, Ted. *Hard Time: Reforming the Penitentiary in Nineteenth-Century Canada*. Edmonton: AU Press, 2012.

McSherry, Peter. *The Big Red Fox: The Incredible Story of Norman "Red" Ryan, Canada's Most Notorious Criminal*. Toronto: Dundurn Press, 1999.

Miller, J.R. *Shingwauk's Vision: A History of Native Residential Schools*. Toronto: University of Toronto Press, 1996.

Milloy, John S. *A National Crime: The Canadian Government and the Residential School System, 1879 to 1986*. Winnipeg: University of Manitoba Press, 1999.

Montigny, Edgar-Andre. *Foisted upon the Government? State Responsibilities, Family Obligations, and the Care of the Dependent Aged in Late Nineteenth-Century Ontario*. Montreal and Kingston: McGill-Queen's University Press, 1997.

Niergarth, Kirk. "Art, Education, and a 'New World Society': Joseph McCulley's Pickering College and Canadian Muralism, 1934–1950." *Journal of Canadian Studies* 41, no. 1 (1950): 172–201.

Osborne, Geraint B. "Scientific Experimentation on Canadian Inmates, 1955 to 1975." *Howard Journal of Criminal Justice* 45, no. 3 (July 2006): 284–306. https://doi.org/10.1111/j.1468-2311.2006.00422.x.

Reiman, Jeffrey, and Paul Leighton. *The Rich Get Richer and the Poor Get Prison: Ideology, Class, and Criminal Justice*. 9th ed. Boston: Allyn and Bacon, 2010.

Richards, Stephen C., Jeffrey Ian Ross, Greg Newbold, Michael Lenza, Richard S. Jones, Daniel S. Murphy, and Robert S. Grigsby. "Convict Criminology, Prisoner Reentry, and Public Policy Recommendations." *Journal of Prisoners on Prisons* 21, nos. 1–2 (2012): 16–34.

Ross, Jeffrey Ian, Richard S. Jones, Mike Lenza, and Stephen C. Richards. "Convict Criminology and the Struggle for Inclusion." *Critical Criminology* 24, no. 2 (July 2016): n.p. https://doi.org/10.1007/s10612-016-9332-9.

Rothman, David J. *The Discovery of the Asylum: Social Order and Disorder in the New Republic*. Boston: Little, Brown, 1971.

Rotman, Edgardo. "The Failure of Reform: United States, 1865–1965." In *The Oxford History of the Prison: The Practice of Punishment in Western Society*, edited by Norval Morris and David J. Rothman, 154–60. New York: Oxford University Press, 1998.

Rusche, Georg, and Otto Kirchheimer. *Punishment and Social Structure*. New Brunswick: Transaction, 2003.

Sellin, J. Thorsten. *Slavery and the Penal System*. New York: Elsevier, 1976.

Sioui, Georges. *For an Amerindian Autohistory: An Essay on the Foundations of a Social Ethic*. Translated by Sheila Fischman. Montreal and Kingston: McGill-Queen's University Press, 1992.

Smith, Dale E. "Crowding and Confinement." In *The Pains of Imprisonment*, edited by Robert Johnson and Hans Toch. Beverly Hills: Sage, 1982.

Strange, Carolyn. "Casting Light on Women in the Shadow of the Law." In *Great Dames*, edited by Elspeth Cameron and Janice Dickin. Toronto: University of Toronto Press, 1997.

Street, T. George. *Handbook on Parole*. Ottawa: National Parole Board, 1960. https://www.publicsafety.gc.ca/lbrr/archives/hv%209308%20s7h%20 1960-eng.pdf.

Sykes, Gresham, and Sheldon Messinger. "The Inmate Social System." *Theoretical Studies in Social Organization of the Prison*, edited by R.A. Cloward et al., 5–19. New York: Social Science Research Council, 1960.

Taylor, Graham D., and Peter A. Baskerville. *A Concise History of Business in Canada*. Toronto: Oxford University Press, 1994.

Taylor, Ian, Paul Walton, and Jock Young. *The New Criminology: For a Social Theory of Deviance*, London: Routledge and Kegan Paul, 1973.

"The Closing of the Prison for Women in Kingston, July 6, 2000: Post-War Decades." Correctional Service Canada. Last modified 6 March 2008. Accessed 22 May 2018. http://www.csc-scc.gc.ca/text/pblct /brochurep4w/6-eng.shtml.

Thompson, John Herd, with Allen Seager. *Canada, 1922–1939: Decades of Discord*. The Canadian Centenary Series, edited by Ramsay Cook. Toronto: McClelland and Stewart, 1985.

Tilly, Charles. "Family History, Social History, and Social Change." In *Family History at the Crossroads: A Journal of Family History Reader*, edited by Tamara Hareven and Andrejs Plakans. Princeton: Princeton University Press, 1987.

Topping, C.W. *Canadian Penal Institutions*. Toronto: The Ryerson Press, 1929.

Tyler, Tracey. "Prisoners Used for 'Frightening' Tests, New Papers Show." *Toronto Star*, 18 December 1999. http://johnmueller.org/Problems/prison.html.

Weber, Max. *The Protestant Ethic and the Spirit of Capitalism*. New York: Scribner, 1930.

White, Hayden V. *Tropics of Discourse: Essays in Cultural Criticism*. Baltimore: Johns Hopkins University Press, 1978.

Winterdyk, John, and Jessica Wood. "An Historical Overview of Adult Corrections in Canada." In *Adult Corrections in Canada*, edited by John Winterdyk and Michael Weinrath. Whitby: deSitter, 2013.

Withrow, Oswald C.J. *Shackling the Transgressor: An Indictment of the Canadian Penal System*. With an introduction by Harry Anderson. Toronto: Thomas Nelson and Sons, 1933.

Zinger, Ivan. "The Psychological Effects of 60 days in Administrative Segregation." PhD diss., Carleton University, 1998.

Index

Page references in italics indicate a figure; page references in bold indicate a table.

www.ingramcontent.com/pod-product-compliance
Lightning Source LLC
Chambersburg PA
CBHW030237030426
42336CB00009B/138